Step-by-Step
GOURMET

Step-by-Step
GOURMET

MEREDITH PRESS®
Des Moines, Iowa

Published by Meredith ® Press
1716 Locust Street,
Des Moines, IA 50309-3023

Meredith ® Press is an imprint of Meredith Books
Director, New Product Development: Ray Wolf
Associate Art Director: Lynda Haupert
Managing Editor: Christopher Cavanaugh

Meredith Publishing Group
President, Publishing Group: Christopher Little
Vice President and Publishing Director: John P. Loughlin

Meredith Corporation
Chairman and Chief Executive Officer: Jack D. Rehm
President and Chief Operating Officer: William T. Kerr

Chairman of the Executive Committee: E.T. Meredith III

ISBN 0-696-20531-9

Library of Congress catalog card No. 95-80274

This book may not be sold outside the
United States of America and Canada

Distributed by Meredith Corporation, Des Moines, Iowa

Printed in France

CREDITS

Recipes by: Pat Alburey, Jo Craig, Linda Fraser, Annette Grimsdale,
Kerenza Harries, Kathryn Hawkins, Lesley Mackley, Janice Murfitt,
Louise Pickford, Lorna Rhodes, Lyn Rutherford, Anne Sheasby,
Louise Steele, Beverley Sutherland Smith, Sally Taylor,
Hilaire Walden, Elizabeth Wolf-Cohen.

Photographs by: Steve Baxter, Simon Butcher, Ken Field, Paul Grater,
David Gill, Ray Joyce, Jon Stewart, Alister Thorpe, Philip Wymant.

CONTENTS

INTRODUCTION

Do you need inspiration for another quick supper to please all the family or for a simple-to-make but special dinner party starter? Are you looking for the perfect, failsafe recipe for a Christmas cake or a low-calorie sauce? Do you plan to try your hand at creating some authentic Thai, Chinese or Indian dishes? Or do you want to delight your family and friends with some home-made food gifts, such as a special preserve or hand-dipped chocolates? With 448 delicious recipes, *Step-by-Step Gourmet* is the only recipe book you need.

For those with a love of food, this is a book to pour over; as well as classic favorites, it also contains recipes from cuisines around the world, ranging from Greek meze dishes, such as Imam Bayaldi, to Chinese salads, such as the traditional Eight Treasure Salad; from Cajun Crabcakes to the alcohol-rich Scottish dessert Atholl Brose; from Indian breads, such as nan and chapati to Japanese Teriyaka Steaks. For those who have been nervous of gourmet cooking, this is a book to ease the fear – the layout of each recipe ensures that the instructions are easy to follow; all the ingredients you will need are given at the beginning of each recipe, each finished dish is beautifully photographed, and step-by-step photographs and accompanying text clearly explain how to achieve a perfect result every time.

SOUPS

CONSOMMÉ

5 cups homemade chicken stock (see Note)
4 ounces chicken breast meat
2 large eggs
4 tablespoons finely chopped fresh parsley
1 teaspoon vegetable oil
salt and pepper

Into a large pan, put stock. Slowly bring to a boil. In a blender or food processor, finely chop chicken. Separate 1 egg and beat white lightly with a fork. Roughly crush shell. Mix together chicken, egg white, shell and 3 tablespoons of the parsley. Add to stock.

Bring stock to just below boiling, stirring. Reduce heat and simmer 25 minutes. Beat remaining egg with remaining yolk and parsley, and season with salt and pepper. In a small omelet pan, heat oil, pour in egg mixture and cook until set. Turn out and roll up like a jellyroll, then cut into thin strips. Strain soup through a sieve lined with cheesecloth. Pour into bowls and add strips of omelet.

Makes 4 servings.

Note: To make your own stock, into a large pan, put bones from a chicken, 1 quartered large onion, 2 halved carrots, 2 halved leeks, 2 sliced celery sticks, 1 bay leaf, some parsley stems, 1 bunch of thyme and 6 peppercorns with enough cold water to cover. Bring to a boil, then reduce heat and simmer 2 to 3 hours. Skim off any foam; strain into a large bowl. Cool as quickly as possible. Refrigerate until chilled, then remove any fat from surface. Use within 2 to 3 days or freeze up to 3 months.

VICHYSSOISE

2 tablespoons butter
3 medium-size leeks, trimmed, sliced, washed
1 shallot, finely chopped
8 ozs. potatoes, sliced
3 cups light chicken stock
Pinch ground mace or grated nutmeg
Salt and pepper to taste
2/3 cup half and half
Snipped chives to garnish

Melt butter in a large saucepan. Cook leeks and shallot in butter, covered, over low heat 10 minutes without browning. Add potatoes, stock and mace. Bring to a boil, cover and simmer 20 minutes.

In a food processor fitted with a metal blade or a blender, process mixture to a puree. Strain puree through a sieve set over a bowl. Season with salt and pepper.

Cool and stir in 2/3 of half and half. Refrigerate until ready to serve. Swirl in remaining half and half. Garnish soup with snipped chives.

Makes 6 servings.

SUMMER AVOCADO SOUP

GAZPACHO

2 medium-size ripe avocados
1 tablespoon lemon juice
1 garlic clove, crushed
2/3 cup half and half
2-1/2 cups cold chicken stock
Dash hot-pepper sauce
Salt and pepper to taste
1/2 medium-size avocado and snipped chives to garnish

Cut 2 avocados in half. Remove seeds and scoop flesh into a food processor fitted with a metal blade or a blender. Add lemon juice, garlic and half and half and process to a puree.

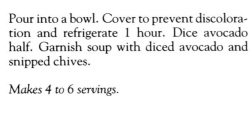

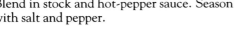

Blend in stock and hot-pepper sauce. Season with salt and pepper.

Pour into a bowl. Cover to prevent discoloration and refrigerate 1 hour. Dice avocado half. Garnish soup with diced avocado and snipped chives.

Makes 4 to 6 servings.

1-1/2 pounds beefsteak tomatoes
1/2 Spanish onion, chopped
1 green bell pepper, chopped
1 red pepper, chopped
2 garlic cloves, chopped
2 slices firm white bread, crusts removed, broken into
   pieces
1-1/4 cups tomato juice
3 tablespoons extra-virgin olive oil
2 tablespoons sherry vinegar
Salt and black pepper
About 8 ice cubes, to serve
ACCOMPANIMENTS:
1 diced small red bell pepper, 1 diced small green bell
   pepper, 1 diced small onion, 1 chopped hard-cooked
   egg and croutons

With a sharp knife, peel, seed and chop tomatoes. In a blender or a food processor with the metal blade, combine tomatoes and remaining soup ingredients, except ice cubes. Process until smooth. Pour soup through a nylon strainer, pressing down well on contents of strainer. If necessary, thin soup with cold water, then cover and refrigerate until chilled.

Place accompaniments in separate bowls. Adjust seasoning of soup, if necessary, then pour into cold soup bowls. Add ice cubes and serve with accompaniments.

Makes 4 servings.

Variation: Do not strain the soup if more texture is preferred.

ZUCCHINI & TOMATO SOUP

2 tablespoons butter
1 medium-size onion, finely chopped
12 ozs. zucchini, coarsely grated
1 garlic clove, crushed
2-1/2 cups vegetable stock
1 (14-oz.) can chopped tomatoes
2 tablespoons chopped fresh mixed herbs, if desired
Salt and pepper to taste
1/4 cup whipping cream and fresh basil leaves to garnish

Melt butter in a large saucepan. Cook onion in butter over medium heat until soft. Stir in zucchini and garlic and cook 4 to 5 minutes.

Stir in stock and tomatoes with juice. Bring to a boil and simmer 15 minutes.

Stir in herbs, if desired, and season with salt and pepper. Garnish with dollops of whipping cream and basil leaves.

Makes 4 servings.

CURRIED PARSNIP SOUP

3 tablespoons butter
1 medium-size onion, chopped
1 teaspoon chopped gingerroot
1 teaspoon curry powder
1/2 teaspoon ground cumin
1 lb. parsnips, chopped
1 medium-size potato, chopped
3-3/4 cups beef stock
2/3 cup plain yogurt
Salt and pepper to taste
Lemon peel strips to garnish
CURRIED CROUTONS
1/2 teaspoon curry powder
Squeeze lemon juice
2 tablespoons butter
2 thick slices bread

Melt butter in a large saucepan. Gently cook onion in butter until soft. Stir in gingerroot, curry powder and cumin and cook 1 minute. Add parsnips and potato and stir over medium heat to coat vegetables with spicy butter. Pour in stock and bring to a boil. Simmer 30 minutes or until vegetables are very tender. In a food processor fitted with a metal blade or a blender, process mixture to a puree. Clean pan and return puree to clean pan. Ladle a small amount of puree into a bowl. Whisk in yogurt, then pour back into puree.

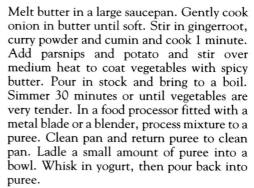

Season soup with salt and pepper and gently reheat. To prepare croutons, preheat oven to 400F (205C). In a small bowl, beat curry powder, lemon juice and butter. Spread on bread. Remove crusts and cut in cubes. Place cubes on a baking sheet and bake in preheated oven until crisp and golden. Garnish soup with croutons and lemon peel strips.

Makes 4 to 6 servings.

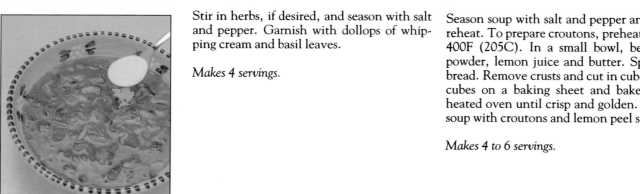

FRENCH ONION SOUP

WINTER VEGETABLE SOUP

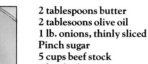

2 tablespoons butter
2 tablesoons olive oil
1 lb. onions, thinly sliced
Pinch sugar
5 cups beef stock
1 bay leaf
Salt and pepper to taste
4 thick slices French bread stick
1 teaspoon Dijon-style mustard
3/4 cup (3 ozs.) shredded Gruyère cheese

Heat butter and oil in a large saucepan. Add onions and sugar.

Cook over medium heat about 20 minutes, stirring occasionally, until onions are a deep golden brown. Add stock and bay leaf and slowly bring to a boil. Simmer 25 minutes. Remove bay leaf and season with salt and pepper.

Toast bread on each side and spread with mustard. Ladle soup into 4 heat-proof bowls and top with toast. Pile cheese onto toast and broil until cheese is melted and bubbling. Serve at once.

Makes 4 servings.

2 tablespoons butter
1 medium-size onion, sliced
8 ozs. carrots, diced
8 ozs. rutabagas, diced
1 medium-size potato, diced
2 large parsnips, diced
2 cups vegetable stock
1 bay leaf
1 tablespoon corstarch
2 cups milk
Salt and pepper to taste
1 cup frozen green peas
2 small bread rolls
1/2 cup (2 ozs.) shredded Cheddar cheese

Melt butter in a large saucepan. Add onion, carrots, rutabagas, potato and parsnips. Cover and cook over low heat 10 minutes. Add stock and bay leaf and simmer 30 minutes. In a small bowl, blend cornstarch with a small amount of milk, then add to soup. Pour remaining milk into soup and heat, stirring until soup thickens. Remove bay leaf and season with salt and pepper.

Stir green peas into soup and simmer over low heat. Cut bread rolls in half. Sprinkle with cheese. Broil until cheese is melted. Serve bread rolls with soup.

Makes 4 servings.

SPICED BLACK BEAN SOUP

HOT & SOUR SOUP

1-1/2 cups dried black beans, soaked, overnight in cold water to cover
2 tablespoons olive oil
1 onion, chopped
1 garlic clove, chopped
1 dried red chile, seeded and chopped
2 carrots, chopped
1 celery stalk, chopped
5 cups vegetable stock
1 teaspoon each toasted coriander seeds, cumin seeds and allspice berries
1 bay leaf
1/2 cup unsalted butter, softened
Grated peel and juice of 1/2 lime
1 tablespoon chopped fresh cilantro
Salt and pepper

5 cups chicken stock
3 tablespoons rice vinegar
1 tablespoon dry sherry
2 teaspoons soy sauce
1 small garlic clove, finely chopped
1/2 teaspoon finely chopped gingerroot
5 dried Chinese mushrooms, soaked in hot water 20 minutes
1 carrot, cut in thin strips
1 (3-oz.) can bamboo shoots, rinsed, cut in thin strips
1/2 teaspoon hot-pepper sauce or chili sauce
2 tablespoons cornstarch
4 ozs. tofu, cut in strips
2 green onions, shredded

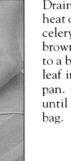

Drain beans; rinse well. In a large saucepan, heat oil. Add onion, garlic, chile, carrots and celery; cook, stirring, 5 minutes or until browned. Add beans and stock. Slowly bring to a boil. Boil 10 minutes. Tie spices and bay leaf in a small piece of cheesecloth. Add to pan. Cover and simmer 1 to 1-1/4 hours or until beans are tender. Discard cheesecloth bag.

Bring stock to a boil in a large saucepan. Stir vinegar, sherry, soy sauce, garlic and gingerroot into stock. Remove stems from mushrooms and slice mushrooms. Add mushrooms, carrot, bamboo shoots and hot-pepper sauce to soup mixture. Bring to a boil, then simmer 10 minutes.

Meanwhile, prepare lime butter. Cream together butter, lime peel, lime juice, chopped cilantro, salt and pepper. Roll into a log shape. Refrigerate until required. To serve, cut log into 12 to 16 slices. In a blender, puree soup. Spoon into bowls and serve topped with 2 slices of lime butter.

Makes 6 to 8 servings.

In a small bowl, blend cornstarch and 3 tablespoons water. Stir cornstarch and water and tofu into soup. Simmer 2 minutes or until thickened. Sprinkle with green onions.

Makes 6 servings.

—CREAM OF MUSHROOM SOUP—

1/4 cup butter
12 ozs. mushrooms, finely chopped
1/2 cup all-purpose flour
2 cups chicken stock
2/3 cup milk
1 tablespoon chopped fresh parsley
1 tablespoon lemon juice
Salt and pepper to taste
2/3 cup half and half
1/4 cup plus 1 tablespoon whipping cream
1 tablespoon finely chopped watercress
Watercress leaves to garnish

Melt butter in a large saucepan. Gently cook mushrooms in butter 5 minutes.

Stir in flour, then gradually add stock and milk. Bring to a boil, then simmer 10 minutes. Add parsley and lemon juice. Season with salt and pepper. Stir in half and half and reheat gently.

In a small bowl, whip cream until soft peaks form. Stir in chopped watercress. Top each portion of soup with watercress chantilly. Garnish with watercress leaves.

Makes 4 servings.

WATERCRESS & ALMOND SOUP

2 large bunches watercress
2 tablespoons butter
1 small onion
2 cups vegetable stock
1/3 cup blanched almonds, toasted, ground
1 tablespoon plus 1 teaspoon cornstarch
2 cups milk
Salt and pepper to taste
Flaked almonds, lightly toasted, to garnish

Wash watercress. Reserve a few sprigs to garnish. Cut away any coarse stalks and chop remainder.

Melt butter in a large saucepan. Saute onion in butter until soft. Add watercress. Cook 2 minutes, then stir in chicken stock. Cover and simmer 10 minutes

In a food processor fitted with a metal blade or a blender, process watercress mixture to a puree. Clean pan and return puree to pan. Stir in ground almonds. In a small bowl, blend cornstarch with a little milk. Add to watercress mixture, then stir in remaining milk. Simmer gently over low heat, stirring constantly, 5 minutes or until smooth. Remove from heat and cool. Refrigerate at least 4 hours or overnight. Garnish soup with flaked almonds and reserved watercress sprigs.

Makes 4 servings.

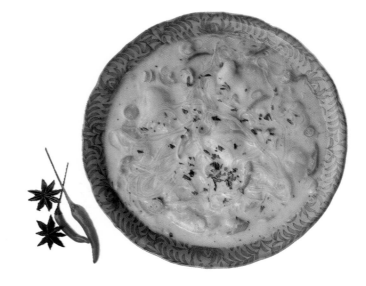

TOMATO, OLIVE & BREAD SOUP

— THAI SHRIMP & NOODLE SOUP —

2 pounds very ripe tomatoes
3 tablespoons olive oil
1 onion, chopped
2 garlic cloves, crushed
4 slices day-old Italian bread, cubed
1 tablespoon chopped fresh sage
2/3 cup dry white wine
2-1/2 cups vegetable stock
1 tablespoon tomato paste
1 teaspoon balsamic vinegar
1/2 cup pitted ripe olives, finely chopped
1 tablespoon finely grated Parmesan cheese

2 cups fish stock
2 stalks lemon grass, crushed and chopped
2 small star anise pods
2 garlic cloves, chopped
2 cups coconut milk
8 large raw shrimp, shelled
4 shelled scallops, halved horizontally
3 ounces clear vermicelli, soaked in cold water 10
    minutes, then drained
2 green onions, thinly sliced
2 fresh red chiles, seeded and sliced
Juice of 1-1/2 limes
1 tablespoon fish sauce
1 tablespoon chopped fresh cilantro

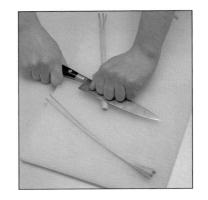

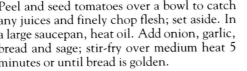

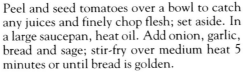

Peel and seed tomatoes over a bowl to catch any juices and finely chop flesh; set aside. In a large saucepan, heat oil. Add onion, garlic, bread and sage; stir-fry over medium heat 5 minutes or until bread is golden.

In a saucepan, bring stock to a boil. Add lemon grass, star anise, and garlic, then simmer, uncovered, 5 minutes. Cover and let stand 30 minutes.

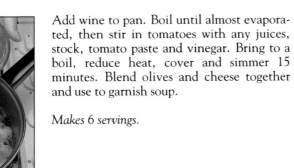

Add wine to pan. Boil until almost evaporated, then stir in tomatoes with any juices, stock, tomato paste and vinegar. Bring to a boil, reduce heat, cover and simmer 15 minutes. Blend olives and cheese together and use to garnish soup.

Makes 6 servings.

To pan, add coconut milk. Heat to simmering point. Add shrimp and scallops. Poach 1 minute, then add noodles, green onions, and chiles and cook 1 minute longer until shrimp are pink. Remove pan from heat and stir in lime juice, fish sauce, and chopped cilantro.

Makes 4 servings.

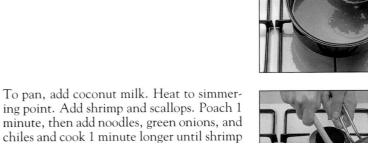

—MEDITERRANEAN FISH SOUP—

2-1/2 pounds mixed fish and shellfish, such as
   monkfish, red mullet, bass, bream, snapper, shrimp,
   and mussels
Pinch saffron threads, toasted and crushed
5 tablespoons olive oil
2 Spanish onions, sliced
1 stalk celery, sliced
3 garlic cloves, chopped
3 large tomatoes, peeled
Bouquet garni of 1 bay leaf, sprig each dried thyme and
   fennel, 3 parsley sprigs, and a strip dried orange peel
5-1/2 cups fish stock
Salt and pepper
Torn basil or chopped fresh parsley to garnish
French bread to serve

Skin and fillet fish and cut into fairly large
pieces. Remove shellfish from their shells.
Soak saffron in 2 tablespoons warm water 10
minutes. In a large saucepan, heat oil. Add
onions, celery, and garlic and cook gently
until softened. Chop tomatoes and add to
pan with bouquet garni. Arrange fish on
vegetables. Add saffron liquid, then pour in
sufficient stock to cover fish. Simmer,
uncovered, 6 minutes.

To the pan, add any shellfish and mussels.
Simmer 3 to 4 minutes longer until shellfish
are just tender and mussels open; discard any
mussels that remain closed. Season with salt
and pepper. Serve garnished with basil or
parsley and accompanied by French bread.

Makes 6 servings.

—CRAB & CORN SOUP—

3-3/4 cups chicken stock
1 small piece gingerroot, peeled
2 teaspoons light soy sauce
1 tablespoon dry sherry
1 (15-oz.) can creamed corn
Salt and pepper to taste
2 teaspoons cornstarch
2 tablespoons water
4 ozs. crabmeat
2 eggs, beaten
2 green onions, finely sliced, to garnish

In a large saucepan, combine stock and
gingerroot. Simmer for 15 minutes.

Remove gingerroot and stir in soy sauce,
sherry and creamed corn. Season with salt
and pepper. Simmer 5 minutes. In a small
bowl, blend cornstarch and water. Stir into
stock mixture. Stir in crabmeat and heat
until mixture thickens.

Bring mixture to a slow simmer and slowly
pour in beaten eggs in a thin stream, stirring
constantly. Do not allow soup to boil.
Garnish soup with sliced green onions.

Makes 4 to 6 servings.

CREAM OF CHICKEN SOUP

MULLIGATAWNY

2 tablespoons butter or margarine
1 small leek, diced
1/3 cup all-purpose flour
3-3/4 cups chicken stock
2/3 cup dry white wine
1 cup finely chopped cooked chicken
Pinch of nutmeg
2/3 cup half and half
2 teaspoons snipped fresh chives
2/3 cup thick sour cream and croutons, to serve

In a saucepan, melt butter over low heat. Add leek; sauté until soft. Stir in flour. Cook over low heat 1 to 2 minutes.

Remove pan from heat. Slowly add stock, a little at a time, stirring well. Return to heat and bring to a boil, stirring until thickened.

1 lb. boneless beef stew meat, cut in pieces
1 (2-inch) piece gingerroot, peeled
2 bay leaves
1 medium-size onion, chopped
1 teaspoon turmeric
1/2 teaspoon chili powder
2 teaspoons coriander seeds, crushed
2 teaspoons cumin seeds, crushed
8 black peppercorns, crushed
1 small cooking apple, peeled, cored, chopped
1 carrot, sliced
2 tablespoons red lentils
2 garlic cloves, chopped
Salt to taste
1 tablespoon lemon juice
GARLIC CROUTONS
2 thick slices bread
1/4 cup plus 2 tablespoons vegetable oil
3 garlic cloves, crushed

In a large saucepan, cover beef with 7-1/2 cups water. Bring to a boil. Skim surface and add remaining ingredients except lemon juice. Simmer very gently 2-1/2 to 3 hours or until beef is tender. Meanwhile, to prepare croutons, cut off crusts from bread and dice bread. Heat oil in a medium-size skillet. Fry diced bread and garlic, turning bread constantly until crisp and golden. Remove with a slotted spoon and drain on a paper towel.

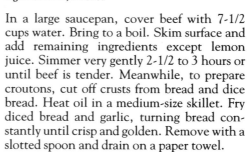

Add wine. Cover and simmer 15 minutes. Add chicken and nutmeg and simmer 5 minutes longer. Pour in half and half and heat until hot without boiling. Stir in chives. Serve in warmed bowls with spoonfuls of sour cream and croutons.

Makes 4 servings.

Remove beef and set aside. Pour stock through a sieve set over a bowl, rubbing vegetables through. Discard pulp. Cool, then refrigerate meat and stock until chilled. Remove solidified fat from surface of soup. Pour into a pan and reheat. Cut beef in small pieces. Add beef and lemon juice to soup and season again with salt, if necessary. Simmer 5 minutes. Garnish soup with croutons.

Makes 4 to 6 servings.

COCK-A-LEEKIE SOUP

6 chicken thighs, skinned
4-1/2 cups chicken stock
3 leeks

In a large pan, put chicken thighs with chicken stock. Simmer 35 to 40 minutes.

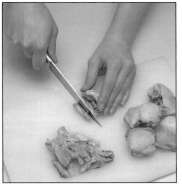

Meanwhile, wash leeks; slice into rings. Remove cooked chicken from stock with a slotted spoon. Remove meat from bones. Cut meat into bite-size pieces. Set aside.

Increase heat and bring stock to a low boil. Add prepared leeks. Cook 3 to 4 minutes until leeks are just tender. Add chicken to pan and simmer 2 to 3 minutes. Serve hot with warm rolls.

Makes 4 servings.

PHEASANT & LENTIL SOUP

1 small pheasant, cleaned
7-1/2 cups water
1 onion, thickly sliced
1 large carrot, thickly sliced
2 stalks celery, chopped
1 bay leaf
8 peppercorns
Fresh thyme sprig
2/3 cup brown lentils
2 small leeks, trimmed, chopped
Salt and pepper to taste

In a large saucepan, cover pheasant with water. Bring slowly to a boil and skim off scum from surface.

Add onion, carrot, celery, bay leaf, peppercorns and thyme sprig. Cover and simmer 45 minutes. Remove pheasant and cool. Remove breast meat. Return carcass to stock and cook 2 hours. Strain stock through a sieve set over a bowl. Cool and refrigerate stock and reserved breast meat and best bits of leg meat overnight. Next day, remove layer of fat from soup. Measure stock and return to pan. Bring to a boil. Reduce stock to 6 cups by simmering, adding water if necessary.

Add lentils and leeks to stock. Cover and simmer 45 minutes or until lentils are tender. Meanwhile, dice reserved meat and add to soup. Season with salt and pepper and simmer a few minutes until heated through.

Makes 6 servings.

SCOTCH BROTH

2 lbs. neck of lamb, cut in pieces
6 cups light stock
1/4 cup pearl barley
Salt and pepper to taste
1 large onion, chopped
2 leeks, trimmed, chopped
2 stalks celery, chopped
1 small turnip, diced
1 large carrot, sliced
Bouquet garni

In a large saucepan, combine lamb and stock. Bring slowly to a boil and skim off any scum that rises to surface.

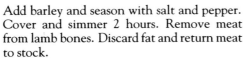

Add barley and season with salt and pepper. Cover and simmer 2 hours. Remove meat from lamb bones. Discard fat and return meat to stock.

Add remaining ingredients to stock and bring back to a simmer. Cook 30 minutes or until vegetables are tender. Discard bouquet garni. Season again with salt and pepper, if necessary.

Makes 6 servings.

GOULASH SOUP

2 tablespoons vegetable oil
1 lb. lean beef stew meat, cut in 1/4-inch cubes
1 large onion, thinly sliced
1 garlic, crushed
1/2 teaspoon ground cumin
2 teaspoons paprika
1 tablespoon all-purpose flour
5 cups beef stock
1 large potato
1 (14-oz.) can tomatoes, chopped, with juice
Salt and pepper to taste
Sour cream and paprika to garnish.

Heat oil in a large saucepan and add beef and onion.

Cook over medium heat 4 minutes or until beef is brown and onion is soft. Stir in garlic, cumin, paprika and flour and cook 1 minute. Gradually add stock. Bring to a boil, then simmer 2 hours.

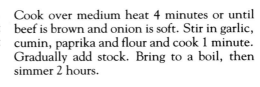

Dice potatoes. Add potatoes and tomatoes with juice to soup. Season with salt and pepper. Cook 30 minutes or until potatoes are tender. Garnish soup with sour cream and sprinkle with paprika.

Makes 6 servings.

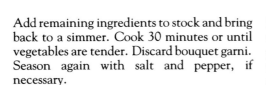

APPETIZERS & STARTERS

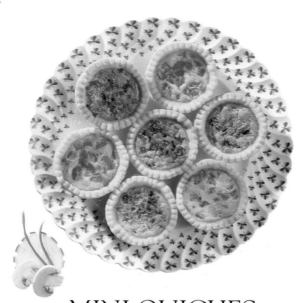

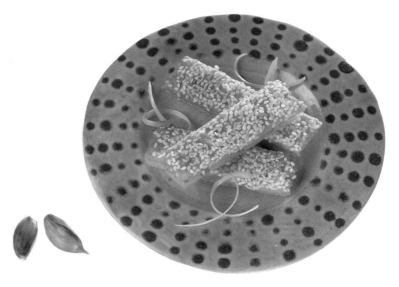

MINI QUICHES

1-1/2 recipes Pie Crust Dough
3 egg yolks
1 egg
Salt and pepper
1-1/4 cups whipping cream
MUSHROOM FILLING:
1 tablespoon butter
1-1/2 cups finely chopped mushrooms
BELL PEPPER FILLING:
1 tablespoon butter
1 red bell pepper, chopped

Preheat oven to 400F (205C). Grease 12 individual 2-1/2-inch quiche pans.

To make mushroom filling, in a small pan, melt the 1 tablespoon butter. Add mushrooms and cook gently until softened and all liquid has evaporated. Set aside. To make bell pepper filling, in another small pan, melt remaining 1 tablespoon butter. Add bell pepper and cook gently until beginning to soften. Set aside. On a floured surface, roll out pastry to 1/8 inch thick. Use to line prepared pans; prick bottoms with a fork.

Press a square of foil into each dough case. Bake blind 15 minutes, removing foil after 12 minutes. In a bowl, beat together egg yolks, egg, salt, pepper and cream. Put half the mixture in a bowl with the mushrooms and half in a bowl with the bell pepper. Divide the 2 fillings among baked pastry shells. Return to oven and cook 15 minutes longer, just until firm. Serve warm or at room temperature.

Makes 12.

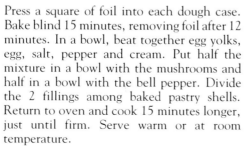

SESAME CHICKEN TOASTS

2 large green onions
2 garlic cloves, crushed
1 (1-inch) piece gingerroot, finely chopped
1/3 pound skinned and boned chicken
2 tablespoons cornstarch
2 teaspoons light soy sauce
2 teaspoons oyster sauce
10 day-old white bread slices
1/3 cup sesame seeds
Vegetable oil, for frying
Green onion strips, to garnish

In a blender or food processor, process onions, garlic, gingerroot, chicken, cornstarch, soy and oyster sauces until smooth.

With a sharp knife, cut crusts off bread and spread each slice with a generous layer of chicken mixture. Sprinkle with a layer of sesame seeds. Place on a tray and refrigerate at least 20 minutes.

Pour 2 inches of oil into a deep pan. Heat to 375F (190C) or until an 1-inch bread cube browns in 40 seconds. Cut each topped bread slice into 3 pieces. Fry, a few at a time, until golden-brown. Drain on paper towels and serve hot. Garnish with green onion strips.

Makes 30 appetizers.

CHICKEN APRICOT BAGS

1/2 tablespoon vegetable oil, for frying, plus extra for brushing
1/2 onion, finely chopped
1/2 cup finely chopped dried apricots
1 cup finely diced cooked chicken
1/4 cup plain yogurt
2 tablespoons chopped fresh cilantro
Salt and pepper
3 sheets filo pastry dough
Watercress, to garnish

Preheat oven to 375F (190C). In a small pan, heat the 1/2 tablespoon oil. Add onion; cook 3 to 4 minutes or until softened. Add chopped apricots and cook 2 minutes.

Into a bowl, put onion mixture. Add chicken, yogurt, cilantro, salt and pepper; mix well. Cut each sheet of filo pastry dough in half, then cut each half into quarters to make 16 (4-inch) squares.

Brush each dough square with a little oil. Place a spoonful of chicken mixture in center. Gather up corners of the square and pinch together to form a loose bag. Place filo bags on 2 baking sheets. Bake 10 to 12 minutes or until the dough is crisp and golden. Serve warm. Garnish with watercress.

Makes 16 appetizers.

ANGELS ON HORSEBACK

4 slices bacon
8 oysters, shelled
4 slices bread
Unsalted butter for spreading
Pepper
Mâche and lemon twists to garnish

Preheat broiler. Cut each bacon slice across in half, then stretch each piece with the back of a knife. Wrap a piece of bacon around each oyster, then place on a broiler tray with ends of bacon underneath.

Toast bread. Broil oysters until crisp, then turn over and crisp the other side.

Meanwhile, cut 2 circles from each slice of toast, then butter circles. Place one oyster on each circle. Grind black pepper over and serve garnished with mâche and lemon twists.

Makes 8.

CHEESE & HERB TRIANGLES

IMAM BAYALDI

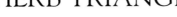

1/4 pound feta cheese
1/2 cup cottage cheese
1/2 beaten egg
1 tablespoon chopped fresh parsley
1 tablespoon chopped fresh mint
1 tablespoon snipped fresh chives
Pepper
4 sheets filo pastry
1/4 cup butter

2 small eggplants
Salt
1/4 cup extra-virgin olive oil
1 large onion, chopped
1 garlic clove, crushed
1 red bell pepper, seeded and chopped
2 tablespoons tomato paste
2 ounces sun-dried tomatoes in oil, drained and
   chopped
1/2 teaspoon sugar
1 teaspoon wine vinegar
Pepper
Toasted pine nuts and cilantro leaves, to garnish

Into a bowl, crumble feta cheese. Add cottage cheese, egg, parsley, mint, chives and pepper. Blend together with a fork.

Cut eggplants into 1/4-inch slices. Sprinkle with salt and put into a colander to drain 30 minutes. Preheat oven to 350F (175C). In a skillet, heat 2 tablespoons of the olive oil, add onion, garlic and bell pepper. Cook about 10 minutes until onion is soft. Add tomato paste, sun-dried tomatoes, sugar, vinegar and pepper.

Preheat oven to 375F (190C). Butter a baking sheet. Lay the sheets of dough in a pile on a work surface. Keep covered while working with one sheet at a time. In a small saucepan melt butter. Brush one sheet of dough with butter. Cut it into 4 long strips.

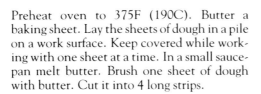

Place a teaspoon of filling in one corner of dough strip. Fold a corner of dough over filling. Turn triangle over and over to the end of the strip. Repeat with remaining dough. Brush tops of triangles with butter. Bake in the oven 10 to 12 minutes or until crisp and brown.

Makes 16.

Pat eggplant slices dry with paper towels. Arrange slices in a baking pan. Put a teaspoonful of tomato mixture onto each eggplant slice. Drizzle remaining olive oil over and around eggplants. Cover pan and bake 40 to 50 minutes until eggplants are tender. Serve garnished with toasted pine nuts and cilantro leaves.

Makes 6 servings.

STUFFED ARTICHOKE BOTTOMS

6 hard-cooked eggs, finely chopped
7 to 9 tablespoons extra-virgin olive oil
2 tablespoons white wine vinegar
1/2 red bell pepper packed in wine vinegar, drained and
  chopped
2 tablespoons capers in wine vinegar, drained and
  chopped
2 tablespoons chopped Italian parsley
Salt and freshly ground pepper
1 (14-oz) can artichoke bottoms, drained
3 tablespoons extra-virgin olive oil
Juice of 1/2 lemon
1 teaspoon coriander seeds, crushed
Italian parsley sprigs to garnish

Place eggs in a bowl then, using a wooden spoon, gradually stir in 4 tablespoons of the oil and the vinegar; the mixture should be stiff enough to hold its shape but if too dry add a little more olive oil. Stir in bell pepper, capers and parsley and season with salt and freshly ground pepper.

Divide egg mixture among artichoke bottoms and arrange on a serving plate. Drizzle with the 3 tablespoons olive oil and lemon juice and sprinkle with coriander seeds. Cover and refrigerate at least 1 hour. Serve garnished with Italian parsley sprigs.

Makes 4 to 6 servings.

LEEKS A LA GRECQUE

8-10 young small leeks
3 tablespoons extra-virgin olive oil
2 tablespoons fresh lemon juice
1 garlic clove, crushed
Salt and pepper
1 tablespoon chopped fresh mint
Slivers of sun-dried tomatoes and mint leaves, to
  garnish

With a sharp knife, cut root ends off leeks and trim tops down to white parts. Wash very carefully.

In a non-reactive saucepan, put olive oil, lemon juice, 1/2 cup water, garlic, salt and pepper. Bring to a boil. Add leeks, cover and cook 10 to 15 minutes or until leeks are tender.

Transfer leeks to a serving dish. If there is a lot of liquid, boil to reduce and thicken slightly, then pour it over the leeks. Scatter chopped mint over the top and leave until cool. Serve garnished with slivers of sun-dried tomatoes and mint leaves.

Makes 8 servings.

Variation: Substitute pearl onions for leeks.

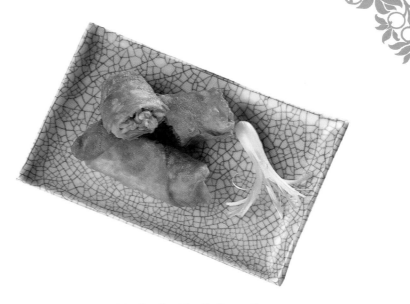

FRITTO MISTO

About 3/4 cup all-purpose flour
Salt and freshly ground pepper
2 eggs, beaten
About 2 cups dry bread crumbs
4 lamb kidneys, halved and cored
8 ounces calves' liver, cut into strips
8 ounces fresh spicy Italian sausages, cut into bite-size
    pieces
1 small eggplant, sliced
2 medium-size zucchini, thickly sliced
Vegetable oil for deep-frying
Italian parsley sprigs to garnish

Put flour into a shallow dish; season with salt and freshly ground pepper. Put eggs into a second shallow dish and bread crumbs into a third dish. Dip kidneys, liver, sausages, eggplant and zucchini first in seasoned flour, then in eggs and finally in bread crumbs to coat evenly.

Half-fill a deep-fat fryer with oil. Preheat to 350F (175C). Deep-fry meats and vegetables, in batches, 2 to 4 minutes, turning once, until crisp and golden. Using a slotted spoon, transfer to paper towels to drain. Serve hot garnished with parsley sprigs.

Makes 6 to 8 servings.

EGG ROLLS

2 tablespoons vegetable oil
1 garlic clove, finely chopped
1 (1-inch) piece gingerroot, finely chopped
4 ounces chicken breast meat, shredded
1/3 cup finely sliced snow peas
2-1/3 cups finely sliced shiitake mushrooms
8 green onions, finely chopped
1/2 cup chopped shelled, cooked shrimp
1 tablespoon soy sauce
1 teaspoon sesame oil
10 ounces filo pastry dough
1 egg white, for brushing
Vegetable oil, for deep frying
Green onion brushes, to garnish
Chile and hoisin sauce dips

In a wok or large skillet, heat the 2 table-spoons oil. Add garlic and gingerroot; stir-fry 15 seconds. Add chicken; stir-fry 2 to 3 minutes. Add snow peas, mushrooms, green onions and shrimp followed by the soy sauce and sesame oil. Mix well and transfer to a bowl to cool. Cut filo pastry dough into 16 (7-inch) squares. On a board, place a square with a corner toward you. Cover with another square of dough to make 2 layers.

Place 1 large tablespoon of mixture just below center of dough. Fold bottom corner over and then 2 side corners in to make an elongated open envelope. Brush dough with egg white and roll up, pressing gently. Repeat with remaining filo pastry dough and filling. Pour about 3 inches of oil into a deep pan; heat to 375F (190C) or until an 1-inch bread cube browns in 40 seconds. Add egg rolls in batches; fry about 4 minutes or until golden. Drain on paper towels. Serve with dips.

Makes 4 servings.

DOLMADES

20 vacuum-packed grape leaves
1 cup boiling water
1/2 cup long-grain rice
3 tablespoons extra-virgin olive oil
1 small onion, finely chopped
1/3 cup pine nuts
1/4 cup raisins
2 tablespoons chopped fresh mint
1/4 teaspoon ground cinnamon
Salt and pepper
2 tablespoons tomato paste
2 teaspoons fresh lemon juice
Lemon slices and fresh mint, to garnish (optional)

Rinse grape leaves and place in a saucepan of boiling water. Simmer 5 minutes. Drain. In a small saucepan, combine the 1 cup boiling water and rice, cover and simmer until rice is almost cooked. Drain, if necessary. In a skillet, heat 2 tablespoons of the oil. Add onion and cook until soft. Add pine nuts and cook until lightly browned. Stir in raisins, mint, cinnamon, salt, pepper and rice. Let cool.

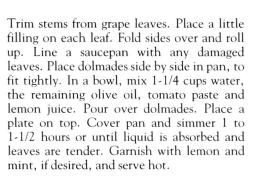

Trim stems from grape leaves. Place a little filling on each leaf. Fold sides over and roll up. Line a saucepan with any damaged leaves. Place dolmades side by side in pan, to fit tightly. In a bowl, mix 1-1/4 cups water, the remaining olive oil, tomato paste and lemon juice. Pour over dolmades. Place a plate on top. Cover pan and simmer 1 to 1-1/2 hours or until liquid is absorbed and leaves are tender. Garnish with lemon and mint, if desired, and serve hot.

Makes 20.

FENNEL WITH FETA & PEARS

2 fennel bulbs
4 tablespoons olive oil
6 ounces vegetarian feta cheese
1 ripe pear
4 sun-dried tomatoes in oil, drained and sliced
1/4 cup pitted ripe olives
Few basil leaves
1 teaspoon lemon juice
1/2 teaspoon honey
Salt and pepper

Preheat broiler. Trim fennel, discarding any damaged outer leaves. Cut each bulb, lengthwise, into 6 thin slices.

Brush each fennel piece with a little olive oil. Place on a baking sheet. Broil 2 to 3 minutes or until browned. Turn fennel, brush with oil and broil 2 to 3 minutes until charred and just tender. Cool slightly.

With a sharp knife, slice feta cheese into thin slabs. Quarter, core and thinly slice pear. Arrange fennel, cheese and pear on serving plates. Top with the tomatoes, olives and basil. In a small bowl, blend remaining oil, lemon juice, honey, salt and pepper together. Drizzle over salad and serve.

Makes 4 servings.

SHRIMP WITH MELON

CRAB & GINGER TRIANGLES

12 cooked jumbo shrimp
1 small Charentais or cantaloupe melon
1 small Galia melon
Juice of 1 small lemon
Salt and freshly ground pepper
Mint leaves to garnish

Peel shrimp leaving the tail tips on, if desired.

1 (7-oz.) can crabmeat, drained
6 green onions, finely chopped
1-inch piece gingerroot, peeled and grated
2 teaspoons soy sauce
Salt and pepper
6 large sheets filo pastry, each about 14 inches square
6 tablespoons butter, melted
TO GARNISH:
Green onion slivers or curls

In a bowl, mix together crabmeat, green onions, gingerroot, soy sauce, salt and pepper. Set aside.

Cut melons into thin wedges and remove skins.

Preheat oven to 350F (175C). Lightly grease a baking sheet. Work with 1 sheet of pastry at a time, keeping remainder covered with a damp cloth. Cut sheet of pastry in half. Brush each half with melted butter and fold in half lengthwise. Brush pastry all over with melted butter. Put a portion of crab mixture in 1 corner of 1 strip of pastry. Fold pastry and filling over at right angles to make a triangle, then continue folding in this way along strip of pastry to make a triangular package.

Arrange shrimp and the two different colored varieties of melon on a platter or individual plates and sprinkle with lemon juice. Season with salt and freshly ground pepper. Serve garnished with mint leaves.

Makes 4 to 6 servings.

Repeat with remaining pastry and crab mixture. Brush each triangle with melted butter. Bake 20 to 25 minutes, until crisp and golden-brown. Serve warm, garnished with green onion slivers or curls.

Makes 12.

SHRIMP & FETA TARTS

6 ounces shelled cooked shrimp
4 ounces feta cheese
Fresh basil leaves, to garnish
PASTRY:
1-1/2 cups all-purpose flour
1/2 teaspoon salt
3 tablespoons extra-virgin olive oil
1 egg, beaten
TOMATO SAUCE:
2 tablespoons extra-virgin olive oil
1 onion, chopped
1 garlic clove, crushed
Half (14-oz.) can chopped tomatoes
1 tablespoon chopped sun-dried tomato
2 teaspoons chopped fresh basil
Salt and pepper

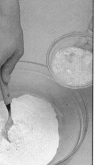

To make Pastry, into a bowl, sift flour and salt. With a fork, mix in olive oil, egg and 1 to 2 teaspoons water to make a firm dough. Knead lightly, wrap in plastic wrap and refrigerate 1 hour. To make Tomato Sauce, in a skillet, heat oil. Add onion and garlic and cook until soft. Add tomatoes. Cook 5 to 10 minutes or until sauce is very thick. Stir in basil, salt and pepper. Preheat oven to 400F (205C).

On a floured surface, roll out dough thinly. Line 4 (4-inch) loose-bottom tart pans with dough and press a piece of foil into each. Bake 10 minutes. Remove foil; bake 5 minutes. Divide shrimp among pastry cases. Crumble cheese over shrimp. Spread Tomato Sauce over cheese and shrimp. Bake 5 minutes. Serve garnished with basil leaves.

Makes 4 servings.

SEAFOOD PARCELS

2/3 cup butter
1/4 cup all-purpose flour
2/3 cup milk
2 tablespoons fresh lemon juice
1 garlic clove, crushed
1 tablespoon each chopped fresh mint, chopped fresh
    cilantro and chopped fresh parsley
Pinch of red (cayenne) pepper
Pinch of paprika
1/2 teaspoon ground cumin
Salt
3 ounces cooked mussels
2 ounces cooked shelled shrimp
2 ounces cooked squid or white fish
6 sheets filo pastry, thawed if frozen

Preheat oven to 375F (190C). In a saucepan, melt 2 tablespoons of the butter. Stir in flour, then gradually stir in milk. Stirring, cook sauce until thick. Stir in lemon juice, garlic, mint, cilantro, parsley, cayenne, paprika, cumin and salt. Remove from heat. Gently stir in mussels, shrimp and squid or white fish.

Melt remaining butter. Brush over 1 sheet filo dough, place another sheet on top and butter it. Repeat with 2 more sheets of dough. Cut into 12 squares. Butter remaining 2 sheets of dough. Place one on top of the other. Cut in half. Pile the 4 sheets together; cut into 6 squares. Place some filling in middle of each square. Draw dough up and pinch together to form pouches. Place on a baking sheet. Bake 30 minutes or until brown and crisp.

Makes 18.

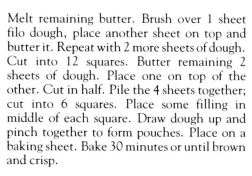

STUFFED MUSSELS

3 pounds large mussels in their shells
1/3 cup dry white wine
1/3 cup olive oil
1/2 cup fresh bread crumbs
3 tablespoon finely chopped fresh parsley
1 tablespoon finely chopped fresh oregano
2 garlic cloves, finely crushed
Pinch of red (cayenne) pepper
Salt and freshly ground black pepper
1 large lemon, quartered
Parsley sprigs, to garnish

Scrub mussels and remove beards. Discard any mussels that remain open when tapped firmly. Into a large saucepan, put mussels and wine.

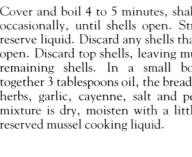

Cover and boil 4 to 5 minutes, shaking pan occasionally, until shells open. Strain and reserve liquid. Discard any shells that do not open. Discard top shells, leaving mussels on remaining shells. In a small bowl, stir together 3 tablespoons oil, the bread crumbs, herbs, garlic, cayenne, salt and pepper. If mixture is dry, moisten with a little of the reserved mussel cooking liquid.

Preheat broiler. Divide bread-crumb mixture among mussels on their shells. Place on a baking sheet. Drizzle with remaining olive oil and broil 1 to 2 minutes or until topping is crisp and golden. Squeeze lemon juice over mussels and serve garnished with parsley sprigs.

Makes 4 to 6 servings.

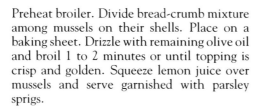

PIQUANT SALMON ROLLS

4 oz. cream cheese
1/4 cup walnuts, chopped
1 tablespoon chopped fresh chives
1 stalk celery, chopped
3 teaspoons lemon juice
Several pinches cayenne pepper
1/4 teaspoon ground coriander
8 (4 × 2 in.) thin slices smoked salmon
8 thin slices whole-wheat bread
Butter
8 thin slices cucumber
Freshly ground pepper
Fresh dill sprigs and chives, if desired

In a bowl, soften cream cheese and stir in walnuts, chives and celery.

Add 2 teaspoons of lemon juice and spices and mix well. Spread cream cheese mixture on each slice of salmon and season with pepper. Roll up to form neat rolls.

Toast slices of bread and cut 8 (2-1/2-inch) rounds, using a biscuit cutter. Spread thinly with butter. Place a cucumber slice on each bread round and place a salmon roll on top of each cucumber. Drizzle with remaining lemon juice and garnish, if desired.

Makes 4 servings.

Note: Salmon rolls can be prepared several hours in advance and refrigerated. Toast bases, however, are better freshly made. Once assembled, serve within 30 minutes.

TUNA PATE

3 tablespoons butter
4 green onions, white part only, chopped
2 celery stalks, finely chopped
1 (7-oz.) can tuna in water, drained
2 tomatoes, peeled, seeded and chopped
2 tablespoons mayonnaise
1 teaspoon lemon juice
1 teaspoon white wine vinegar
Salt and freshly ground pepper
Chopped Italian parsley, parsley leaves and pitted green
    olives to garnish
Crusty bread or toast to serve

Melt butter in a small skillet over low heat. Add green onions and celery; cook 5 minutes to soften. Let cool.

Put green onion mixture in a blender or food processor with remaining ingredients, except garnish and bread. Process until fairly smooth. Transfer to a serving dish, cover and refrigerate at least 30 minutes. Garnish with chopped parsley, parsley leaves and green olives and serve with crusty bread or toast.

Makes 4 to 6 servings.

SIZZLING SHRIMP

1/2 cup olive oil
4 garlic cloves, finely crushed
1 small fresh red chile, seeded and chopped
3/4 pound raw shrimp, shelled
Sea salt
2 tablespoons chopped fresh parsley
Lemon wedges and bread, to serve

In 4 individual flameproof dishes over high heat, heat oil. Add garlic and chile and cook 1 to 2 minutes, then add shrimp and sea salt.

Cook 2 to 3 minutes, stirring occasionally. Stir in parsley. Serve quickly so the shrimp are sizzling in the oil, and accompany with lemon wedges and bread to mop up the juices.

Makes 4 servings.

Note: One large dish, or a skillet, can be used instead of individual dishes.

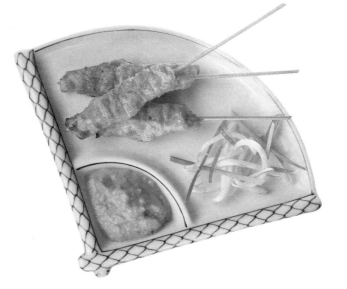

CHICKEN & HAM MOUSSE

1-1/3 cups finely ground cooked chicken
1 cup finely ground cooked ham
1 tablespoon fresh lemon juice
1 tablespoon chopped fresh parsley
1 tablespoon snipped fresh chives
2/3 cup mayonnaise
2 teaspoons unflavored gelatin powder
3 tablespoons chicken stock
2/3 cup whipping cream
Chives and lemon wedges, to garnish

In a bowl, mix chicken with ham, lemon juice, chopped herbs and mayonnaise.

In a small pan, sprinkle gelatin over chicken stock; leave 5 minutes to soften. Over low heat, melt very gently until gelatin dissolves, Remove from heat; cool. Fold into ham and chicken mixture.

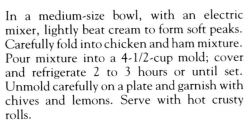

In a medium-size bowl, with an electric mixer, lightly beat cream to form soft peaks. Carefully fold into chicken and ham mixture. Pour mixture into a 4-1/2-cup mold; cover and refrigerate 2 to 3 hours or until set. Unmold carefully on a plate and garnish with chives and lemons. Serve with hot crusty rolls.

Makes 4 servings.

CHICKEN SATE

12 ounces skinned and boned chicken breasts, cut into
    long, thin strips
1 tablespoon grated gingerroot
1 teaspoon ground coriander
1 teaspoon turmeric
1-1/2 teaspoons chile powder
1 teaspoon brown sugar
2 tablespoons light soy sauce
2 tablespoons sesame oil
2 garlic cloves, crushed
Juice of 1 lime
1/2 cup chopped onion
2 ounces creamed coconut
2/3 cup boiling water
3 tablespoons crunchy peanut butter

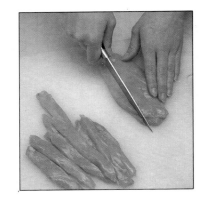

Arrange chicken in a shallow bowl. In a blender or food processor, blend together gingerroot, coriander, turmeric, 1/2 teaspoon of the chile powder, sugar, soy sauce, 1 tablespoon of the sesame oil, garlic and lime juice. Pour over chicken, cover and refrigerate 3 to 4 hours. To make sauce: In a skillet, heat remaining 1 tablespoon sesame oil. Add half of the onion; cook until softened. Preheat broiler.

In a blender or food processor, blend remaining onion, creamed coconut and chile powder and boiling water. Add this paste to cooked onion. Stir in peanut butter and 2 tablespoons of the marinade. Simmer 5 minutes, stirring occasionally, or until thickened. Thread chicken onto skewers. Broil 15 to 20 minutes, turning frequently. Serve with peanut sauce for dipping.

Makes 4 servings.

BROILED FIVE-SPICE CHICKEN

CHICKEN LIVER TOASTS

2 boneless, skinless chicken breasts, each weighing
   6 oz., trimmed
2 small red bell peppers, halved
2 small yellow bell peppers, halved
Chopped fresh chives, to garnish
MARINADE:
1 garlic clove, crushed
1 fresh red chile, seeded and chopped
3 tablespoons light soy sauce
1 teaspoon five-spice powder
1 teaspoon brown sugar
2 teaspoons sesame oil

3 tablespoons olive oil
1 celery stalk, finely chopped
2 garlic cloves, crushed
8 ounces chicken livers, chopped
1 teaspoon chopped fresh sage
1/4 cup marsala wine
2 anchovy fillets canned in oil, drained
1 tablespoon capers in wine vinegar, drained
Freshly ground pepper
1 medium-size loaf French bread
Capers and fresh sage leaves to garnish

Preheat oven to 375F (190C). Heat oil in a
large skillet. Add celery and garlic and cook 2
minutes to soften.

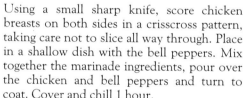

Using a small sharp knife, score chicken
breasts on both sides in a crisscross pattern,
taking care not to slice all way through. Place
in a shallow dish with the bell peppers. Mix
together the marinade ingredients, pour over
the chicken and bell peppers and turn to
coat. Cover and chill 1 hour.

Add chicken livers and fry over high heat
about 3 minutes, stirring occasionally, until
crisp and brown on outside but still pink
inside. Using a wooden spoon, stir in sage
and marsala, scraping up all the cooking
juices. Transfer to a blender or food processor
and add anchovy fillets and capers. Season
with freshly ground pepper and process until
fairly smooth. Transfer to a warmed plate,
cover and place over a saucepan of hot water
to keep warm.

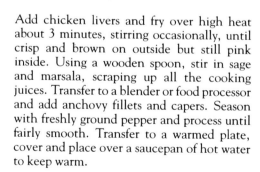

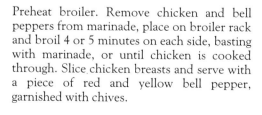

Preheat broiler. Remove chicken and bell
peppers from marinade, place on broiler rack
and broil 4 or 5 minutes on each side, basting
with marinade, or until chicken is cooked
through. Slice chicken breasts and serve with
a piece of red and yellow bell pepper,
garnished with chives.

Makes 4 servings.

Cut bread diagonally into thick slices and lay
on a baking sheet. Bake in preheated oven 6
to 7 minutes until golden. Serve the chicken
liver paste on the baked bread, and garnish
with capers and sage leaves.

Makes 6 to 8 servings.

SOUVLAKIA

2 garlic cloves, crushed
1/4 cup fresh lemon juice
2 tablespoons extra-virgin olive oil
4 tablespoons chopped fresh oregano
Salt and pepper
1 pound lean lamb
6 bay leaves
Fresh oregano sprigs, to garnish
RED PEPPER SAUCE:
1 tablespoon extra-virgin olive oil
1 small onion, chopped
2 red bell peppers, chopped
1 cup chicken stock

In a bowl, mix together garlic, lemon juice, olive oil, oregano, salt and pepper. Cut lamb into 3/4-inch cubes. Add lamb to marinade and stir to coat lamb with marinade. Cover and refrigerate 2 hours. To make the sauce, in a saucepan, heat oil, add onion and cook until soft. Add bell peppers and cook 5 minutes. Pour in stock and simmer 10 minutes. Press through a strainer or puree in a blender or food processor.

Thread lamb onto skewers, placing bay leaves on skewers at intervals. Preheat grill or broiler. Cook, turning occasionally, 10 minutes or until lamb is brown and crisp on the outside and pink and juicy inside. Garnish with oregano and serve with the sauce.

Makes 6 servings.

PORK & LIVER PATE

12 ounces bacon slices
8 ounces lean pork, chopped
8 ounces pork liver, chopped
8 ounces pork sausage
1 small onion, finely chopped
2 garlic cloves, chopped
1 tablespoon chopped thyme
1 tablespoon chopped oregano
3 tablespoons marsala wine
Salt and freshly ground pepper
Thyme and oregano sprigs to garnish

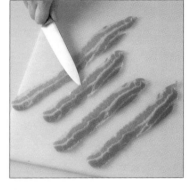

Preheat oven to 325F (165C). Grease an 8″ × 4″ loaf pan. Lay bacon slices flat on a board and stretch using the back of a knife.

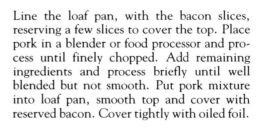

Line the loaf pan, with the bacon slices, reserving a few slices to cover the top. Place pork in a blender or food processor and process until finely chopped. Add remaining ingredients and process briefly until well blended but not smooth. Put pork mixture into loaf pan, smooth top and cover with reserved bacon. Cover tightly with oiled foil.

Place loaf pan in a roasting pan half-filled with boiling water. Cook in preheated oven 1-1/2 to 1-3/4 hours until firm. Remove foil. Cover pate with waxed paper, then put a plate or board and a heavy weight on top; refrigerate overnight before turning out. Slice to serve and garnish with herb sprigs.

Makes 6 to 8 servings.

PORK SATAY

12 ounces lean pork, cubed
Juice of 1 lime
1 stalk lemon grass, finely chopped
1 garlic clove, finely chopped
2 tablespoons vegetable oil
SAUCE:
4 tablespoons vegetable oil
1/2 cup raw shelled peanuts
2 stalks lemon grass, chopped
2 fresh red chiles, seeded, sliced
3 shallots, chopped
2 garlic cloves, chopped
1 teaspoon fish paste
2 tablespoons sugar
1-1/2 cups coconut milk
Juice of 1/2 lime

Meanwhile, make sauce. Over a high heat, heat 1 tablespoon of the oil in a wok, add nuts and cook, stirring constantly, 2 minutes. Using a slotted spoon, transfer nuts to paper towels to drain. Using a pestle and mortar or small food processor, grind nuts to a paste. Remove and set aside.

Divide pork among 4 skewers and lay in a shallow dish. In a bowl, mix together lime juice, lemon grass, garlic and oil. Pour over pork, turn to coat, cover and refrigerate 1 hour, turning occasionally.

Using a pestle and mortar or small food processor, pound or mix to a smooth paste lemon grass, chiles, shallots, garlic and fish paste.

Preheat broiler. Remove pork from dish, allowing excess liquid to drain off. Broil pork, turning frequently and basting, 8 to 10 minutes.

Heat remaining oil in wok, add spice mixture and cook, stirring, 2 minutes. Stir in peanut paste, sugar and coconut milk. Bring to a boil, stirring. Reduce heat so sauce simmers, add lime juice and simmer, stirring, 5 to 10 minutes, until thickened. Serve in a bowl to accompany pork.

Makes 4 servings.

CARPACCIO

LAYERED COUNTRY TERRINE

1 (10-oz.) piece beef tenderloin
1 (3-oz.) piece Parmesan cheese, thinly sliced
3 cups thinly sliced button mushrooms (8 ounces)
Leaves from about 8 Italian parsley sprigs
DRESSING:
1/2 cup extra-virgin olive oil
Juice of 2 lemons
1 garlic clove, chopped
Salt and freshly ground pepper

8 bacon slices
4 ounces chicken livers
4 ounces ground pork
4 ounces pork sausage
1 garlic clove
1 onion, finely chopped
3 tablespoons chopped fresh parsley
1/2 cup fresh white bread crumbs
1/4 cup brandy
1 egg, beaten
1/4 teaspoon freshly grated nutmeg
1 teaspoon finely grated lemon peel
Salt and pepper
2 skinned and boned chicken breast halves
1 bay leaf
Parsley, to garnish

Put beef in freezer 30 minutes. Using a very sharp knife, cut beef into wafer-thin slices.

Preheat oven to 350F (175C). On a chopping board, place bacon. Stretch with the back of a knife. Use 4 of the slices to line a 5-cup loaf pan, reserving 4 slices for top. With a sharp knife, roughly chop chicken livers. Mix together with pork, sausage, garlic, onion and parsley. In a small bowl, soak bread crumbs in brandy, then add to meat mixture. Beat in egg, nutmeg, lemon peel, salt and pepper.

Lay beef slices in the center of a large serving plate and arrange Parmesan slices, mushrooms and parsley around edge.

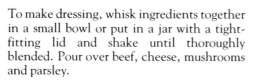

To make dressing, whisk ingredients together in a small bowl or put in a jar with a tight-fitting lid and shake until thoroughly blended. Pour over beef, cheese, mushrooms and parsley.

Makes 6 servings.

Over bacon in pan, spread one-third of the meat mixture. Cut chicken into thin slices; layer half over meat mixture. Cover with half the remaining meat mixture, then cover with remaining chicken and remaining meat mixture. Lay reserved bacon on top and add bay leaf. Cover with foil. In a baking pan three-quarters full of boiling water, place terrine. Bake 1-1/2 hours. Remove from oven and cool. Cut into slices; garnish with parsley. Serve with crusty bread.

Makes 4 to 6 servings.

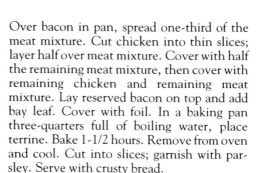

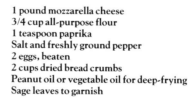

FONDUTA

1 pound fontina cheese, diced
1-1/4 cups milk
1/4 cup unsalted butter, melted
4 large egg yolks
Freshly ground pepper
Breadsticks, crusty bread or toast for dipping
Italian parsley sprig to garnish

Place cheese and milk in a bowl. Refrigerate at least 2 hours to soften. Transfer to a double boiler or heatproof bowl set over a pan of simmering water; heat until cheese melts and becomes stringy. Stir in butter and remove from heat.

Beat egg yolks in a small bowl. Stir in a little of the hot cheese mixture, then pour back into the remaining cheese mixture. Return to the heat and beat vigorously until smooth, creamy and thickened. Season with freshly ground pepper.

Transfer to a serving dish (the dish is usually kept hot at table over a candle or small burner), and serve with Breadsticks, crusty bread or toast for dipping. Garnish with parsley sprig.

Makes 6 servings.

Note: If fontina cheese is not available a mixture of 8 ounces Gruyeré cheese and 8 ounces Edam cheese is a good substitute.

MOZZARELLA FRITTERS

1 pound mozzarella cheese
3/4 cup all-purpose flour
1 teaspoon paprika
Salt and freshly ground pepper
2 eggs, beaten
2 cups dried bread crumbs
Peanut oil or vegetable oil for deep-frying
Sage leaves to garnish

Cut mozzarella cheese into 1-1/2-inch cubes. Mix flour, paprika, salt and freshly ground pepper in a shallow dish. Put eggs into a second shallow dish and bread crumbs into a third dish.

Coat cheese cubes lightly in the seasoned flour. Dip into eggs, then into bread crumbs to coat evenly. Repeat once more with eggs and bread crumbs.

Half-fill a deep-fat fryer with oil. Preheat to 350F (175C). Deep-fry a few cheese cubes at a time about 2 minutes until golden. Using a slotted spoon, transfer to paper towels to drain. Serve hot garnished with sage leaves.

Makes 4 to 6 servings.

GOAT CHEESE TARTS

1 to 2 teaspoons extra-virgin olive oil
2 tablespoons butter
2 cups fresh bread crumbs
1 tablespoon sesame seeds
6 ounces goat cheese
4 sun-dried tomatoes preserved in oil, drained
Salt and freshly ground pepper
4 basil leaves
1 teaspoon finely chopped mint
Mixed lettuce leaves and chives to garnish

Preheat oven to 400F (205C). Use olive oil to grease 4 (3- to 4-inch) tart pans.

Melt butter in a small saucepan, and stir in bread crumbs and sesame seeds. Divide among prepared tart pans, pressing firmly onto bottoms and sides. Bake in preheated oven 12 to 15 minutes until crisp and light golden. Carefully remove tart shells from pans and place on a baking sheet.

Divide goat cheese among tart shells and top each with a sun-dried tomato. Season with salt and freshly ground pepper. Return to oven 8 to 10 minutes to heat through. Put a basil leaf and a sprinkling of chopped mint on each tart and garnish with mixed lettuce leaves and chives.

Makes 4 servings.

RICOTTA MOLDS

1-1/2 cups ricotta cheese (12 ounces)
1 tablespoon finely chopped Italian parsley
1 tablespoon chopped fennel tops
1 tablespoon snipped fresh chives
1 tablespoon unflavored gelatin powder
3 tablespoons water
2/3 cup mayonnaise
Salt and freshly ground pepper
Fresh herb sprigs to garnish
BELL PEPPER SAUCE
2 large red bell peppers, broiled, peeled and chopped, page 42
3 tablespoons extra-virgin olive oil
Few drops of balsamic vinegar
Salt and freshly ground pepper

In a bowl, mix together cheese and herbs. Oil 6 (about 1/2-cup) molds. In a small bowl, soften gelatin in water 5 minutes. Place bowl over a saucepan of simmering water and stir until dissolved. Cool slightly, then stir into cheese mixture with mayonnaise, salt and freshly ground pepper. Divide among oiled molds, cover and refrigerate until set.

To make sauce, put bell peppers and oil in a food processor or blender and process until smooth. Add balsamic vinegar to taste, and season with salt and freshly ground pepper. Pour into a small bowl, and refrigerate until required. Turn out ricotta molds onto individual plates and serve with sauce. Garnish with herb sprigs.

Makes 6 servings.

MOZZARELLA TOASTS

12 thick slices French or Italian bread
1/3 cup extra-virgin olive oil
1 teaspoon finely chopped Italian parsley
14 anchovy fillets canned in oil, drained
1 pound mozzarella cheese, cut into 12 slices
Freshly ground pepper
Italian parsley sprigs to garnish

Preheat broiler. Arrange bread in 1 layer on a baking sheet, then toast both sides under preheated broiler until golden.

Meanwhile put oil, parsley and 2 of the anchovy fillets in a small saucepan. Heat gently to warm, stirring with a fork to break up anchovies. Drizzle oil mixture over toasted bread and put a slice of cheese on each one. Season with freshly ground pepper.

Garnish with remaining anchovy fillets and return to broiler 2 to 3 minutes until cheese is hot and bubbling. Serve at once garnished with Italian parsley sprigs.

Makes 6 servings.

ASPARAGUS & EGG SALAD

2 pound asparagus
Salt and freshly ground pepper
7 hard-cooked eggs
6 tablespoons olive oil
2 tablespoons white wine vinegar
2 small dill pickles, finely chopped
Freshly ground pepper
Chopped Italian parsley and Italian parsley sprig
  to garnish

Snap off and discard woody ends of asparagus stems. Using a small sharp knife, scrape stems. Rinse asparagus, then tie into small bundles using string.

Stand bundles in a deep pan of boiling salted water so tips are above water. Cover, making a dome of foil, if necessary. Boil 15 minutes until tips are crisp-tender. Drain, refresh under cold running water, drain, untie bundles and cool.

Finely chop 4 of the eggs and place in a bowl. Using a wooden spoon, gradually stir in oil, vinegar and pickles. Season with salt and freshly ground pepper. Set aside. Quarter remaining eggs and arrange with asparagus around edge of a serving plate. Pour egg sauce into center and sprinkle with chopped Italian parsley. Garnish with Italian parsley sprig.

Makes 4 to 6 servings.

HOT ANCHOVY DIP

2 (1-3/4-oz.) cans anchovy fillets, drained and coarsely chopped
1-1/4 cups whipping cream
2 garlic cloves, crushed
4 tablespoons unsalted butter, diced
TO SERVE:
Cubes of crusty bread
Bread sticks
Vegetables pieces for dipping such as fennel, celery, bell peppers, radishes, endive and broccoli
Italian parsley leaves to garnish

Put anchovies in a small saucepan with cream and garlic. Bring to a boil, then reduce heat and simmer, uncovered and stirring occasionally, 12 to 15 minutes until smooth and thickened.

Stir in butter. Transfer to a serving dish. Garnish with Italian parsley leaves and serve with cubes of bread, bread sticks and vegetables.

Makes 4 servings.

Note: Traditionally, the serving dish is kept hot at the table like a fondue over a candle or burner.

CANNELINI BEAN PASTE

1-1/4 cups dried cannelini beans, soaked overnight, drained
4 cups water
1/2 teaspoon hot red pepper flakes
2 teaspoons tomato paste
2 rosemary sprigs
2 tablespoons butter
2 tablespoons extra-virgin olive oil
1 garlic clove, finely chopped
1 tablespoon finely chopped oregano or 1 teaspoon dried leaf oregano
3/4 to 1 cup hot chicken stock
Juice of 1 small lemon
Salt and freshly ground pepper
Rosemary sprigs to garnish
Toasted bread or vegetable sticks to serve

Combine beans in a saucepan with the water, red pepper flakes, tomato paste and rosemary sprigs. Bring to a boil, then reduce heat, cover and simmer 2 hours until most of the water has been absorbed and beans are very tender. Discard rosemary. In a blender or food processor fitted with the metal blade, puree beans and remaining liquid until very smooth.

Heat butter and oil in a medium-size saucepan. Add garlic and oregano. Cook 2 minutes. Stir in bean puree and hot stock and simmer 10 to 12 minutes, stirring frequently, until mixture is very thick. Remove from heat, stir in lemon juice and season with salt and freshly ground pepper. Garnish with rosemary sprigs. Serve either hot spread on toasted crusty bread or cold with fresh vegetable sticks or warmed crusty bread.

Makes 6 servings.

SALADS

BELL PEPPER SALAD

1 large red bell pepper
1 large green bell pepper
1 large yellow bell pepper
1 small red onion, sliced
16 ripe olives
2 teaspoons chopped basil or 2/3 teaspoon dried leaf
    basil
2 teaspoons chopped thyme or 2/3 teaspoon dried leaf
    thyme
DRESSING:
3 tablespoons extra-virgin olive oil
1 tablespoon red wine vinegar
1 garlic clove, finely chopped
Pinch of sugar
Salt and freshly ground pepper

To make dressing, mix all ingredients together in a small bowl, or shake together in a jar with a tight-fitting lid. Set aside. Preheat broiler. Place whole peppers under hot broiler about 10 minutes, turning occasionally, until skins are evenly blistered and blackened. Transfer peppers to a plastic bag a few minutes, then peel away and discard skins.

Cut peppers in half, remove and discard seeds and cut peppers into strips. Place in a salad bowl with onion and olives. Stir or shake dressing and pour over salad. Toss gently to mix and sprinkle with herbs.

Makes 4 servings.

ZUCCHINI SALAD

2 tablespoons pine nuts
1 pound zucchini
2 tablespoons extra-virgin olive oil
1 garlic clove, crushed
2 tablespoons dried currants
2 teaspoons chopped fresh mint
Juice of 1/2 lemon
Salt and pepper
2 green onions

In a large skillet, cook pine nuts, stirring, until just beginning to brown. Remove pine nuts and reserve. Trim zucchini and slice thinly.

In a medium-size skillet, heat oil and add zucchini, garlic, currants and pine nuts. Cook, stirring, until zucchini are just beginning to soften and brown slightly.

Stir in mint, lemon juice, salt and pepper. Transfer to a serving dish and leave until cold. Slice the green onions and scatter them over the top.

Makes 8 servings.

BEAN & ONION SALAD

12 ounces green beans
1 onion, thinly sliced
2 tablespoons capers in wine vinegar, drained
6 tablespoons extra-virgin olive oil
Juice of 1 lemon
1/2 teaspoon hot red pepper flakes
Pinch of sugar
Salt and freshly ground pepper
2 teaspoons chopped Italian parsley
1 teaspoon chopped mint

Add beans to a saucepan of boiling salted water and cook 4 minutes until tender. Drain and refresh under cold running water. Place in a bowl with onion and capers.

Beat olive oil, lemon juice, red pepper flakes, sugar, salt and freshly ground pepper in a small bowl or shake together in a jar with a tight-fitting lid.

Pour over salad, add herbs and mix well.

Makes 4 to 6 servings.

MUNG BEAN SPROUT SALAD

1 cup mung beans
2 green chiles, seeded, chopped
1 (1-inch) piece fresh gingerroot, grated
2/3 cup shredded fresh coconut
1/2 cucumber, diced
Juice of 1 lemon
Salt and pepper to taste
1 mango
2 tablespoons vegetable oil
1/2 teaspoon mustard seeds
Cilantro (fresh coriander) leaves and shredded lemon peel, to garnish, if desired

Rinse beans, put in a bowl and cover with cold water.

Soak in warm water 30 minutes. Drain, then place in a sprouting tray and leave about two days, rinsing thoroughly every 12 hours, until beans germinate. Rinse well and drain. Place sprouts in a bowl and stir in chiles, gingerroot, coconut, cucumber, lemon juice and salt and pepper.

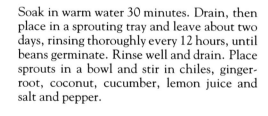

Peel and seed mango and dice flesh, stir into salad. Heat oil in a small pan. Add mustard seeds; cook 1 minute, until they begin to pop. Pour contents of pan over the salad and toss well to combine. Refrigerate at least 30 minutes, then serve, garnished with cilantro leaves and lemon peel.

Makes 4 to 6 servings.

Variation: Other beans, seeds and grains that sprout easily can be used for this salad – try whole-wheat kernels or alfalfa seeds.

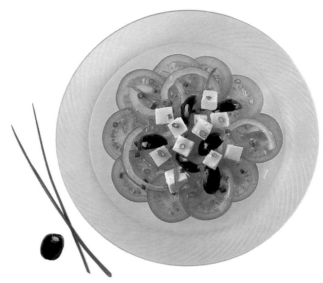

THREE BEAN SALAD

TOMATO SALAD

3 ounces dried flageolet beans
3 ounces dried red kidney beans
2 fresh thyme sprigs
1 pound fresh fava beans, shelled
1 small onion, finely chopped
Red bell pepper rings, to garnish
DRESSING:
1/2 cup extra-virgin olive oil
Juice of 1 lemon
1 tablespoon chopped fresh mint
1 tablespoon chopped fresh parsley
Salt and pepper

Put flageolet and kidney beans in 2 separate bowls.

Cover each with water to come well above top of beans. Let soak at least 6 hours. Drain. Put flageolet and kidney beans in 2 separate saucepans each with a sprig of thyme. Cover with water, bring to a boil and boil briskly 10 minutes. Cover pans, reduce heat and simmer 1 to 1-1/2 hours or until beans are tender. In a pan of boiling water, cook fava beans 5 to 10 minutes or until tender. Drain all the beans and put together into a bowl.

To make the dressing, in a bowl, mix together oil, lemon juice, mint, parsley, salt and pepper. Pour dressing over warm beans. Add chopped onion and mix well. Cover and refrigerate until chilled, then transfer to a serving dish. Serve garnished with bell pepper rings.

Makes 6 servings.

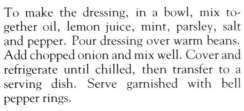

1/2 pound small tomatoes
1/2 small red onion
10 to 12 ripe olives
Greek bread, to serve
DRESSING:
1/4 cup extra-virgin olive oil
1 tablespoon fresh lemon juice
1 teaspoon chopped fresh mint
2 teaspoons snipped fresh chives
1 teaspoon honey
Salt and pepper

To make dressing, in a small bowl, mix together olive oil, lemon juice, mint, chives, honey, salt and pepper.

With a sharp knife, cut tomatoes into slices. Slice onion thinly. Place in a serving bowl with olives.

Stir dressing and pour over tomatoes, onions and olives. Toss together to coat tomatoes with dressing. Serve with Greek bread.

Makes 4 servings.

Variation: Add cubes of feta cheese.

TOMATO & RED ONION SALAD

4 beefsteak tomatoes, sliced
4 sun-dried tomatoes packed in oil, drained and
    chopped
1 red onion, chopped
Salt and freshly ground pepper
3 tablespoons extra-virgin olive oil
2 tablespoons oil from the sun-dried tomatoes
2 tablespoons red wine vinegar
Pinch of sugar
4 tablespoons chopped mixed fresh herbs such as basil,
    oregano, parsley, chives, dill and cilantro
Herb sprigs to garnish

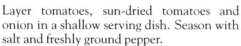
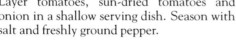

Layer tomatoes, sun-dried tomatoes and
onion in a shallow serving dish. Season with
salt and freshly ground pepper.

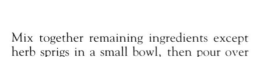

Mix together remaining ingredients except
herb sprigs in a small bowl, then pour over
salad. Garnish with herb sprigs.

Makes 4 to 6 servings.

COUNTRY SALAD

2 heads leaf lettuce
6 tomatoes
1/2 cucumber
1 bunch green onions
2 tablespoons chopped fresh mint
2 teaspoons chopped fresh oregano
1/4 cup extra-virgin olive oil
2 tablespoons fresh lemon juice
Salt and pepper
6 ounces feta cheese
12 ripe olives

Wash and dry lettuce. Roll up the leaves and
slice across to make shreds. Arrange them on
a serving dish.

Cut tomatoes into quarters and arrange on
lettuce. Score down side of cucumber with a
fork or knife to make grooves, then slice
cucumber and arrange on lettuce. Chop
green onions and sprinkle them over the
salad with mint and oregano.

In a bowl, mix together oil, lemon juice, salt
and pepper. Pour over salad. Cut feta cheese
into cubes and arrange on the salad with
olives. Serve immediately.

Makes 6 servings.

TRICOLOR SALAD

LENTIL SALAD

1 avocado
2 tablespoons lemon juice
2 large beefsteak tomatoes, sliced
6 ounces Italian mozzarella cheese, preferably made
 from buffalo milk
Salt and freshly ground pepper
Few drops balsamic vinegar
1/4 cup extra-virgin olive oil
6 fresh basil leaves, shredded
Basil sprigs to garnish

Seed and peel avocado, slice thinly and brush with lemon juice.

Arrange tomatoes, cheese and avocado on a large plate. Season with salt and freshly ground pepper.

Drizzle balsamic vinegar and oil over salad; sprinkle with shredded basil. Garnish with basil sprigs.

Makes 4 to 6 servings.

1-1/4 cups green lentils
1/4 cup extra-virgin olive oil
1 onion, finely chopped
3 tomatoes, peeled and chopped
Salt and pepper
1 tablespoon chopped fresh parsley
2 tablespoons fresh lemon juice
Onion rings, chopped fresh parsley and lemon slices, to
 garnish

Put lentils into a bowl, cover with cold water and let soak 3 to 4 hours. Drain well.

In a large saucepan, heat oil, add onion and cook until soft. Add tomatoes and cook 1 minute, then add lentils. Cover with water, cover pan and simmer 30 minutes, adding water if necessary, or until lentils are tender, yet still hold their shapes and all water has been absorbed.

Add salt, pepper, parsley, lemon juice and remaining oil to lentils. Mix carefully, then transfer to a serving dish and let cool. Serve garnished with onion rings, chopped parsley and lemon slices.

Makes 4 to 6 servings.

ROASTED VEGETABLE SALAD

OLIVE & TOMATO SALAD

2 Spanish onions, unpeeled
1 pound small eggplants
2 red bell peppers
3 firm but ripe beefsteak tomatoes
8 garlic cloves
1-1/2 teaspoons cumin seeds
Juice of 1 lemon
1/4 cup extra-virgin olive oil
3 tablespoons white-wine vinegar
Salt
2 tablespoons finely chopped fresh parsley (optional)

Preheat oven to 350F (175C). Place onions on a baking sheet and bake 10 minutes. Add eggplants.

Bake another 10 minutes, then add peppers. Bake 10 minutes before adding tomatoes and 6 of the garlic cloves, then bake 15 minutes or until all vegetables are tender. If necessary, remove vegetables from oven as they are done. When vegetables are cool enough to handle, peel them with your fingers.

Remove and discard cores and seeds from peppers, then cut into strips. Halve tomatoes and discard seeds, then slice. Slice eggplants into strips and onions into rings. Arrange in a serving dish. Using a mortar and pestle, pound the roasted and the raw garlic and the cumin seeds to a paste. Beat in lemon juice, oil and vinegar. Add salt to taste. Pour over vegetables and sprinkle with parsley, if desired. Serve warm or cold.

Makes 4 servings.

1-1/2 pounds mixed yellow and green zucchini
1 tablespoon olive oil
3/4 cup halved cherry tomatoes
1/3 cup chopped pitted ripe olives
1 small head oak leaf lettuce
1 tablespoon pine nuts, toasted
GARLIC DRESSING:
3 tablespoons olive oil
1 teaspoon balsamic vinegar
1/2 garlic clove, crushed
1/2 teaspoon chopped fresh thyme
Salt and pepper

Preheat oven to 425F (220C). Wash and trim zucchini and cut into 1-inch slices. Into a roasting pan, place zucchini. Toss with oil. Bake on top rack 20 minutes or until tender.

In a large bowl, place tomatoes and olives. Stir in cooked zucchini. In a small bowl, blend dressing ingredients together. Add to bowl and stir well. Leave until zucchini are cool. Rinse and trim lettuce, discarding tough outer leaves. Tear into bite-size pieces. Arrange lettuce on 4 serving plates. Spoon zucchini mixture over lettuce. Sprinkle pine nuts over. Serve at once.

Makes 4 servings.

MEDITERRANEAN POTATO SALAD —ORIENTAL CARROT SALAD—

1 pound new potatoes
4 ounces green beans
1 fennel bulb
1/4 cup pitted ripe olives
2 tablespoons capers, drained
2 tablespoons snipped fresh chives
2 teaspoon chopped fresh tarragon
1/4 cup virgin olive oil
Juice of 1/2 lemon
2 eggs
1 (14-oz.) can artichoke hearts, drained and halved

3/4 pounds carrots
3 tablespoons peanut oil
1/2 teaspoon sesame oil
1 teaspoon grated peeled gingerroot
1 small garlic clove, sliced
1 dried red chile, seeded and crushed
2 tablespoons lemon juice
1 teaspoon sugar
1/3 cup peanuts, toasted and chopped
Salt and pepper
Cilantro leaves, to garnish

Into a large bowl, finely grate carrot.

In a pan of lightly salted boiling water, cook potatoes 10 to 12 minutes or until just tender. Drain and place in a large bowl. Blanch beans in boiling water 1 to 2 minutes or until just tender. Drain and refresh under cold water. Pat dry. Very thinly slice fennel and halve olives. Add to potatoes with beans, capers and herbs. Stir in oil and lemon juice. Set aside until potatoes are cool.

In a skillet, heat 1 tablespoon of the peanut oil and the sesame oil. Add gingerroot, garlic and chile; cook until just turning golden. Beat in remaining oil, lemon juice and sugar. Remove from heat.

Meanwhile, hard cook eggs. Plunge into cold water, then peel. Rough chop and add to salad with the artichoke hearts. Toss well and serve at once.

Makes 4 to 6 servings.

Pour dressing over carrots. Add nuts and toss well until evenly combined. Cover and let marinate 30 minutes. Stir again, season to taste and serve garnished with cilantro leaves.

Makes 4 servings.

PEA TABBOULEH

1-1/4 cups bulgur wheat
2/3 cup olive oil
1 garlic clove, crushed
1 tablespoon red-wine vinegar
1 tablespoon chopped fresh cilantro
1 tablespoon chopped fresh mint
1 teaspoon ground coriander
1/2 teaspoon ground cumin
4 ounces sugarsnap peas
1 cup frozen green peas, thawed
1 large ripe peach, chopped
1 red onion, finely chopped
Salt and pepper

VEGETABLE SALAD

1 pound potatoes
1 large carrot, halved or quartered
1/3 cup shelled green peas
4 ounces green beans
2 tablespoons chopped Spanish onion
1 small red bell pepper, chopped
4 small pickles, chopped
1-1/2 tablespoons capers
8 to 12 anchovy-stuffed olives
2/3 cup mayonnaise
1 hard-cooked egg, sliced
Chopped fresh parsley, to garnish

In a large bowl, cover bulgur wheat with plenty of cold water. Let soak 30 minutes. Drain well and squeeze out excess liquid. In a small bowl, mix together oil, garlic, vinegar, herbs and spices. Pour over bulgur wheat. Stir well, cover and set aside 30 minutes.

In a saucepan of lightly salted water, boil potatoes in their skins until tender. Cool, peel, then dice. Boil carrot, peas and beans separately in boiling salted water until tender; drain and cool. Dice carrot and cut beans into short pieces.

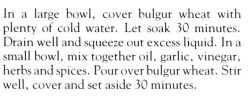

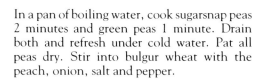

In a pan of boiling water, cook sugarsnap peas 2 minutes and green peas 1 minute. Drain both and refresh under cold water. Pat all peas dry. Stir into bulgur wheat with the peach, onion, salt and pepper.

Makes 4 to 6 servings.

Into a bowl, put potatoes, carrot, peas and beans. Stir in onion, pepper, pickles, capers, olives and mayonnaise while vegetables are still warm. Refrigerate until chilled. Arrange egg and chopped parsley on top before serving.

Makes 4 servings.

—WILD & BROWN RICE SALAD—

—EIGHT-TREASURE SALAD—

1 cup wild rice
1-1/4 cups brown rice
2/3 cup pecans
6 green onions, trimmed
1/3 cup dried cherries, cranberries or raisins
2 tablespoons chopped fresh cilantro
1 tablespoon chopped fresh parsley
DRESSING:
1/2 cup olive oil
2 teaspoons raspberry vinegar
1/4 teaspoon honey or sugar
Salt and pepper

12 oz. lean cooked skinless turkey
1 red, 1 green and 1 yellow bell pepper
4 oz. snow peas
2 oz. oyster mushrooms
1 bunch green onions
2 teaspoons sesame oil
1 tablespoon white rice vinegar
1 teaspoon honey
Freshly ground pepper
1/3 cup salted cashew nuts, crushed, to garnish

Cut turkey into 1/4-inch slices and arrange in center of 4 serving plates.

In a pan of lightly salted boiling water, cook wild rice 35 to 40 minutes or until just tender. In another pan of lightly salted boiling water, cook brown rice 25 minutes or until just tender. Drain well. Place both rices in a large bowl.

Halve and seed bell peppers. Cut into thin slices and arrange around turkey. Diagonally slice snow peas. Shred oyster mushrooms and green onions. Arrange on serving plates.

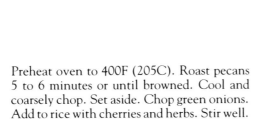

Preheat oven to 400F (205C). Roast pecans 5 to 6 minutes or until browned. Cool and coarsely chop. Set aside. Chop green onions. Add to rice with cherries and herbs. Stir well. Blend the dressing ingredients well together. Pour over salad, stir once, cover and let rice cool. Just before serving, toss in pecans and season with salt and pepper.

Makes 4 to 6 servings.

Mix together oil, vinegar, honey and pepper. Pour dressing over each salad, garnish with cashew nuts and serve.

Makes 4 servings.

SUMMER NOODLE SALAD

TUNA SALAD

6 oz. egg noodles
1 teaspoon sesame oil
2 tablespoons crunchy peanut butter
2 tablespoons light soy sauce
2 teaspoons sugar
Pinch of chile powder
1 lb. tomatoes, thinly sliced
1 bunch green onions, finely chopped
4 oz. bean sprouts
1 large carrot, grated
8 pitted dates, finely chopped

Cook noodles in boiling water 4 or 5 minutes or until tender but firm to the bite. Drain well and rinse in cold water. Leave in cold water until required.

Mix together oil, peanut butter, soy sauce, sugar and chile powder. Drain noodles well, place in a large bowl and mix in peanut sauce. Arrange tomato slices on a serving plate.

Using chopsticks or 2 forks, toss the green onions, bean sprouts, grated carrot and dates into the noodles and mix well. Pile on top of the sliced tomato and serve.

Makes 4 servings.

3 small carrots, thickly sliced
1-1/3 cups diced potatoes (about 8 ounces)
1 (7-oz.) can tuna in olive oil, drained and flaked
1 (1-3/4-oz.) can anchovy fillets in oil, drained and chopped
About 12 pitted ripe olives, halved
2 tablespoons capers in wine vinegar, drained
2 hard-cooked eggs, quartered
1/4 cup extra-virgin olive oil
Juice of 1 small lemon
1 garlic clove, crushed
Salt and freshly ground pepper
1 tablespoon chopped Italian parsley
Italian parsley sprigs to garnish

Cook carrots in a saucepan of boiling salted water 4 minutes until tender. Cook potatoes in a separate saucepan of boiling salted water about 7 minutes until tender. Drain and refresh both vegetables under cold running water, then drain and cool completely.

Put carrots, potatoes, tuna, anchovies, olives, capers and eggs into a large serving dish. Mix olive oil, lemon juice, garlic and salt and pepper together in a small bowl or put in a jar with a tight-fitting lid and shake until blended. Pour over salad, toss lightly to mix, then sprinkle with chopped Italian parsley. Garnish with Italian parsley sprigs.

Makes 4 servings.

SESAME SHRIMP SALAD

MINTY SEAFOOD SALAD

8 oz. snow peas
2 oz. oyster mushrooms, thinly sliced
1 (4-oz.) can water chestnuts, rinsed and sliced
8 oz. cooked, peeled large shrimp, thawed and
    dried, if frozen
2 tablespoons sesame seeds
DRESSING:
1 tablespoon sesame oil
1 tablespoon light soy sauce
2 teaspoons white rice vinegar
1 teaspoon brown sugar
Salt and freshly ground pepper

2/3 cup dry white wine
1 shallot, chopped
5 peppercorns
1/3 cup water
1 pound shelled scallops, fresh or frozen and thawed
1 pound cooked large shrimp
4 celery stalks
2 medium-size carrots
About 16 mint leaves
1/2 teaspoon finely grated lemon peel
DRESSING:
Juice of 2 lemons
1/2 cup extra-virgin olive oil
1 tablespoon white wine vinegar
2 tablespoons chopped Italian parsley
Salt and freshly ground pepper

Remove ends from snow peas and string if necessary. Bring a saucepan of water to a boil and cook 2 minutes or until just softened. Drain and rinse under cold water. Drain and leave to cool completely.

Put white wine, shallot, peppercorns and water in a shallow pan. Heat until boiling then add scallops. Reduce heat and poach 5 to 6 minutes, until scallops are just firm and opaque. Using a slotted spoon transfer scallops to paper towels to drain and cool. Discard cooking liquid. Slice scallops in half horizontally. Put in a serving dish. Peel shrimp and add to dish.

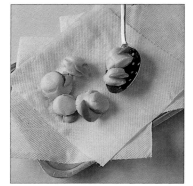

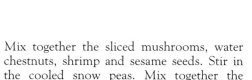

Mix together the sliced mushrooms, water chestnuts, shrimp and sesame seeds. Stir in the cooled snow peas. Mix together the dressing ingredients and pour over the salad just before serving.

Makes 4 servings.

Cut celery and carrots into thin matchsticks and add to seafood with mint leaves and lemon peel. Toss lightly to mix. To make dressing, mix ingredients together in a small bowl or put in a jar with a tight-fitting lid and shake until blended. Pour over salad and toss. Cover and refrigerate 30 minutes before serving.

Makes 4 to 6 servings.

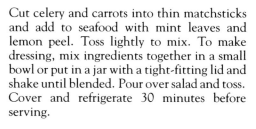

WARM CHICKEN LIVER SALAD

6 ounces small spinach leaves
1 small radicchio, separated into leaves
2 oranges, cut into segments
1 red onion, sliced into rings
2 tablespoons butter or margarine
1 tablespoon hazelnut oil
1 pound chicken livers, membranes removed and livers halved
1 garlic clove, crushed
1 tablespoon sherry vinegar
1-1/2 teaspoons whole-grain mustard
3 tablespoons dry sherry
1 teaspoon honey
Salt and pepper
2 tablespoons coarsely chopped toasted hazelnuts, to garnish

Arrange spinach and radicchio leaves on 4 plates. Arrange orange segments and onion rings over greens.

In a heavy-bottomed skillet, heat butter and oil. Add chicken livers and cook, stirring, over high heat until well browned. Push livers to side of pan, then add garlic, vinegar, mustard, sherry, honey, salt and pepper. Bring to a boil; cook until reduced slightly. Stir in livers. Spoon livers over salad. Sprinkle with chopped toasted hazelnuts.

Makes 4 servings.

CHICKEN & GRAPE SALAD

1 pound cooked chicken breasts
1-1/4 cups walnut halves
1 cup seedless green grapes, halved
16 stuffed green olives, sliced
3 green onions, sliced
Salt and freshly ground pepper
1 head romaine lettuce, separated into leaves
DRESSING:
2/3 cup mayonnaise
1 garlic clove, chopped
1 teaspoon paprika
2 tablespoons chopped Italian parsley
Few drops of hot pepper sauce
2 tablespoons milk

Cut chicken into thin strips, and place in a bowl with walnuts, grapes, olives and green onions. Season with salt and freshly ground pepper.

To make dressing, mix all ingredients together in a small bowl. Pour over salad and toss gently to mix. Arrange lettuce on a serving plate. Pile chicken salad in center and serve at once.

Makes 4 to 6 servings.

CURRIED CHICKEN SALAD

WALDORF SALAD

1 tablespoon olive oil
1 small onion, diced
2 teaspoons mild curry paste
1 (7-oz.) can chopped tomatoes
1/4 cup dry white wine
2 tablespoons hot mango chutney, chopped if necessary
2 teaspoons apricot jam
2 teaspoons fresh lemon juice
2/3 cup mayonnaise
2/3 cup plain yogurt
1 pound cooked chicken
2 cups cooked, long-grain rice
1 red bell pepper, diced
2 tablespoons chopped fresh mint
3 tablespoons prepared Italian salad dressing

1/4 cup mayonnaise
2 tablespoons plain yogurt
1 tablespoon honey
Few drops of lemon juice
Salt and pepper
2 teaspoons snipped fresh chives
1 pound cooked chicken
6 ounces green seedless grapes
2 apples
2 celery stalks
1-1/3 cups walnut halves, toasted
Mixed salad greens
VINAIGRETTE:
1/4 cup olive oil
1 tablespoon lemon juice

In a small saucepan, heat oil. Add onion; cook until softened but not browned. Stir in curry paste, tomatoes and wine. Bring to a boil. Reduce heat and simmer 15 minutes. Stir in chutney, jam and lemon juice; cook, stirring occasionally, 5 minutes or until thick and syrupy.

In a medium-size bowl, mix together mayonnaise, yogurt and honey. Add lemon juice. Season with salt and pepper; stir in chopped chives. Remove skin from chicken and cut into thin strips. Cut grapes in half. Core and slice apples; chop celery. Add chicken, grapes, apples, celery and walnuts to mayonnaise mixture; stir gently to combine.

Remove from heat. Strain into a small bowl; set aside to cool. When completely cold, stir in mayonnaise and yogurt and mix well. Cut the chicken into large pieces and stir into sauce. In a medium-size bowl, combine rice, bell pepper, mint and dressing. Spoon rice mixture into a large serving dish; arrange chicken in center of rice.

Make Vinaigrette: In a small bowl, beat together oil, lemon juice, salt and pepper. In a medium-size bowl, arrange salad greens. Add Vinaigrette; toss until greens are coated in dressing. Arrange salad greens on 4 plates and top with chicken mixture.

Makes 4 servings.

Makes 4 servings.

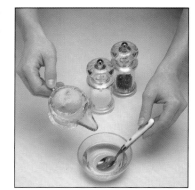

FISH & SHELLFISH

SCALLOPS WITH CASHEWS

1/4 cup dry sherry or rice wine
3 tablespoons ketchup
1 tablespoon oyster sauce
1 tablespoon white-wine vinegar
1 tablespoon sesame oil
1 teaspoon Chinese chili sauce (or to taste)
1 tablespoon each grated orange zest and orange juice
1 teaspoon cornstarch
1 tablespoon vegetable oil
1/2 pound bay scallops, with roe (optional)
2 garlic cloves, finely chopped
4 green onions, thinly sliced
6 ounces asparagus, cut into 1-inch pieces
5 ounces cashew nuts, lightly rinsed

In a medium-size bowl, combine sherry, ketchup, oyster sauce, vinegar, sesame oil, chili sauce, orange zest, orange juice and cornstarch. Heat a wok until hot, add oil and swirl to coat wok. Add scallops and stir-fry 1 or 2 minutes or until they begin to turn opaque. Remove to a bowl.

Add garlic, green onions and asparagus to wok and stir-fry 2 or 3 minutes or until asparagus is bright green and tender but still crisp. Stir sauce ingredients and pour into wok. Bring to a simmer. Return scallops to wok and add the cashews. Stir-fry 1 minute or until scallops are heated through, tossing to coat all ingredients. Serve with rice garnished with strips of orange peel.

Makes 4 servings.

SQUID WITH RED WINE

1-1/2 pounds squid
1/4 cup extra-virgin olive oil
1 large onion, chopped
2 garlic cloves, crushed
1 pound tomatoes, peeled and coarsely chopped
2/3 cup red wine
Salt and pepper
1/2 teaspoon sugar
1-inch cinnamon stick
1 tablespoon chopped fresh parsley
6 bread slices, crusts removed, and 3 tablespoons olive oil, to serve

Clean squid, see page 34. Cut into rings. Dry thoroughly with paper towels. In a large saucepan, heat oil. Add onion and garlic and cook until soft. Add squid and fry until lightly browned. Add tomatoes, wine, salt, pepper, sugar and cinnamon. Simmer, uncovered, 30 minutes, or until squid is tender. Stir in parsley.

Sauce should be thick and rich. If not, transfer squid to a hot dish and boil sauce to reduce. Cut bread into triangles. In a skillet, heat oil and fry bread until golden on both sides. Serve squid in individual dishes, with fried bread tucked around the sides.

Makes 6 servings.

— SHRIMP & FISH BALL CURRY —

1 pound white fish fillets, such as sole, cod, whiting or monkfish, skinned
4 ounces cooked peeled shrimp
1-1/2 cups fresh white bread crumbs
2 eggs, beaten separately
2 tablespoons chopped cilantro (fresh coriander)
2 teaspoons lemon juice
Salt and pepper to taste
2 tablespoons vegetable oil plus extra for deep-frying
1 large onion, finely chopped
2 green chiles, seeded, chopped
4 garlic cloves, crushed
1/2 teaspoon ground turmeric
2/3 cup Coconut Milk
1 (14-oz.) can chopped tomatoes

Rinse fish and remove any bones. Mince fish and shrimp, then transfer to a large bowl. Stir in 1 cup of bread crumbs, 1 egg, cilantro, lemon juice, salt and pepper. Mix well and form into 24 balls. Roll balls in remaining egg, then in remaining bread crumbs to coat completely. Cover and refrigerate 30 minutes. Meanwhile, heat 2 tablespoons oil in a heavy saucepan, add onion and cook, stirring, 5 minutes to soften.

Add chiles, garlic and turmeric; cook 2 minutes more. Stir in Coconut Milk and tomatoes and cook, uncovered 20 minutes, until reduced and thickened, stirring occasionally. Half-fill a deep pan or deep-fryer with oil and heat to 375F (190C), or until a 1-inch bread cube browns in 50 seconds. Fry fish balls 3 to 5 minutes, until golden brown. Drain on paper towels and serve with the sauce.

Makes 4 servings.

— SHRIMP WITH RADICCHIO —

2 tablespoons olive oil
4 garlic cloves, finely chopped
2 shallots, finely chopped
2 prosciutto slices, diced
1-1/2 pounds raw medium-size shrimp, shelled and deveined
1/2 cup grappa or brandy
1/2 pound radicchio, thinly shredded
1 cup whipping cream
Salt and freshly ground pepper
3 or 4 tablespoons chopped fresh parsley
1 pound linguine

Heat a wok until hot. Add oil; swirl to coat wok. Add garlic, shallots and prosciutto.

Stir-fry 2 minutes or until prosciutto is crisp. Add shrimp and stir-fry 2 minutes or until shrimp turn pink and feel firm to the touch. With a Chinese strainer or slotted spoon, remove shrimp mixture to a bowl. Add grappa and bring to a boil, stirring frequently. Stir in radicchio, cream, salt and pepper and bring to a simmer; cook 1 minute or until sauce thickens slightly. Return shrimp to wok and stir to coat. Stir in half of the parsley.

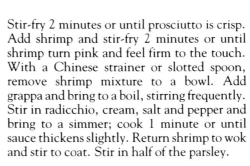

In a large saucepan of boiling water, cook linguine according to package directions. Drain and divide among 4 large bowls. Top with equal amounts of shrimp and sauce and sprinkle with remaining parsley.

Makes 4 servings.

Variation: Cooked shrimp can be substituted for raw shrimp. Add to thickened sauce and heat until hot before adding parsley.

PACIFIC SHRIMP

2 tablespoons peanut oil
1 pound raw medium-size shrimp, shelled and deveined
2 garlic cloves, finely chopped
1-inch piece gingerroot, peeled and finely chopped
2 celery stalks, sliced
1 red bell pepper, sliced
4 green onions, cut into thin strips
1 (8-oz.) can unsweetened pineapple chunks, drained, juice reserved
2 teaspoons cornstarch
2 teaspoons soy sauce
1 tablespoon lemon juice
Dash of hot pepper sauce
1 cup macadamia nuts, rinsed lightly if salted

Heat a wok until hot. Add 1 tablespoon of the oil and swirl to coat wok. Add shrimp and stir-fry 2 minutes or until shrimp turn pink and feel firm to the touch. Remove to a bowl. Add remaining oil to wok. Add garlic and gingerroot and stir-fry 30 seconds. Stir in celery, bell pepper and green onions and stir-fry 3 or 4 minutes or until vegetables are tender but still crisp. Stir in the pineapple chunks.

Dissolve cornstarch in the reserved pineapple juice. Stir in soy sauce, lemon juice and hot pepper sauce. Stir into the vegetable mixture and bring to a simmer. Add reserved shrimp and macadamia nuts and stir-fry until sauce thickens and shrimp are heated through.

Makes 4 servings.

HOT MUSSELS WITH CUMIN

3 pounds mussels
2 tablespoons vegetable oil
1 large onion, finely chopped
1 (1-inch) piece fresh gingerroot, grated
6 garlic cloves, crushed
2 green chiles, seeded, finely chopped
1/2 teaspoon ground turmeric
2 teaspoons ground cumin
1 cup water
1-3/4 cups shredded fresh coconut
2 tablespoons chopped cilantro (fresh coriander)
Cilantro (fresh coriander) leaves, to garnish

Scrub mussels clean in several changes of fresh cold water and pull off beards.

Discard any mussels that are cracked or do not close tightly when tapped. Set other mussels aside. Heat oil in a large saucepan and add onion. Cook, stirring, 5 minutes until soft, then add gingerroot, garlic, chiles, turmeric and cumin. Cook 2 minutes, stirring constantly.

Add mussels, coconut and water; bring to a boil. Cover and cook over high heat, shaking pan frequently, about 5 minutes or until mussels have opened. Discard any that remain closed. Spoon mussels into a serving dish, pour cooking liquid over mussels and sprinkle with chopped cilantro. Garnish with cilantro leaves and serve at once.

Makes 4 servings.

CURRIED CRAB

1-1/2 lbs. cooked large crab claws, thawed and dried,
    if frozen
1 tablespoon sunflower oil
2 garlic cloves, thinly sliced
1 large green bell pepper, shredded
8 oz. small broccoli flowerets
5 tablespoons vegetable stock
1 tablespoon Madras curry paste
1 tablespoon light soy sauce
1 teaspoon brown sugar

Wrap the end of a rolling pin in plastic wrap and tap the main part of the crab claws until the shell cracks, leaving pincers intact. Peel away hard shell to expose crab flesh, leaving shell on pincers. Heat oil in a nonstick or well-seasoned wok and stir-fry crab and garlic for 1 or 2 minutes until crab is lightly browned. Drain on paper towels and set aside.

Mix together remaining ingredients and add to wok. Simmer 5 minutes, stirring occasionally. Return crab and garlic to wok and simmer 2 to 3 minutes, stirring to coat crab with sauce. Serve immediately with rice, vegetables and lemon wedges.

Makes 4 servings.

CAJUN CRABCAKES

1 small clove garlic, finely chopped
2 tablespoons finely chopped white and green parts of
    green onions
2 tablespoons finely chopped red bell pepper
1 egg, beaten
1-1/2 tablespoons mayonnaise
1 pound fresh white crab meat, chopped
1 tablespoon chopped fresh parsley
2 cups fresh bread crumbs
Squeeze lemon juice
Salt and red (cayenne) pepper
Olive oil for shallow frying
Sour cream and snipped chives and crisp green salad to
    serve

In a mortar or small bowl, put garlic, green onions, bell pepper, and a pinch salt. Crush together using a pestle or end of a rolling pin. Stir in egg, mayonnaise, crab meat, parsley, and about half the bread crumbs to bind together. Add lemon juice, salt, and cayenne to taste.

Form crab mixture into 8 cakes, 3/4 inch thick and 2 1/2 inches round. Lightly press in remaining bread crumbs. Chill 1 hour. In a nonstick skillet, heat a thin layer oil. Add crab cakes in batches and fry 3 to 4 minutes on each side until golden. Serve warm with sour cream and chives, and a crisp green salad.

Makes 8.

FISH & PESTO PACKAGES

2 sheets phyllo pastry dough, about 2 ounces
Melted butter for brushing
2 fish fillets, such as turbot or salmon, about 5 ounces
    each, skinned
2 ounces cooked shelled shrimp, finely chopped
1 cup chopped button mushrooms
5 tablespoons fromage frais or low-fat cream cheese
2 to 3 teaspoons pesto sauce
Salt and pepper
Tossed salad to serve

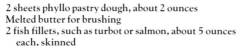

Preheat oven to 400F (205C). Butter a baking sheet. Brush 1 sheet of phyllo pastry with butter. Place the other sheet on top and brush with butter, then cut in half. Place 1 fish fillet in center of each phyllo pastry square. Top with shrimp and mushrooms. Mix together fromage frais or cream cheese and pesto sauce. Season with salt and pepper. Spoon one-quarter of the pesto mixture onto each portion of mushrooms. Reserve remaining mixture.

Bring together 2 opposite edges of phyllo pastry and fold down over fish. Fold remaining edges over and tuck ends under fish. Brush with melted butter and place on baking sheet. Bake 15 minutes or until browned. Using a pancake turner, transfer fish to a warmed serving plate. Split open top of pastry and spoon in remaining pesto mixture. Serve with a tossed salad.

Makes 2 servings.

SOLE WITH CHIVE SAUCE

1/2 cup cottage cheese, drained and pressed through a
    fine strainer
Grated peel and juice of 1 lemon
Salt and pepper
3-1/2 ounces cooked shelled shrimp, finely chopped
8 sole or flounder fillets, skinned
1 cup fish stock
1 small shallot, finely chopped
1 tablespoon dry white vermouth
6 tablespoons dry white wine
3/4 cup whipping cream, fromage frais, or cream cheese
1-1/2 tablespoons finely snipped fresh chives
Shrimp and snipped fresh chives to garnish
Broccoli to serve

Preheat oven to 350F (175C). Grease a shallow baking dish. In a bowl, beat together cottage cheese and lemon peel and juice. Season with salt and pepper. Stir in shrimp. Spread mixture on skinned side of fillets, then roll up neatly. Secure with wooden picks. Place fish in a single layer in dish, pour in stock to come halfway up the rolls, and add chopped shallot. Cover dish and cook in the oven about 20 minutes or until fish begins to flake. Meanwhile, in a small saucepan, boil vermouth and wine until reduced by half.

Transfer fillets to a warm plate and keep warm. Add stock and shallot to wines and boil until reduced by three-quarters. Stir in cream, if using, and simmer to a light creamy consistency. If using fromage frais or cream cheese, stir in and heat without boiling. Quickly pour sauce into a blender and mix until frothy. Add chives and seasoning. Pour some sauce over fish and serve rest separately. Garnish fillets with shrimp and chives and serve with broccoli.

Makes 4 servings.

SOLE WITH GREEN DRESSING

HALIBUT WITH ZUCCHINI

Flour for coating
Salt and pepper
4 (6-oz.) sole or flounder fillets
1 egg, lightly beaten
About 1-1/2 cups fresh bread crumbs
1/4 cup olive oil
Lemon wedges and fresh herbs, to garnish
GREEN DRESSING:
3 garlic cloves
6 canned anchovy fillets, drained and chopped
3 tablespoons finely chopped fresh parsley
1/2 teaspoon chopped fresh oregano
1-1/2 tablespoons finely chopped capers
1-1/2 tablespoons fresh lemon juice
2/3 cup extra-virgin olive oil

2-2/3 cups thinly sliced small zucchini
4 halibut fillets, 5 to 6 ounces each
4 tablespoons unsalted butter (optional)
Finely grated peel and juice of 1 lemon
Salt and pepper
4 sprigs chervil
Lemon wedges and chervil sprigs to garnish

Preheat oven to 350F (175C). Generously butter 4 pieces of parchment paper or foil large enough to loosely enclose each fillet.

To make the dressing, using a mortar and pestle, crush garlic with anchovies, then mix in parsley, oregano, capers and lemon juice. Beat in oil very slowly; set aside. Put flour on a plate and season with salt and pepper. Put egg and bread crumbs in separate shallow bowls. Coat fish in seasoned flour; dip in egg. Allow excess to drain off, then coat fish lightly and evenly in bread crumbs. Set aside 5 minutes.

Bring a saucepan of salted water to a boil. Add zucchini and boil 1 minute. Drain and refresh under cold running water. Pat dry. Make a bed of zucchini in center of each piece of paper or foil. Place a piece of fish on each bed of zucchini. Place about 1 tablespoon of butter, if using, on each fillet. Sprinkle with lemon peel and juice, season with salt and pepper, and top with a chervil sprig.

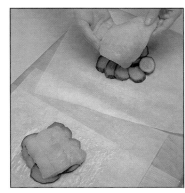

In a large skillet, heat oil. Add fish and cook until golden and crisp, about 3 minutes each side. Cook fish in batches if necessary so pan is not crowded. Using a spatula, transfer fish to paper towels to drain. Garnish with lemon wedges and herbs. Stir dressing and serve with hot fish.

Makes 4 servings.

Fold paper or foil over fish and seal edges tightly. Place fish packages on a baking sheet and bake about 15 minutes. Either serve fish and zucchini in the packages or transfer, with cooking juices, to warm plates. Garnish with lemon wedges and sprigs of chervil.

Makes 4 servings.

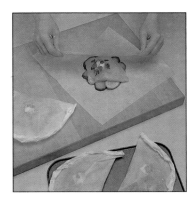

HALIBUT IN WINE SAUCE

INDONESIAN-STYLE HALIBUT

4 tablespoons olive oil
Flour for coating
Salt and pepper
2 pounds halibut, cut into 1-inch-thick slices
1/2 Spanish onion, finely chopped
2 canned anchovy fillets, drained and coarsely chopped
3 tablespoons chopped fresh parsley
3/4 cup dry white wine
Squeeze of lemon juice

4 halibut fillets, about 6 ounces each
Juice of 1 lime
2 teaspoons ground turmeric
1/2 cup vegetable oil
1 garlic clove, finely chopped
1/2-inch piece gingerroot, peeled and finely chopped
1 fresh red hot chile, seeded and chopped
1 onion, sliced lengthwise into thin wedges
2 teaspoons ground coriander
2/3 cup unsweetened coconut milk
1 teaspoon sugar
1/2 teaspoon salt
6 ounces snow peas
Cilantro sprigs, to garnish

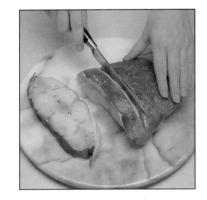

In a large skillet, heat 3 tablespoons of the oil. Season flour with salt and pepper. Coat fish evenly in the seasoned flour. Add fish slices to pan, making sure they are not crowded. Cook 5 minutes on each side.

Place fish fillets in a shallow dish. Sprinkle with lime juice and rub the turmeric into both sides of each fillet. Set aside. In a wok, heat half of the oil until hot, but not smoking; swirl to coat wok. Gently slide 2 of the fish fillets into the oil and fry 4 to 5 minutes, carefully turning once during cooking. Remove and drain on paper towels. Add remaining oil to wok and fry remaining fish fillets in the same way. Drain as before and keep fish fillets warm.

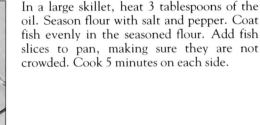

Meanwhile, in a small saucepan, heat remaining oil. Add onion and cook over low heat about 7 minutes until lightly colored. Add anchovies and parsley and cook, stirring and mashing anchovies with a wooden spoon, until anchovies are blended in. Stir in wine and boil until reduced by half. Add pepper and lemon juice to taste. Spoon or pour surplus oil from skillet; pour sauce over the fish. Cook over medium heat 2 minutes, basting occasionally. Serve.

Makes 4 servings.

Pour off all but 1 tablespoon oil from wok. Add garlic, gingerroot and chile and stir-fry 1 minute. Add onion and coriander and stir-fry 2 minutes until onion begins to soften. Stir in coconut milk, sugar and salt and bring to a boil, adding a little more water if sauce is too thick. Stir in snow-peas and cook 1 minute, until they turn bright green. Spoon sauce over fish fillets and garnish with cilantro.

Makes 4 servings.

— BAKED COD WITH LENTILS —

— FLOUNDER WITH PROSCIUTTO —

3 tablespoons olive oil
3 shallots, finely chopped
2 garlic cloves, finely crushed
1 cup green or brown lentils
3-1/2 teaspoons crushed coriander seeds
1-1/4 cups fish stock
1-1/4 cups dry white wine
2 tablespoons chopped fresh cilantro
1-1/2 pounds cod fillet, cut into 4 pieces
Pinch saffron threads, toasted and crushed
4 tomatoes, peeled, seeded, and chopped
Salt and pepper
Cilantro sprigs to garnish

2-1/2 large slices prosciutto
8 small flounder fillets
8 small sage leaves
2 tablespoons lemon juice, plus extra for seasoning
Salt and pepper
1-1/2 to 2 tablespoons light olive oil
1 tablespoon unsalted butter, diced
Hot cooked pasta to serve
Lemon peel shreds to garnish

Cut prosciutto into 8 strips lengthwise. On each piece of prosciutto, lay a flounder fillet.

In a saucepan, heat 1-1/2 tablespoons oil. Add 2 of the shallots and the garlic and cook over low heat until softened. Stir in lentils and 3 teaspoons coriander seeds. Cook 2 minutes, stirring, then stir in stock and wine. Bring to a boil, then reduce heat and simmer, covered, 30 to 45 minutes until lentils are tender. Stir in chopped cilantro. Meanwhile, preheat oven to 450F (230C). In a nonstick roasting pan, heat 1 tablespoon oil. Add cod, skin sides down; cook 2 minutes. Transfer to oven and bake 8 minutes.

Put a sage leaf at one end of each fillet and season with lemon juice and pepper. Roll up each fillet. Secure each with a wooden pick.

In a saucepan, heat remaining oil. Add remaining shallot and coriander seeds and the saffron and cook over low heat until softened. Add tomatoes and a little lentil cooking liquid, then season with salt and pepper. Simmer 5 minutes. Drain lentils and season. Serve cod on lentils, garnished with sprigs of cilantro and accompanied by the tomato relish.

Makes 4 servings.

In a nonstick skillet, heat oil. Add flounder rolls, seam sides down, then cook until lightly browned all over. Transfer fish rolls to a warm serving plate. Stir 2 tablespoons lemon juice into pan and bring to a boil. Remove pan from heat and swirl in butter. Season with salt and pepper, then pour over flounder rolls. Serve on a bed of pasta, garnished with lemon peel.

Makes 4 servings.

—FRIED FISH WITH SKORDALIA—

2 pounds fish fillets, such as cod
Flour seasoned with salt and pepper
Vegetable oil for deep-frying
BATTER:
1 cup all-purpose flour
1 teaspoon chopped fresh parsley
2 tablespoons butter, melted
3/4 cup lukewarm water
1 egg white
SKORDALIA:
3 garlic cloves, crushed
2-inch thick slice white bread
1-1/4 cups ground blanched almonds
1/2 cup extra-virgin olive oil
2 teaspoons fresh lemon juice

To make the batter, into a large bowl, sift flour and a pinch of salt. Stir in parsley. Add melted butter and gradually add water, beating to form a smooth, creamy batter. Let stand 1 hour. Meanwhile, make the Skordalia. Put garlic in a blender or food processor fitted with the metal blade. Remove crust from bread. Squeeze bread in a little cold water, then add to garlic with ground almonds and a little olive oil.

With the motor running, gradually add remaining oil. Stir in lemon juice and salt and pepper to taste. In a bowl, whisk egg white, then fold into batter mixture. Heat oil in a deep-fryer. Cut fish into 6 pieces. Dip in seasoned flour, then in batter. Fry 8 to 10 minutes, according to thickness of fish. Drain on paper towels, then serve with the Skordalia.

Makes 6 servings.

—CHUNKY FISH CASSEROLE—

1 cup pasta shells
3 tablespoons olive oil
2 garlic cloves, finely crushed
1/2 cup pearl onions, halved
2 cups halved button mushrooms
1 pound firm, white fish, such as cod or monkfish
8 ounces trout fillets
3 tablespoons well-seasoned all-purpose flour
1-1/3 cups fava beans
1/2 cup dry white wine
1-1/4 cups fish stock
Large bouquet garni
Grated peel and juice of 1 lemon
5 ounces cooked shelled shrimp or cooked shelled
   mussels or clams
Chopped fresh herbs to garnish

Preheat oven to 350F (175C). In a large saucepan of boiling water, cook pasta three-quarters of time recommended on package. Drain and rinse under cold running water; set aside. In a skillet, heat half the oil. Add garlic, onions, and mushrooms and cook 3 to 4 minutes. Using a slotted spoon, transfer vegetables to a large, deep baking dish. Meanwhile, skin fish, if needed, and cut into 1-inch chunks. Toss in seasoned flour.

Heat remaining oil in a skillet. Add fish, in batches if necessary, and fry 2 to 3 minutes, turning pieces carefully. Transfer to dish. Add pasta and beans. Stir wine, stock, bouquet garni, and lemon peel and juice into skillet. Bring to a boil. Reduce heat and simmer a few minutes, then pour into dish. Cover and bake about 30 minutes. Add shrimp, mussels or clams, cover again, and bake about 5 minutes. Garnish with plenty of chopped herbs.

Makes 4 servings.

COD WITH PARSLEY CRUST

FISH IN GREEN SAUCE

1-1/2 pounds cod, haddock or hake fillets, skinned
Salt and pepper
2 garlic cloves, crushed
1/3 cup olive oil
1 cup fresh bread crumbs
2 tablespoons chopped fresh parsley
1/4 cup fresh lemon juice
Parsley and lime wedges, to garnish

Season fish with salt and pepper and put in a shallow baking dish.

3 tablespoons olive oil
4 hake or cod steaks, about 6 ounces each
1/2 Spanish onion, finely chopped
3 garlic cloves, chopped
1/2 cup fish stock
2 tablespoons chopped fresh parsley
3/4 cup slivered, toasted almonds
Salt and pepper
Fennel sprigs, to garnish

In a skillet, heat oil. Add fish and cook 2 minutes on each side.

In a bowl, mix together garlic and 4 tablespoons of the oil. Pour over fish, cover and refrigerate 1 hour. Meanwhile, preheat oven to 350F (175C).

Using a spatula, transfer fish to a warmed plate, cover and keep warm. Add onion to oil remaining in pan and fry 3 minutes. Stir in garlic and fry 3 minutes, then stir in stock, parsley and almonds. Simmer about 3 minutes or until slightly thickened.

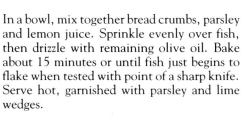

In a bowl, mix together bread crumbs, parsley and lemon juice. Sprinkle evenly over fish, then drizzle with remaining olive oil. Bake about 15 minutes or until fish just begins to flake when tested with point of a sharp knife. Serve hot, garnished with parsley and lime wedges.

Makes 4 servings.

Transfer almond mixture to a blender or food processor with the metal blade and process until smooth. Season with salt and pepper. Return fish to pan, pour the sauce over the top and heat through 1 to 2 minutes. Garnish with fennel.

Makes 4 servings.

COCONUT SPICED COD

FISH GRATINS

4 (6- to 8-oz.) cod steaks
Salt and pepper to taste
2 tablespoons vegetable oil
1 onion, chopped
1-1/3 cups shredded coconut
1 (2-inch) piece fresh gingerroot, grated
2 garlic cloves, crushed
2 green chiles, seeded, chopped
1/2 teaspoon chile powder
Grated peel and juice of 1 lemon
2 tablespoons chopped cilantro (fresh coriander)
2 tomatoes, peeled, seeded and diced
Oregano sprigs, to garnish

1/2 teaspoon Dijon mustard
1 tablespoon lemon juice
1 tablespoon olive oil
Pinch freshly grated nutmeg
Salt and pepper
4 cod or haddock steaks, about 5 ounces each
1/2 cup finely shredded sharp Cheddar cheese
3 tablespoons freshly grated Parmesan cheese
2 tablespoons fine fresh bread crumbs
Paprika
Pattypan squash to serve
Basil sprigs to garnish

Rinse cod steaks; pat dry with paper towels. Place in a greased baking dish; sprinkle with salt and pepper. Heat oil in a skillet, add onion and cook, stirring, about 5 minutes, or until soft. Stir in coconut, gingerroot, garlic, chiles and chile powder; cook, stirring, 3 to 5 minutes, until golden brown.

Preheat broiler. In a small bowl, beat together mustard and lemon juice using a fork, then gradually beat in oil. Add nutmeg and season with salt and pepper. Place fish in a broiler pan. Brush 1 side of each fish with mustard mixture, then broil, coated sides up, 2 minutes. Turn fish over, brush tops with mustard mixture, and broil 2 minutes longer.

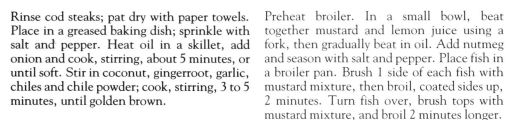

Stir in lemon peel and juice, cover and simmer 10 minutes to soften coconut. Preheat oven to 325F (160C). Stir cilantro and tomatoes into coconut mixture and spoon over steaks. Bake 20 to 25 minutes, until fish just begins to flake. Serve hot, garnished with oregano.

Cover fish with Cheddar cheese. Mix together Parmesan cheese and bread crumbs, then sprinkle evenly over fish. Season generously with pepper. Broil until the top is golden and bubbling. Lightly sprinkle with paprika. Serve with pattypan squash, garnished with sprigs of basil.

Makes 4 servings.

Makes 4 servings.

Note: Cover fish with foil during cooking if coconut begins to brown too much.

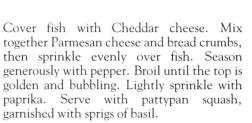

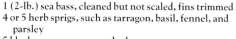

FISH CAKES

1 pound potatoes, cut into pieces and boiled
1 pound cooked mixed fresh and smoked fish, such as
    haddock or cod, flaked
2 tablespoons butter, diced
3 tablespoons chopped fresh parsley
1 egg, separated
Salt and pepper
1 egg, beaten
About 1 cup bread crumbs made from day-old bread
Olive oil for frying
Lemon wedges and onion and avocado salad to serve
Dill sprigs to garnish

Drain potatoes. Gently heat potatoes in saucepan a few minutes over low heat, shaking pan occasionally.

Remove pan from heat. Mash potatoes, then beat in fish, butter, chopped parsley, and egg yolk. Season with salt and pepper. Transfer to a large bowl and mix well. Chill if the mixture is too soft to handle.

Divide fish mixture into 8 equal portions. With floured hands, form each portion into a flat cake. In a bowl, beat egg white with whole egg. Spread bread crumbs on a plate. Dip each fish cake in egg, then in bread crumbs. In a skillet, heat a thin layer of oil. Fry fish cakes about 3 minutes on each side until crisp and golden. Drain on paper towels. Serve hot with lemon wedges and salad, garnished with sprigs of dill.

Makes 4 servings.

SEA BASS UNDER A CRUST

1 (2-lb.) sea bass, cleaned but not scaled, fins trimmed
4 or 5 herb sprigs, such as tarragon, basil, fennel, and
    parsley
5 black peppercorns, crushed
4 pounds coarse sea salt
Tomato, basil, red onion, and caper salad to serve
Lemon wedges and basil sprigs to garnish

Preheat oven to 425F (220C). In cavity of sea bass, place herb sprigs and peppercorns. In a deep baking dish that fish will fit without too much space around, spread a layer of salt about 1 inch deep.

Place fish on salt. Pack salt around fish until it is completely buried and there is a 1-inch layer on top. Bake fish about 25 minutes.

To serve, crack open salt crust and remove pieces carefully to expose whole fish. Remove skin from top of fish and serve the fish with salad, garnished with lemon wedges and sprigs of basil.

Makes 2 or 3 servings.

—BASS WITH GINGER & LIME—

—TROUT WITH TOMATO SAUCE—

2 shallots, finely chopped
1 (1-1/2-inch) piece gingerroot, finely chopped
Juice of 2 limes
1/4 cup rice wine vinegar
1 cup olive oil
2 tablespoons Chinese sesame oil
2 tablespoons soy sauce
Salt and pepper
6 to 8 bass fillets, about 1/2 inch thick each
Leaves from 1 bunch cilantro
Toasted sesame seeds to garnish
Stir-fried baby corn and sun-dried tomatoes to serve

In a bowl, mix together first 8 ingredients. Set aside.

Preheat broiler. Brush fish lightly with ginger mixture. Place fish on a large baking sheet. Broil 2 to 3 minutes on each side.

Before serving, bring remaining ginger mixture to a full boil, then remove from heat. Chop cilantro, reserving a few leaves for garnish. Mix chopped cilantro into ginger mixture. Spoon some onto serving plates at room temperature, then place fish on top. Sprinkle with sesame seeds and garnish with reserved cilantro leaves. Serve with stir-fried baby corn and sun-dried tomatoes.

Makes 6 to 8 servings.

2-1/2 ounces sun-dried tomatoes
2 teaspoons capers, drained
1 large garlic clove, crushed
8 basil leaves
Leaves from 2 small sprigs rosemary
Leaves from 2 sprigs oregano
1/4 cup butter, plus extra for brushing
1 tablespoon crème fraîche or sour cream
1-1/4 cup fish stock
Salt and pepper
6 to 8 trout fillets
Sugar snap peas and sun-dried tomatoes to serve
Lemon wedges and oregano sprigs to garnish

In a blender or food processor, process sun-dried tomatoes, capers, garlic, herbs, 1/4 cup butter, crème fraîche, and stock until smooth. Season with pepper and just a little salt. Pour mixture into a saucepan.

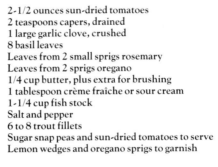

Preheat broiler. Brush trout with butter and season with pepper. Place on a baking sheet and broil 3 to 4 minutes on each side. Meanwhile, heat sauce over low heat, stirring occasionally. Transfer fish to warm plates, season with salt and spoon sauce over the fish. Serve with sugar snap peas and sun-dried tomatoes, garnished with lemon wedges and sprigs of oregano.

Makes 3 or 4 servings.

TROUT WITH PROSCIUTTO

4 trout, about 10 ounces each
Pepper
1 lemon, quartered
4 sprigs basil or tarragon
4 slices prosciutto
Lemon wedges and chervil sprigs to garnish
Tomato, lime, red chicory, and asparagus salad to serve

Preheat oven to 400F (205C). Season trout with pepper and a squeeze of lemon juice. Inside each fish, place a sprig of basil or tarragon.

Wrap a slice of prosciutto around each fish and season with pepper. Place fish into a large shallow baking dish with loose ends of prosciutto underneath.

Bake fish 15 to 20 minutes or until cooked through and flesh flakes. Garnish with lemon wedges and sprigs of chervil and serve with salad.

Makes 4 servings.

BAKED TROUT WITH GINGER

2 trout, each weighing 10 oz., cleaned
Salt and freshly ground pepper
2 green onions, finely shredded
1 tablespoon chopped fresh cilantro
Strips of fresh red chile, to garnish
SAUCE:
1 garlic clove, finely chopped
1/2-inch piece fresh ginger root, peeled and finely chopped
2 tablespoons white rice vinegar
2 tablespoons light soy sauce
2 tablespoons dry sherry
1 teaspoon salt
1 teaspoon chile powder
2 teaspoons sugar

Preheat oven to 350F (175C). Rinse trout and pat dry with paper towels. Season trout inside and out with salt and pepper. Fill the cavities with green onions and cilantro. Using a sharp knife, score flesh lightly in diagonal lines. Place trout in a nonstick roasting pan.

Mix together sauce ingredients and pour over trout. Cover loosely with oiled foil and bake 20 minutes, basting halfway through. Remove foil, baste, and bake, uncovered, 10 minutes. Skin trout and remove flesh from bones to give 4 fillets. Brush with cooking juices, garnish with strips of chile and serve with noodles and vegetables.

Makes 4 servings.

SALMON WITH AVOCADO SALSA

SALMON STIR-FRY

4 salmon fillets with skin, about 6 ounces each
2-1/2 tablespoons olive oil
Sea salt and pepper
Lime wedges and cilantro leaves to garnish
SALSA:
1 ripe but firm avocado
2 large ripe tomatoes, peeled, seeded, and finely chopped
1/2 small red onion, finely chopped
1/2 to 1 fresh red chile, seeded and thinly sliced
1 garlic clove, finely chopped
2 tablespoons lime juice
2 tablespoons chopped fresh cilantro
Salt and pepper

1 pound small asparagus, trimmed
2 tablespoons peanut oil
10 ounces salmon, skinned, boned, and cut into thin strips 1 inch long
Squeeze of lemon juice
1 tablespoon soy sauce
2 teaspoons sesame oil
Salt and pepper
Lightly toasted sesame seeds to garnish
Chinese egg noodles to serve

Slice asparagus diagonally into 1/2-inch pieces. Bring a saucepan of salted water to a boil. Add asparagus and cook 1-1/2 minutes. Drain and rinse.

To make salsa, halve avocado, then discard seed, quarter each half, and remove skin. Dice avocado flesh, and in a bowl mix with remaining salsa ingredients. Cover and refrigerate about 1 hour.

In a wok or large skillet, heat peanut oil. Add asparagus and stir-fry 1-1/2 minutes.

Pat fish dry with paper towels, then brush skin with some of the olive oil. In a heavy skillet, heat remaining oil until hot. Add salmon, skin sides down, and cook 10 to 15 minutes depending on thickness of fillets, until skin is quite crisp, sides are opaque, and top is slightly soft as it should be rare. Season salmon with sea salt and pepper, garnish with lime wedges and cilantro leaves, and serve with salsa.

Makes 4 servings.

Add salmon, lemon juice, soy sauce, and sesame oil. Stir-fry 2 minutes. Add pepper and a little salt. Serve immediately, sprinkled with sesame seeds, accompanied by egg noodles.

Makes 4 servings.

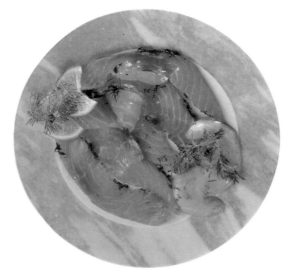

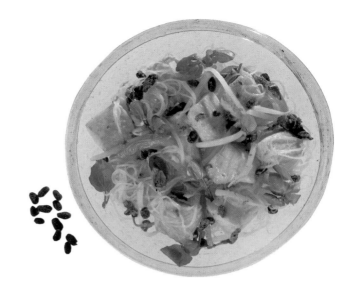

GRAVLAX

3 tablespoons sea salt
2 to 3 teaspoons light brown sugar
2 teaspoons crushed black peppercorns
6 tablespoons lime juice
Large bunch dill
1 (3- to 4-lb.) salmon, filleted, with skin
Lime slices and dill sprigs to garnish
DILL & MUSTARD SAUCE:
3 tablespoons Dijon mustard
2 tablespoons white-wine vinegar
1 tablespoon sugar
2/3 cup grapeseed oil
2 tablespoons finely chopped fresh dill
Salt and pepper

In a small bowl, mix together sea salt, sugar, peppercorns, and lime juice. In a shallow, nonmetallic dish, spread some dill. Add one-quarter of salt mixture. Lay one salmon fillet, skin side down, in dish. Cover with plenty of dill and sprinkle with half remaining salt mixture. Place remaining salmon on top, skin side up. Cover salmon with remaining dill and sprinkle with remaining salt mixture. Cover with parchment paper, then plastic wrap.

Place a 2-pound weight on top and refrigerate 3 days, turning occasionally and spooning liquid back between fillets occasionally. To make sauce, in a bowl, mix together mustard, vinegar, and sugar, then gradually beat in oil. Add chopped dill, salt, and pepper. Drain salmon well, pat dry, and trim off any hard edges. Very thinly slice salmon on the diagonal, discarding skin. Garnish with lime slices and sprigs of dill and serve with sauce.

Makes 8 servings.

CHINESE SALAD WITH SALMON

12 ounces Chinese noodles
1 tablespoon salted black beans, coarsely chopped
3 ounces bean sprouts
1 tablespoon peanut oil
1 pound salmon fillets, cut into 1-inch cubes
2 teaspoons grated gingerroot
2 tablespoons rice wine or medium-dry sherry
2 teaspoons sesame oil
3 ounces watercress leaves and fine stems
1/2 red bell pepper, seeded and chopped

Cook noodles according to package directions, drain, and rinse well with cold water. Drain again, then put into a serving bowl, cover and refrigerate while preparing remaining ingredients. Soak black beans in 1 to 2 tablespoons hot water. Bring a pan of water to a boil, add bean sprouts and boil 1 minute. Drain, rinse under cold running water, then set aside. In a skillet, heat peanut oil. Add salmon, in batches if necessary, and fry until just cooked and pale gold. Drain on paper towels.

Add gingerroot, rice wine or sherry, sesame oil, and half the watercress. Boil a few seconds, then add black beans and remove from heat. Add bean sprouts, bell pepper, and salmon to noodles. Pour warm dressing over noodle mixture and garnish with remaining watercress.

Makes 4 servings.

TUNA & GINGER VINAIGRETTE

TUNA WITH SPICY SALSA

1 (1-inch) piece gingerroot, finely chopped
2 large green onions, white and some green parts thinly
    sliced
1 cup olive oil
Juice of 2 limes
2 tablespoons soy sauce
2 tablespoons sesame oil
1 bunch cilantro, finely chopped
Pepper
6 tuna steaks, 5 to 6 ounces each
Leeks and red bell peppers stir-fried with sesame seeds
Cilantro sprigs to garnish

2 tablespoons sesame oil
1 tablespoon light soy sauce
1 garlic clove, finely chopped
1-1/2 pounds tuna steaks, 1 inch thick, cut into chunks
2 tablespoons vegetable oil
8 ounces daikon, diced
1 small cucumber, peeled, seeded and diced
1 red bell pepper, diced
1 red onion, finely chopped
1 fresh hot red chile, seeded and finely chopped
2 tablespoons lime juice
1 teaspoon sugar
1 tablespoon sesame seeds, toasted
Lime wedges and cilantro sprigs, to garnish
Oriental noodles, to serve

Preheat broiler. To make vinaigrette, in a bowl, stir together gingerroot, green onions, olive oil, lime juice, and soy sauce. Beat in sesame oil. Add chopped cilantro and season with pepper. Set aside.

In a shallow dish, combine 1 tablespoon of the sesame oil, soy sauce and garlic. Add tuna chunks and toss gently to coat. Allow to stand 15 minutes. Heat a wok until very hot; add 1 tablespoon of the vegetable oil and swirl to coat. Add daikon, cucumber, bell pepper, onion and chile and stir-fry 2 to 3 minutes or until vegetables begin to soften and turn a bright color. Stir in lime juice, sugar and remaining sesame oil and cook 30 seconds or until sugar dissolves. Remove to a bowl.

Place tuna on a broiler pan. Broil tuna 3-1/2 to 4 minutes on each side, or a little longer for well-done fish. Spoon some dressing onto 6 serving plates. Add tuna. Serve with leeks and red bell peppers, garnished with sprigs of cilantro. Serve any remaining dressing separately.

Makes 6 servings.

Add remaining vegetable oil to wok and, working in batches, if necessary, add fish chunks and stir-fry gently 2 to 3 minutes or until firm. Arrange fish on 4 dinner plates and sprinkle with the sesame seeds. Spoon some of the warm relish onto each plate and garnish with lime wedges and cilantro sprigs. Serve with noodles.

Makes 4 servings.

LAYERED FISH TERRINE

1 pound salmon, skinned and boned
Salt and white pepper
2/3 cup medium-dry white wine
2 small bunches watercress, trimmed
1 tablespoon butter
1 shallot, finely chopped
1 pound firm white fish, such as hake, monkfish, or cod, skinned, boned, and cubed
2 egg whites
1 cup whipping cream, chilled
Lime slices and mint sprigs to garnish

In a small saucepan, melt butter. Add shallot and cook over low heat until softened but not browned. In a blender or food processor, puree shallot with fish. Add egg whites and season with salt and pepper. Process 1 minute, then, with motor running, slowly pour in cream. Remove and reserve two-thirds of fish mixture. Add watercress to blender or food processor and puree briefly. Chill both mixtures 30 minutes.

Cut salmon into long strips. Put salmon strips into a dish. Season with salt and white pepper and pour wine over salmon. Cover and refrigerate about 1 hour.

Preheat oven to 350F (175C). Lightly oil a 10″ × 3-1/2″ terrine pan. Spread half the plain fish mixture in the bottom of the pan, then half the salmon strips followed by all the green mixture. Cover this with remaining salmon strips, then remaining white mixture.

Meanwhile, bring a saucepan of lightly salted water to a boil. Add watercress and blanch 1 minute. Drain watercress, rinse under cold running water, and drain again. Dry on paper towels; set aside.

Cover terrine with foil. In a roasting pan, place terrine and pour in enough boiling water to come halfway up sides of terrine. Bake about 40 minutes until a skewer inserted in center comes out clean. Transfer terrine to a wire rack to cool slightly, then refrigerate. Cut into slices and serve garnished with lime slices and sprigs of mint.

Makes 4 to 6 servings.

ESCABECHE

6 to 8 red snapper or catfish fillets, cleaned and scaled
3 tablespoons seasoned flour
3 tablespoons olive oil
2 to 3 tablespoons chopped fresh cilantro
MARINADE:
Large pinch saffron threads, toasted
2 tablespoons olive oil
2 red onions, thinly sliced
2 red bell peppers, seeded and sliced
1/2 teaspoon dried chile flakes
1-1/2 teaspoons cumin seeds, lightly crushed
Finely grated peel and juice of 1 orange
2 to 3 tablespoons rice vinegar
Pinch sugar
Salt and pepper

To make marinade, crush saffron. In a bowl, soak in warm water 10 minutes. In a skillet, heat oil. Gently cook onions 2 minutes. Add bell peppers, chile flakes, and cumin. Fry until vegetables are soft. Stir in saffron and liquid, orange peel and juice, vinegar, sugar, salt, and pepper. Bubble a few minutes, then set aside and let cool.

Toss fish in flour. In a skillet, heat 3 table-spoons oil. Add fish and fry 2 to 3 minutes on each side until just cooked through and browned. In a shallow, nonmetallic dish, place fish in a single layer. Pour marinade over it. Cover and refrigerate 4 to 12 hours. Return to room temperature 15 minutes before serving. Stir in cilantro.

Serves 6 to 8 as an appetizer.

Note: Garnish with orange slices and sprigs of cilantro, if wished.

SKATE WITH ANCHOVY SAUCE

4 small skate wings
Salt and pepper
1 tablespoon olive oil
1 tablespoon unsalted butter
Sugar snap peas and new potatoes to serve
Basil sprigs to garnish
SAUCE:
1 large clove garlic
6 anchovy fillets, chopped
2-1/2 tablespoons capers
2-1/2 teaspoons whole-grain mustard
1-1/2 tablespoons chopped fresh basil
3 tablespoons chopped fresh parsley
3 tablespoons lime juice
3 tablespoons virgin olive oil
Black pepper

To make sauce, in a small bowl, crush garlic with anchovies. Stir in capers, mustard, basil, parsley, and lime juice, then gradually beat in oil. Season with black pepper and set aside.

Season skate wings. In a large nonstick skillet, heat oil and melt butter. Add 2 skate wings and fry about 4 minutes on each side until lightly browned. Transfer skate wings to paper towels, then fry remaining skate in same way. Return skate to pan, pour in sauce, and heat briefly until warmed through. Serve with sugar snap peas and new potatoes, garnished with sprigs of basil.

Makes 4 servings.

FISH PLAKI

about 2-1/2 pounds fish, such as porgy, sea bass, gray
   mullet, red snapper, or pompano, scaled
Juice of 1/2 lemon
2 tablespoons olive oil
1 onion, chopped
1 carrot, finely chopped
1 stalk celery, chopped
2 garlic cloves, chopped
1 teaspoon coriander seeds, crushed
1 pound tomatoes, peeled, seeded, and chopped
3 sun-dried tomato halves, finely chopped
1/3 cup dry white wine
Leaves from bunch parsley, finely chopped
Salt and pepper
Parsley sprigs to garnish

Preheat oven to 375F (190C). Into a baking
dish, put fish. Squeeze lemon juice over. In a
saucepan heat oil. Add onion, carrot, and
celery and cook, stirring occasionally, until
onion has softened but not colored. Stir in
garlic and cook about 3 minutes longer. Stir
in coriander seeds, tomatoes, sun-dried
tomatoes, wine, and parsley. Season with salt
and pepper and simmer a few minutes until
well blended.

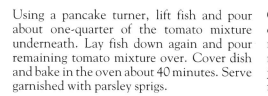

Using a pancake turner, lift fish and pour
about one-quarter of the tomato mixture
underneath. Lay fish down again and pour
remaining tomato mixture over. Cover dish
and bake in the oven about 40 minutes. Serve
garnished with parsley sprigs.

Makes 4 servings.

SEAFOOD GUMBO

2 tablespoons olive oil
2 onions, chopped, and 2 garlic cloves, crushed
1 green bell pepper, cored and chopped
1 stalk celery, chopped
2 tablespoons seasoned flour
3 cups fish stock
1 (14-1/2-oz.) can chopped tomatoes
2/3 cup chopped cooked ham
Bouquet garni
8 ounces fresh okra, sliced
8 ounces each white crab meat and cooked shelled
   shrimp
14 ounces firm white fish fillets, cut into chunks
Lemon juice and dash hot-pepper sauce
2-1/2 cups boiled long-grain rice to serve

In a heavy flameproof casserole, heat oil.
Add onions and cook until softened. Add
garlic, bell pepper, and celery and cook,
stirring frequently, 5 minutes. Sprinkle flour
over and stir 1 minute longer. Stir in stock,
tomatoes, ham, and bouquet garni. Partially
cover and simmer 30 minutes longer. Add
okra and simmer, covered, 30 minutes.

Chop crab meat and shrimp. Add fish to
casserole and cook about 7 minutes. Add crab
meat and shrimp and cook about 2-1/2
minutes until shrimp are hot. Add lemon
juice and hot-pepper sauce to taste. Spoon
rice into warm serving bowls and ladle gumbo
over it.

Makes 4 to 6 servings.

Note: Sprinkle chopped fresh parsley over
the top, if wished.

—SMOKED SALMON SCRAMBLE— —KEDGEREE—

4 ounces smoked salmon trimmings, chopped
2 tablespoons light cream
3 tablespoons unsalted butter
4 large eggs, beaten
Black pepper
Snipped fresh chives and lime slices to garnish
Buttered toasted bagels or English muffins to serve

In a small bowl, mix together smoked salmon and cream. Leave to stand 10 to 15 minutes.

1-1/4 pounds smoked haddock or salmon
1/2 cup long-grain rice
2 tablespoons lemon juice
2/3 cup light or sour cream
Pinch freshly grated nutmeg
Red (cayenne) pepper
2 hard-cooked eggs, shelled and chopped
4 tablespoons butter, diced
2 tablespoons chopped fresh parsley
Parsley sprigs and sliced hard-cooked eggs to garnish

In a saucepan, melt half the butter. Stir in eggs. Cook over low heat, stirring with a wooden spoon, until beginning to set. Add salmon and cream and season with pepper. Continue to stir until eggs are almost set.

In a large skillet that will take fish in a single layer, poach fish just covered by water about 10 minutes. Lift fish from cooking liquid and discard bones and skin. Flake flesh. Measure fish cooking liquid to twice volume of rice; top up with water if necessary. Into a saucepan, put liquid and rice. Bring to a boil. Add rice, and stir, then cover and simmer about 15 minutes until rice is tender and liquid absorbed. Meanwhile, preheat oven to 350F (175C). Butter a baking dish.

Remove pan from heat and immediately stir in remaining butter. Garnish with snipped chives and lime slices and serve with buttered toasted bagels or English muffins.

Makes 2 servings.

Remove rice from heat. Stir in lemon juice, cream, fish, nutmeg, and a pinch of cayenne. Gently fold in eggs. In an openproof serving dish, put rice mixture. Dot with butter and bake about 25 minutes. Stir chopped parsley into kedgeree and garnish with parsley sprigs and sliced hard-cooked egg. Sprinkle a little cayenne over top, if wished.

Makes 4 servings.

POULTRY & GAME

CHICKEN & HAM CROQUETTES

1/4 cup butter or margarine
1 onion, finely chopped
1/2 cup all-purpose flour
1-1/4 cups milk
2-1/2 cups finely chopped cooked chicken
1/2 cup finely chopped ham
2 tablespoons chopped fresh parsley
1 teaspoon Dijon-style mustard
Salt and pepper
1-1/2 cups fresh white bread crumbs
Vegetable oil, for frying
Lemon wedges and green salad, to serve

In a saucepan, melt butter. Add onion; cook 3 to 4 minutes or until softened.

Add flour. Cook 1 minute, stirring. Gradually blend in milk and bring to a boil, stirring constantly. Reduce heat and simmer 2 minutes until sauce is a thick paste. Add chopped chicken, ham, parsley and mustard. Season with a little salt and pepper. Mix well and set aside to cool. Place bread crumbs on a plate. Drop tablespoons of chicken mixture onto bread crumbs.

Roll mixture in crumbs to give an even coating. Refrigerate 30 minutes. In a skillet, heat 2 tablespoons oil. Fry croquettes, a few at a time, until golden-brown. Drain on paper towels. Serve with lemon wedges and salad.

Makes 12 to 14 croquettes.

CHICKEN BURGERS

3 ounces stuffing mix
1/2 pound ground chicken
1 small egg, beaten
1 apple, peeled, cored and grated
Salt and pepper
1 to 2 tablespoons vegetable oil
4 sesame seed buns
Iceberg lettuce, shredded
2 tomatoes, sliced
4 processed Cheddar cheese slices
Mayonnaise and relish, to serve

In a bowl, prepare stuffing mix according to package directions.

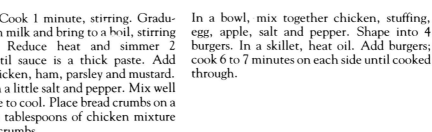

In a bowl, mix together chicken, stuffing, egg, apple, salt and pepper. Shape into 4 burgers. In a skillet, heat oil. Add burgers; cook 6 to 7 minutes on each side until cooked through.

Split buns in half. Cover bottoms with shredded lettuce and tomato slices. Cover each burger with a cheese slice and place over lettuce and tomato. Top with relish or mayonnaise. Place bun top in position.

Makes 4 servings.

CHICKEN KIEV

1/2 cup unsalted butter, softened
3 garlic cloves, crushed
Finely grated peel of 1/2 lemon
1 tablespoon chopped fresh parsley
Salt and pepper
4 skinned and boned chicken breast halves
2 eggs, beaten
3 cups fresh white bread crumbs
Vegetable oil, for deep frying

In a bowl, beat together butter, garlic, lemon peel, parsley, salt and pepper. Transfer to a pastry bag fitted with a plain 1/4-inch tip.

On a cutting board, lay chicken breasts. Insert a sharp knife into breast to form a pocket. Pipe butter into pocket; do not overfill or butter will burst through flesh. Refrigerate 25 minutes.

Dip a filled chicken breast half into beaten eggs, then roll in bread crumbs. Repeat, making sure chicken is well coated. Repeat with remaining chicken. Half-fill a deep-fryer or pan with oil. Heat to 375F (190C) or until an 1-inch bread cube browns in 40 seconds. Add chicken, 2 pieces at a time, and fry 8 to 10 minutes or until the chicken is cooked through and golden-brown. Drain on paper towels. Serve immediately with a squeeze of lemon juice.

Makes 4 servings.

HONEY CHICKEN DRUMSTICKS

8 chicken drumsticks
1/4 cup honey
2 teaspoons Dijon-style mustard
2 teaspoons whole-grain mustard
1 teaspoon soy sauce
1 teaspoon dried rosemary
4 tablespoons mayonnaise (optional)
Lemon juice to taste (optional)

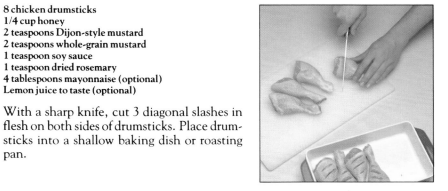

With a sharp knife, cut 3 diagonal slashes in flesh on both sides of drumsticks. Place drumsticks into a shallow baking dish or roasting pan.

In a small bowl, mix together honey, mustards and soy sauce. Pour over drumsticks. Cover and marinate 1 hour, turning occasionally.

Preheat oven to 400F (205C). Sprinkle rosemary over drumsticks. Roast 25 minutes. Increase heat to 450F (230C) and cook 10 minutes longer, basting and turning the drumsticks several times. If desired, any juices from pan can be added to the mayonnaise with a squeeze of lemon juice to make a sauce to serve with drumsticks.

Makes 4 servings.

LEMON CHICKEN

1 egg white
12 ounces chicken breasts, sliced
3 teaspoons cornstarch
Finely grated peel and juice of 1 lemon
2 tablespoons dry sherry
1 teaspoon soy sauce
2 teaspoons honey
3 tablespoons vegetable oil
4 green onions, sliced
2 ounces snow peas, topped and tailed
1/2 red bell pepper, finely sliced
2 ounces bean sprouts

In a bowl, beat egg white until frothy. Add chicken and 2 teaspoons of the cornstarch.

Mix well. Mix in lemon peel. In a small bowl, mix together remaining cornstarch, sherry, lemon juice, soy sauce and honey. Set aside. In a wok or large skillet, heat oil. Add chicken pieces, a few at a time to prevent them from sticking together. Stir-fry 2 minutes or until chicken is cooked through.

Add green onions, snow peas, bell pepper and bean sprouts; stir-fry 1 minute longer. Add lemon juice and cornstarch mixture. Stir-fry 1 to 2 minutes, stirring until the sauce thickens and coats chicken and vegetables.

Makes 4 servings.

CHICKEN IN CAPER SAUCE

1 onion, quartered, and 1 carrot, quartered
1 teaspoon finely grated orange peel
1 orange, peeled and sliced
4 bay leaves
1/4 cup dry white wine
1 cup chicken stock
4 skinned and boned chicken breast halves
2 tablespoons butter or margarine
1/4 cup all-purpose flour
2/3 cup half and half
1 tablespoon chopped fresh parsley
2 teaspoons capers, drained
Salt and pepper

Put onion, carrot, orange peel, orange and bay leaves into a skillet.

Add wine and stock. Bring to a boil. Add chicken, reduce heat to a simmer, then cover and poach 20 minutes or until cooked through. Remove chicken, drain well on paper towels and keep warm. Strain and reserve poaching liquid.

In a pan, melt butter. Stir in flour; cook, stirring, 1 minute, remove from heat and slowly stir in poaching liquid, stirring well between each addition. Return to heat and bring to a boil, stirring constantly, until thickened. Stir in half and half, parsley and capers; season with salt and pepper. Spoon sauce over chicken. Serve with wild rice.

Makes 4 servings.

Note: Garnish with orange peel and parsley, if desired.

TANDOORI CHICKEN

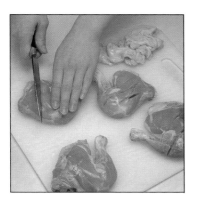

4 chicken leg quarters, skinned
Juice of 1 lemon
Salt
2 teaspoons ground turmeric
2 teaspoons paprika
1 teaspoon curry powder
1 teaspoon ground cardamom
1/2 teaspoon chili powder
Pinch of saffron powder
2 garlic cloves, crushed
2 teaspoons chopped gingerroot
1 tablespoon olive oil
3/4 cup plain yogurt
Lemon wedges, parsley and salsa, to garnish

Cut deep diagonal cuts in flesh.

Sprinkle chicken with lemon juice and a little salt. In a bowl, mix together remaining ingredients. Use to coat chicken quarters, cover and refrigerate 4 hours or overnight.

Preheat broiler. Cook chicken 25 minutes, brushing with any excess marinade and turning frequently until the chicken is tender and juices run clear when chicken leg is pierced with a knife. A slight blackening of the chicken gives an authentic look. Garnish with lemon wedges, parsley and salsa.

Makes 4 servings.

SPICY FRIED CHICKEN

4 chicken breasts
Salt and pepper
3 tablespoons paprika
2 tablespoons ground coriander
1 tablespoon ground cumin
Finely grated peel and juice of 1 lemon
3 tablespoons dark soy sauce
2 tablespoons chopped fresh cilantro
1 teaspoon chopped fresh thyme
1 onion, finely chopped
2 garlic cloves, crushed
1 red chile, seeded and chopped
Vegetable oil, for frying
3/4 cup all-purpose flour
Lemon wedges, to garnish

Remove skin from chicken. Into a shallow dish, place chicken. Make several incisions in chicken pieces. Season well with salt and pepper. In a small bowl, mix together 2 tablespoons of the paprika, 1 tablespoon of the coriander and 2 teaspoons of the cumin. Sprinkle over chicken. In a small bowl, mix lemon peel and juice with soy sauce. Stir in cilantro, thyme, onion, garlic and chile. Pour over chicken, making sure chicken is well covered. Cover dish with plastic wrap and refrigerate 3 hours or overnight.

Half-fill a deep-fryer or pan with oil. Heat to 375F (190C) or until an 1-inch bread cube browns in 40 seconds. Put flour on a plate; season with salt and pepper. Add remaining paprika, cumin and coriander; mix well. Dip chicken pieces in flour to coat. Deep-fry chicken 15 minutes or until golden-brown and cooked through. Garnish with lemon wedges.

Makes 8 servings.

JAMBALAYA

1 tablespoon olive oil
1 tablespoon butter or margarine
12 ounces skinned and boned chicken
6 ounces andouille or chorizo sausage
1 onion, thinly sliced
2 garlic cloves, sliced
1 red bell pepper, sliced
1 yellow bell pepper, sliced
1 green bell pepper, sliced
4 ounces mushrooms, sliced
1 cup long-grain white rice
1/2 teaspoon ground allspice
1-1/4 cups chicken stock
2/3 cup white wine
4 ounces shelled jumbo shrimp
Lime wedges and parsley, to garnish

In a large skillet, heat oil and butter. Cut chicken into thick strips. Fry until well browned, then remove from pan and set aside. Cut sausage into chunks. Fry 1 minute, stirring well, then, using a slotted spoon, add to chicken. Add onion and garlic; cook until slightly softened. Stir in bell peppers, mushrooms, rice and allspice. Cook, stirring, 1 minute longer.

Pour in stock and wine. Bring to a boil. Return chicken and sausage to pan and simmer, uncovered, 15 to 20 minutes until the liquid is absorbed and rice is tender. Stir in shrimp. Cook 5 minutes longer, then season to taste. Garnish with lime wedges and parsley.

Makes 4 servings.

CHICKEN FAJITAS

1/4 cup dry white wine
Finely grated peel and juice of 2 limes
1 tablespoon Worcestershire sauce
2 teaspoons brown sugar
1/2 teaspoon dried leaf basil
1/2 teaspoon dried leaf oregano
1 garlic clove, crushed
4 skinned and boned chicken breast halves
2 tablespoons vegetable oil
8 green onions, sliced
1 red bell pepper, sliced
1 green bell pepper, sliced
8 flour tortillas, warmed
2/3 cup dairy sour cream
Avocado, chopped
Oregano sprigs, to garnish

First prepare marinade for chicken. In a bowl, mix together wine, lime peel and juice, Worcestershire sauce, sugar, basil, oregano and garlic. Slice chicken breast into thin strips. Add to marinade. Mix well and marinate 30 to 40 minutes, stirring occasionally. In a skillet, heat 1 tablespoon of the oil. Add green onions and bell peppers; cook until onions are starting to brown, but the vegetables are still crisp. Remove from skillet and set aside. Drain chicken, reserving marinade.

In a skillet, heat remaining oil over medium-high heat. Add chicken (in several batches, if necessary) and fry quickly until golden-brown. Remove from pan with a slotted spoon and set aside. Add reserved marinade to pan and boil until thickened. Return chicken and peppers to skillet; mix well until all ingredients are coated. Put tortillas on a plate. Place spoonfuls of chicken mixture in middle of each tortilla; top with sour cream and avocado. Fold, garnish and serve.

Makes 4 servings.

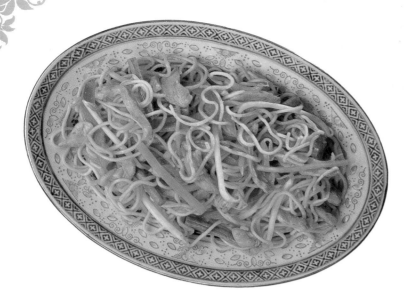

CHICKEN CHOW MEIN

3 tablespoons dark soy sauce
2 tablespoons dry sherry
1 teaspoon brown sugar
1 teaspoon sweet chili sauce
1/2 pound skinned and boned chicken, shredded
1/2 pound egg thread noodles
1 teaspoon cornstarch
6 tablespoons chicken stock or water
3 tablespoons vegetable oil
1 (1-inch) piece gingerroot, finely chopped
1 garlic clove, finely chopped
4 green onions, sliced
1 cup (1-inch pieces) green beans
1 small carrot, cut into matchstick strips
1 red pepper, seeded and finely sliced
6 ounces bean sprouts

In a bowl, mix together soy sauce, sherry, brown sugar and chili sauce. Add chicken and marinate 30 minutes. Drain chicken, reserving marinade. Cook noodles according to package directions. Drain well and set aside. Mix reserved marinade with cornstarch and chicken stock. Set aside.

In a wok or large skillet, heat oil. Add gingerroot and garlic. Stir-fry 15 to 20 seconds, then add chicken and stir-fry 2 to 3 minutes longer until chicken is cooked. Add green onions, beans, carrot and pepper. Stir-fry 1 minute. Add noodles and bean sprouts. Stir-fry 30 seconds, then add marinade mixture and stir-fry until sauce thickens and coats ingredients. Serve immediately.

Makes 4 servings.

SWEET & SOUR CHICKEN

1-1/2 pounds skinned and boned chicken breasts
Salt
5 tablespoons cornstarch
2 cups self-rising flour
3 large eggs, beaten
1 (1-inch) piece gingerroot, finely chopped
1 tablespoon vegetable oil, plus extra for frying
1/2 cup white-wine vinegar
1/4 cup dry sherry
1/2 cup orange juice
3 tablespoons soy sauce
1/4 cup tomato paste
1 garlic clove, finely chopped
1 small onion, finely chopped
1 red bell pepper, sliced
1 green bell pepper, sliced

Cut chicken into 1-inch cubes. Sprinkle with salt and 2 tablespoons cornstarch; mix thoroughly. Meanwhile, make batter. Into a bowl put flour. Gradually add eggs and 1-1/4 cups water to make a smooth batter. Add half of the gingerroot. Add chicken cubes and coat thoroughly. Half-fill a deep pan or deep-fat fryer with oil. Heat to 375F (190C) or until an 1-inch bread cube browns in 40 seconds. Add chicken, in batches, and fry 4 to 5 minutes or until golden and crispy. Drain well on paper towels. Transfer to a plate to keep warm.

In a small bowl, mix remaining 3 tablespoons cornstarch with 2/3 cup water, then add vinegar, sherry, orange juice, soy sauce and tomato paste. In a wok or large skillet, heat the 1 tablespoon oil. Add garlic and remaining gingerroot. Stir-fry 15 seconds. Add onion and bell peppers and stir-fry 1-1/2 minutes. Stir in cornstarch mixture; cook, stirring, until thickened. Put chicken into a warm serving dish; top with vegetables and sauce.

Makes 4 to 6 servings.

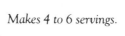

CHICKEN BIRYANI

TIKKA KABOBS

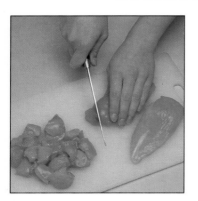

8 tablespoons vegetable oil
1 cinnamon stick
8 whole cloves
6 cardamom pods, bruised
1 (1-inch) piece gingerroot, finely chopped
1-1/2 pounds skinned and boned chicken, cubed
2 garlic cloves, crushed
1 teaspoon chili powder
1-1/4 cups plain yogurt
2/3 cup chicken stock
Pinch of saffron threads
1/4 cup boiling water
2-1/4 cups basmati rice
1/4 cup golden raisins
1/4 cup slivered almonds
1 onion, sliced

2/3 cup plain yogurt
1 tablespoon grated gingerroot
2 garlic cloves, crushed
1 teaspoon chili powder
1 teaspoon ground cumin
1 teaspoon turmeric
1 tablespoon coriander seeds
Juice of 1 lemon
1/2 teaspoon salt
2 tablespoons chopped fresh cilantro
12 ounces skinned and boned chicken, cubed
RAITA:
2/3 cup plain yogurt
2 teaspoons mint jelly
3/4 cup finely chopped cucumber
2 green onions, finely chopped

Preheat oven to 375F (190C). In a Dutch oven, heat 4 tablespoons of the oil. Add spices and fry 15 seconds. Add chicken, garlic and chili powder and fry, stirring, 4 minutes. Add yogurt, 1 tablespoon at a time, stirring between each addition until yogurt is absorbed by spices. Add stock and simmer 20 to 25 minutes. Transfer to a bowl. In a small bowl, soak saffron in boiling water and set aside. Rinse rice under cold running water until water runs clear. In a medium-size saucepan, cook rice in 5 cups boiling salted water 3 minutes, then drain, if necessary.

In a blender or food processor, process yogurt, gingerroot, garlic, chili powder, cumin, turmeric, coriander seeds, lemon juice, salt and cilantro until smooth. Pour into a bowl. Stir in chicken, cover and refrigerate overnight.

Wash Dutch oven. Add 2 tablespoons of the oil. Spoon in a layer of rice, sprinkle with a little saffron water and cover with a layer of chicken. Repeat, ending with a layer of rice. Add any cooking juices left from chicken, cover tightly and cook 25 to 30 minutes. In a small pan, heat remaining oil. Fry golden raisins and almonds until golden; remove. Add onion; fry until crisp and golden. Sprinkle biryani with almonds, onion and golden raisins.

Makes 4 servings.

Preheat broiler. Thread chicken cubes onto skewers. Broil 15 to 20 minutes, turning frequently and brushing with any remaining marinade. In a small bowl, mix together Raita ingredients. Serve kabobs on a bed of pilaf rice. Garnish with mint sprigs. Pass Raita separately.

Makes 4 servings.

CHICKEN POTPIE

1-1/2 pounds chicken pieces
1 large onion, thickly sliced
1/3 cup dry white wine
3/4 cup chicken stock
1 bouquet garni
2 tablespoons butter or margarine
2-1/2 cups halved button mushrooms
1/4 cup all-purpose flour
1 (8-oz.) whole-kernel corn, drained
2 tablespoons chopped fresh parsley
1 teaspoon fresh lemon juice
1/4 cup whipping cream
2 pounds potatoes
1/2 cup milk
3/4 cup shredded Cheddar cheese
1 ounce salted potato chips

In a large pan, place chicken, onion, wine, stock and bouquet garni. Bring to a boil. Reduce heat and simmer 25 to 30 minutes or until chicken is tender. Drain liquid; reserve liquid and onion. Discard bouquet garni. Remove skin and bones from chicken; coarsely chop flesh. In a pan, melt butter. Add mushrooms; cook until softened. Stir in flour; cook 1 minute. Add reserved liquid and onion.

Bring to a boil, stirring constantly. Stir in chicken, corn, parsley, lemon juice and cream. Season to taste with salt and pepper. Boil potatoes until tender. Drain and mash with milk and 1/2 cup of the cheese; season to taste. Preheat broiler. Cover casserole with potatoes. Crush potato chips and mix with remaining cheese. Sprinkle over potatoes. Broil until golden.

Makes 4 servings.

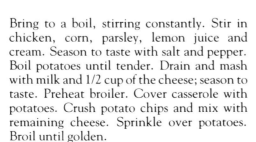

CHICKEN & HAM POTPIE

2 tablespoons butter or margarine
1/2 pound cooked ham, cut into 1-inch cubes
3/4 pound skinned and boned chicken, cut into 1-inch cubes
1 onion, chopped
1-1/3 cups sliced leeks
6 ounces button mushrooms
1/4 cup all-purpose flour
1-1/4 cups chicken stock
2/3 cup half and half
Finely grated peel of 1/2 lemon
Salt and pepper
1 prepared flat pie crust
Milk, for glazing
2 tablespoons grated Parmesan cheese

Preheat oven to 400F (205C). In a pan, melt butter, add ham and chicken and cook 2 to 3 minutes. Remove from pan and reserve. Add vegetables and cook 2 to 3 minutes or until softened. Return ham and chicken to pan. Stir in flour and cook 1 to 2 minutes. Remove from heat. Gradually stir in stock and half and half. Return to heat and cook, stirring, 2 minutes until thickened. Add lemon peel and season with salt and pepper.

Transfer chicken mixture to a deep 9-inch-round ovenproof dish. Cut off an 1-inch strip from pastry to fit edge of dish. Position dough strip on edge and brush with a little water. Cover with remaining pastry. Pinch edges together to seal. Brush pastry with milk to glaze. Sprinkle with cheese. Bake 25 minutes or until the pastry is golden-brown.

Makes 4 servings.

CHICKEN WITH APPLES

CHICKEN PROVENÇAL

1 (3-1/4- to 3-1/2-lb.) chicken
Peel and 1 teaspoon juice from 1 lemon
1/2 cinnamon stick
1 onion, quartered
Salt and pepper
1/2 cup butter or margarine
1 tablespoon vegetable oil
3 tablespoons brandy
1 pound Golden Delicious apples
2/3 cup apple juice
1 cup half and half
1 tablespoon each chopped fresh chives and parsley

Place peel, cinnamon stick and onion in cavity of chicken. Season.

Preheat oven to 350F (175C). In a Dutch oven, melt 1/4 cup of the butter and the oil. Add chicken; brown on all sides. Add brandy and ignite. Peel and thinly slice 1 apple; add to pan when flames die down. Add apple juice; bring to a boil. Cover and cook 1-1/4 hours.

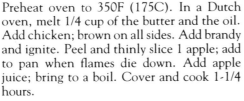

In a pan, melt remaining butter. Peel remaining apples; cut into thick slices. Add to butter; cook until just tender. Remove chicken from pan; place on a warmed platter. Surround with cooked apples. Add half and half to pan. Stir well and simmer to reduce slightly. Season well and pour over chicken. Sprinkle with chopped herbs and serve at once.

Makes 4 to 6 servings.

2 tablespoons butter or margarine
1 tablespoon vegetable oil
6 garlic cloves, unpeeled
4 chicken legs, cut in half
1/2 cup medium-dry sherry
1 (7-oz.) can chopped tomatoes
2 tablespoons tomato paste
2 tablespoons chopped fresh herbs
Salt and pepper
Oregano sprigs, to garnish

In a large skillet, heat butter and oil. Add garlic and chicken. Cook 15 minutes on one side until the chicken is half cooked through.

Add sherry and boil rapidly until reduced by half. Turn chicken pieces over. Continue to cook on high heat until sherry is reduced to a syrup.

Add tomatoes and tomato paste. Continue cooking 15 minutes longer until chicken is tender and sauce has reduced to a glaze. Add chopped herbs and season with a little salt and pepper. Serve with saffron rice and green beans. Garnish with oregano sprigs.

Makes 4 servings.

CHICKEN WITH WALNUT SAUCE —— CHICKEN WITH SHERRY —

6 chicken breast halves
Salt and pepper
Juice of 1 orange
1-1/4 cups walnut halves
2 garlic cloves, chopped
2 tablespoons water
1/3 cup walnut oil
1/3 cup olive oil
Squeeze of lemon juice
Chopped fresh parsley and orange slices, to serve

Preheat oven to 400F (205C). Season chicken breast halves with salt and pepper and place in a large shallow bowl. Pour orange juice over chicken; set aside.

On a baking sheet, spread out walnuts. Bake until lightly browned, 5 to 10 minutes. Transfer to a blender or food processor with the metal blade. Add garlic, water and a pinch of salt. Process to a paste. With motor running, slowly pour in walnut and olive oils to make a smooth, mayonnaise-like sauce. Transfer to a bowl; add lemon juice and pepper to taste; set aside.

Preheat broiler. Broil chicken 5 to 7 minutes on each side until juices run clear when thickest part is pierced with a sharp knife. Sprinkle orange slices with chopped parsley; use to garnish chicken, then serve with the sauce.

Makes 6 servings.

1/4 cup raisins
1 cup oloroso sherry
3 tablespoons olive oil
1 (3-1/2-lb.) chicken, cut into 8 pieces
1 Spanish onion, finely chopped
1 garlic clove, finely chopped
1 cup chicken stock
Salt and pepper
4 tablespoons pine nuts

In a small bowl, soak raisins in sherry 30 minutes.

In a large pan, heat 2 tablespoons of the oil, add chicken and cook until lightly and evenly browned, about 10 minutes. Transfer to paper towels to drain. Add onion and garlic to pan and cook over low heat, stirring occasionally, until softened and lightly colored, about 7 minutes. Strain raisins, reserving sherry, and set aside.

Stir sherry into pan. Simmer until reduced by half. Add stock, chicken, salt and pepper, bring to a boil, then reduce heat and simmer until chicken is tender, about 35 minutes. In a small pan, heat remaining oil. Add pine nuts and cook until lightly colored. Drain on paper towels, then stir into pan with raisins. Transfer chicken to a warm serving dish. Boil liquid in pan to reduce slightly. Pour over chicken.

Makes 4 servings.

LEMON & CORIANDER CHICKEN

4 chicken thighs, skinned
4 chicken drumsticks, skinned
1/4 cup vegetable oil
1 (2-inch) piece fresh gingerroot, grated
4 garlic cloves, crushed
1 green chile, seeded, finely chopped
1/2 teaspoon ground turmeric
1 teaspoon ground cumin
1 teaspoon ground coriander
Salt and red (cayenne) pepper to taste
1/2 cup water
Grated peel and juice of 1 lemon
4 oz. cilantro (fresh coriander), chopped
Cilantro (fresh coriander) leaves and lemon slices,
    to garnish

Rinse chicken; pat dry with paper towels. Heat oil in a large skillet and add chicken. Fry, turning frequently, until browned all over. Remove from pan with a slotted spoon; set aside. Add gingerroot and garlic to skillet, cook 1 minute. Stir in chile, turmeric, cumin, coriander, salt and cayenne; cook 1 minute more.

Return chicken to pan, add water and lemon peel and juice. Bring to a boil, then cover and cook over medium heat 25 to 30 minutes, or until chicken is tender. Stir in chopped cilantro. Serve hot, garnished with cilantro leaves and lemon slices.

Makes 4 servings.

Variation: Substitute fresh parsley, or a mixture of parsley and mint for the cilantro, if preferred.

—APRICOT & CHICKEN CURRY—

2-1/2-lbs. chicken pieces, skinned
1/2 teaspoon chile powder
1 tablespoon Garam Masala
1 (1-inch) piece fresh gingerroot, grated
2 garlic cloves, crushed
1 cup dried apricots
2/3 cup water
2 tablespoons vegetable oil
2 onions, finely sliced
1 (14-oz.) can chopped tomatoes
Salt to taste
1 tablespoon sugar
2 tablespoons white wine vinegar

Rinse chicken; pat dry with paper towels. Cut each piece into four pieces and put in a large bowl. Add chile powder, Garam Masala, gingerroot and garlic; toss well to coat chicken pieces. Cover and refrigerate 2 to 3 hours to allow chicken to absorb flavors. In a separate bowl, combine apricots and water; soak 2 to 3 hours.

Heat oil in a large heavy saucepan; add chicken pieces. Cook over high heat about 5 minutes, or until browned all over. Remove from pan and set aside. Add onions to pan and cook, stirring, about 5 minutes, until soft. Return chicken to pan with tomatoes, cover and cook over low heat 20 minutes. Drain apricots, add to pan with salt, sugar and vinegar. Simmer, covered, 10 to 15 minutes, until tender. Serve hot.

Makes 4 servings.

— GOLDEN STEAMED CHICKEN —

1 (3-1/2-lb.) chicken
3/4 cup basmati rice
3 tablespoons vegetable oil
1/2 teaspoon chile powder
1/3 cup raisins
1/2 cup sliced almonds
1 tablespoon chopped fresh thyme
Salt to taste
1/2 teaspoon ground cumin
1/2 teaspoon ground turmeric
1 teaspoon ground coriander
2 teaspoons Garam Masala
Salt and red (cayenne) pepper to taste
1/2 cup hot water
Thyme sprigs, to garnish

Rinse chicken, pat dry with paper towels and set aside. Wash rice thoroughly and soak in cold water 30 minutes, then drain. Heat 1 tablespoon oil in a saucepan, add rice and fry, stirring, 2 to 3 minutes, until golden brown. Stir in chile powder, raisins, almonds, thyme, 3/4 cup water and salt. Bring to a boil, then reduce heat, cover and simmer 10 to 12 minutes, until rice has absorbed all the liquid. Cool completely. Stuff chicken with rice.

Truss chicken neatly, then place in a steamer and steam 1 hour. Heat remaining oil in a large saucepan. Add cumin, turmeric, coriander, Garam Masala, salt and cayenne; cook 1 minute. Transfer chicken to this pan and cook 5 minutes, turning chicken with two wooden spoons until well coated in spice mixture. Pour hot water down side of pan, cover and cook over low heat 15 to 20 minutes, until chicken is tender. Serve hot, garnished with thyme sprigs.

Makes 4 servings.

— CHICKEN WITH LENTILS —

8 oz. boneless chicken breasts
1-1/4 cups red split lentils
1/2 teaspoon ground turmeric
4 tablespoons vegetable oil
6 green cardamon pods, bruised
1 onion, finely sliced
1 (1/2-inch) piece fresh gingerroot, grated
Salt and red (cayenne) pepper to taste
2 tablespoons lemon juice
2/3 cup water
1 teaspoon cumin seeds
2 garlic cloves, finely sliced

Rinse chicken, pat dry with paper towels and cut into cubes. Set aside.

Wash lentils, place in a large saucepan and add 3 cups water and turmeric. Bring to a boil, then reduce heat, cover and simmer 20 to 30 minutes, or until tender. Drain thoroughly. Meanwhile, heat half the oil in a large saucepan, add cardamom pods and fry 1 minute. Add onion and fry, stirring frequently, about 8 minutes, until golden brown. Add chicken and fry 5 minutes, until browned all over. Add gingerroot and fry 1 minute more. Season with salt and cayenne.

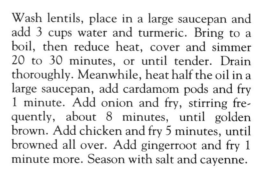

Stir in lemon juice and 2/3 cup water. Cover and simmer 25 to 30 minutes, or until chicken is tender. Stir in lentil mixture and cook, stirring, 5 minutes more. Meanwhile, heat remaining oil in a small pan, add cumin seeds and garlic and fry, stirring, over medium heat 1 to 2 minutes, until garlic is golden. Transfer chicken and lentil mixture to a serving dish and pour garlic mixture over the top. Serve hot.

Makes 4 servings.

-CHICKEN WITH GARLIC SAUCE-

4 chicken portions
Salt and pepper
6 tablespoons olive oil
3 tablespoons fresh lemon juice
2 tablespoons finely chopped green onions
2 tablespoons chopped fresh parsley
1 recipe Garlic Sauce (page 159)
2 lemons, quartered

Rub chicken with salt and pepper, then place in a single layer in a non-metallic dish.

Pour oil and lemon juice over the chicken and let stand for 1 hour, turning chicken over once or twice.

Preheat broiler. Place chicken on a broiler rack and broil slowly 8 to 10 minutes on each side, basting occasionally with the oil and lemon mixture, until crisp on the outside and tender throughout. Transfer to a warm serving plate and sprinkle onions and parsley over the top. Serve with Garlic Sauce and lemon quarters.

Makes 4 servings.

CHICKEN IN BALSAMIC VINEGAR

Mixed salad leaves
2 tablespoons olive oil
1 onion, finely chopped
2 garlic cloves, finely minced or crushed
1-1/2 pounds skinless boneless chicken breasts, cut into 1-inch strips
3 tablespoons balsamic vinegar
1 tablespoon Dijon-style mustard
Freshly ground pepper
2 tablespoons shredded fresh basil
Basil leaves, to garnish

Arrange salad leaves on 4 dinner plates and set aside.

Heat a wok until hot. Add olive oil and swirl to coat wok. Add onion and garlic and stir-fry 1 or 2 minutes or until onion begins to soften. Add chicken strips, working in 2 batches, and stir-fry 3 or 4 minutes or until golden and chicken feels firm to the touch. Return all chicken to wok.

Stir in vinegar and mustard and stir-fry 2 or 3 minutes or until chicken is cooked through and coated with vinegar and mustard. Season with pepper and sprinkle with shredded basil. Spoon onto salad-lined plates and garnish with basil leaves.

Makes 4 servings.

CHICKEN & BASIL STIR-FRY

1 lb. boneless chicken thighs
1 tablespoon dark soy sauce
1 tablespoon cornstarch
1 tablespoon peanut oil
2 garlic cloves, thinly sliced
1 fresh red chile, seeded and thinly sliced
1 teaspoon chile powder
1 tablespoon hoisin sauce
Small bunch basil leaves, shredded
Basil leaves and blanched red chile strips, to garnish

Remove skin and fat from chicken. Cut meat into 1-inch strips and place in a bowl. Stir in soy sauce and cornstarch.

Heat oil in a nonstick or well-seasoned wok and stir-fry chicken with garlic and chile 7 or 8 minutes.

Add chile powder and hoisin sauce and cook another 2 minutes. Remove from heat and stir in shredded basil. Garnish with basil leaves and chile strips and serve on a bed of rice.

Makes 4 servings.

BANG BANG CHICKEN

4 tablespoons peanut oil
3 carrots, cut into julienne strips
1 fresh hot red chile, seeded and chopped
1/2 pound bean sprouts, trimmed
1/2 cucumber, seeded and cut into julienne strips
1-3/4 pounds skinned and boned chicken breasts, cut into shreds
1-inch fresh gingerroot, cut in julienne strips
2 garlic cloves, finely chopped
4 green onions, thinly sliced
3 tablespoons cider vinegar or rice vinegar
2 tablespoons dry sherry or rice wine
1 tablespoon sugar
1 teaspoon Chinese chili sauce
2/3 cup chicken stock
3 tablespoons each light soy sauce and tahini

Heat wok until hot. Add 2 tablespoons of the peanut oil and swirl to coat wok. Add carrots and chile and stir-fry 2 or 3 minutes. Remove to a bowl. Stir-fry bean sprouts 1 minute and remove to bowl. Add cucumber to bowl. Heat remaining oil in wok and add chicken. Working in 2 batches, stir-fry 2 or 3 minutes or until the chicken is white and the juices run clear. Remove to another bowl. Increase heat, add gingerroot and garlic to wok and stir-fry 1 minute. Add green onions and stir-fry 1 minute. Add remaining ingredients and stir-fry until sauce is smooth and thick.

Pour half the sauce over carrot mixture and remaining sauce over chicken; toss each mixture well. Spoon chicken onto center of a serving dish, then spoon vegetables around chicken.

Makes 6 servings.

COQ AU VIN

2-1/2 cups dry red wine
3 garlic cloves, sliced
1 small onion, chopped
2 tablespoons olive oil
1 teaspoon brown sugar
1 teaspoon mixed peppercorns, crushed
1 teaspoon coriander seeds, crushed
1 bouquet garni
1 (3-1/4-lb.) chicken, cut into 8 pieces
3 tablespoons all-purpose flour, seasoned
4 bacon slices, diced
6 ounces pearl onions
6 ounces button mushrooms
2 cups chicken stock
2 tablespoons chopped parsley
Fried bread croutons, to garnish

In a bowl, mix together wine, garlic, onion, 1 tablespoon of the oil, the sugar, peppercorns and coriander. Add bouquet garni and chicken pieces. Cover and refrigerate 2 to 3 hours, turning regularly. Remove chicken from marinade, reserving marinade, and pat chicken dry with paper towels. Toss in seasoned flour. In a Dutch oven, heat remaining oil. Add bacon; fry until browned. Remove with a slotted spoon; set aside. Add chicken to pan; fry on all sides until browned. Set aside with bacon.

Add onions. Cook until browned, then add mushrooms and remaining flour. Cook, stirring, 1 minute. Slowly stir in stock and marinade; cook, stirring, until thickened. Return chicken and bacon to pan. Cover and simmer 40 minutes. Transfer chicken and vegetables to a serving dish. Keep warm. Boil sauce until thickened. Taste for salt and stir in parsley. Spoon sauce over chicken. Garnish with croutons.

Makes 4 servings.

BOMBAY CHICKEN THIGHS

2 tablespoons vegetable oil
1-inch piece gingerroot, peeled and finely chopped
2 garlic cloves, finely chopped
1 fresh hot red chile, seeded and chopped
1-1/2 pounds skinless boneless chicken thighs,
    cut into pieces
1 onion, coarsely chopped
2 teaspoons curry paste
1 (14-oz.) can chopped tomatoes
1 teaspoon ground coriander
Grated peel and juice of 1/2 lemon
2 bay leaves
Freshly ground pepper
2/3 cup unsweetened coconut milk
Cilantro or lemon leaves, to garnish

Heat a wok until hot. Add oil and swirl to coat wok. Add gingerroot, garlic and chile and stir-fry 1 minute or until very fragrant. Add chicken pieces and stir-fry 3 or 4 minutes or until chicken begins to color. Stir in onion and curry paste and stir to coat. Add tomatoes and their juice, coriander, lemon peel, lemon juice, bay leaves and pepper. Bring to a simmer and cook 3 or 4 minutes or until sauce is slightly thickened.

Stir in coconut milk and reduce heat. Simmer 5 to 6 minutes or until sauce is thickened and chicken pieces are tender. Remove bay leaves and garnish with cilantro or lemon leaves. Serve with steamed basmati rice.

Makes 4 servings.

SMOKED CHICKEN KEDGEREE

2 tablespoons butter or margarine
1 teaspoon coriander seeds, crushed
1 onion, sliced
1 teaspoon ground coriander
2 teaspoons ground cumin
1/2 cup long-grain rice
1/2 cup red lentils
2-1/2 cups chicken stock
3 cups coarsely chopped smoked chicken
Juice of 1/2 lemon
1/2 cup plain yogurt
2 tablespoons chopped fresh parsley
2 hard-cooked eggs, coarsely chopped
1 lemon, sliced, to garnish
Mango chutney and poppadoms, to serve

In a large pan, melt butter. Add coriander seeds and onion. Cook over low heat until slightly softened. Stir in ground coriander, cumin, rice and lentils and coat well with butter. Pour in stock. Bring to a boil, then cover and simmer 10 minutes.

Remove lid. Add chicken and cook 10 minutes longer until all liquid is absorbed and rice and lentils are tender. Stir in lemon juice, yogurt, parsley and eggs. Heat until hot. Spoon into a warmed serving dish and garnish with lemon. Serve with mango chutney and poppadoms.

Makes 4 servings.

KLEFTIKO

1 (3-lb.) chicken
1 lemon, quartered
2 teaspoons dried leaf oregano
Salt and pepper
2 tablespoons extra-virgin olive oil
1 red onion, thinly sliced
1/2 cup dry white wine
Lemon zest and oregano sprigs, to garnish

Preheat oven to 325F (165C). With a sharp knife, cut chicken into 4 quarters. Rub each chicken quarter all over with lemon.

In a bowl, mix together dried oregano, 1 teaspoon salt and pepper to taste. Rub mixture over each chicken quarter. Cut 4 squares of foil large enough to wrap around a chicken quarter. Brush foil with olive oil. Place a piece of chicken in the middle of each foil square. Scatter sliced onion over chicken. Pour 2 tablespoons wine over each piece of chicken.

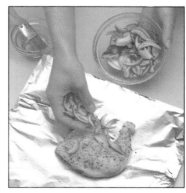

Seal edges of foil to make a package. Place packages on a baking sheet and bake in the oven 1 to 1-1/2 hours or until chicken is cooked and the juices run clear when the thickest part is pierced with a knife. To serve, open each package and slide contents onto a warmed plate. Garnish with lemon zest and oregano.

Makes 4 servings.

TURKEY CHILI

1-1/2 pounds small turkey thighs
2 or 3 tablespoons vegetable oil
1 onion, chopped
4 garlic cloves, finely chopped
1 or 2 fresh hot red chiles, seeded and chopped
4 teaspoons chili powder
Red (cayenne) pepper, to taste
1-1/2 teaspoons ground cumin
1 (14-oz.) can peeled tomatoes
1-1/2 teaspoons brown sugar
Salt
2 (14-oz.) cans red kidney beans
Dairy sour cream and chopped fresh parsley, to garnish

With a small, sharp knife, remove skin from thighs and discard. Slice meat from thigh bones; cut into small pieces. Heat a wok until hot. Add 1 tablespoon of the oil and swirl to coat wok. Add half the turkey meat and stir-fry 4 or 5 minutes or until brown. Remove to a bowl; repeat with remaining turkey meat, adding a little more oil if necessary. Remove meat to bowl. Add remaining oil to wok and add onion and garlic. Stir-fry 3 or 4 minutes or until onion softens. Stir in chile, chili powder, cayenne and cumin.

Stir in tomatoes with their liquid, then add the sugar and season with salt. Add turkey and kidney beans to wok. Bring mixture to a boil and reduce heat. Simmer, covered, 45 to 55 minutes. Remove cover and cook 15 minutes more or until chili is thick. Taste and adjust seasoning, if necessary. Garnish with sour cream and chopped parsley and serve with rice.

Makes 6 to 8 servings.

TURKEY WITH APPLE

1-1/2 pounds turkey cutlets, cut into strips
3 or 4 tablespoons seasoned all-purpose flour
3 or 4 tablespoons vegetable oil
1/3 cup chicken stock
2 tablespoons cider vinegar
1/2 teaspoon chili powder
Red (cayenne) pepper to taste
2 or 3 plum tomatoes, peeled, seeded and chopped
1 red onion, finely chopped
1 fresh hot red chile, seeded and chopped
1 Golden Delicious apple, cored and chopped
Cooked spinach noodles, to serve
2 tablespoons chopped fresh cilantro
1 tablespoon chopped peanuts

Dredge turkey strips in the seasoned flour.

Heat a wok until hot. Add 2 tablespoons of the oil and swirl to coat wok. Add half the turkey strips and stir-fry 1 or 2 minutes. Remove turkey to a serving plate; keep warm. Add 1 or 2 tablespoons of the remaining oil and cook remaining strips. Remove to the platter and keep warm.

Add stock and stir to deglaze wok. Add vinegar, chili powder, cayenne, tomatoes, onion, chile and chopped apple. Cook 1 or 2 minutes or until sauce thickens. Return turkey strips to wok and stir them into the sauce. Spoon over noodles. Sprinkle with cilantro and nuts.

Makes 4 servings.

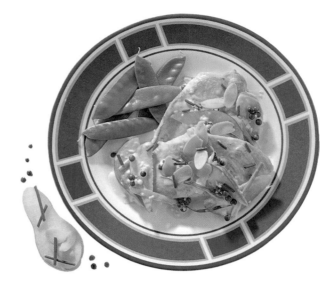

TURKEY MARSALA

1/3 cup sweet Marsala
3 tablespoons raisins
2 tablespoons butter
4 leeks (pale green and white parts only), cut in half lengthwise and sliced
1 cup chicken stock
1 bay leaf
1/2 teaspoon dried leaf thyme
1/4 teaspoon dried rubbed sage
1-1/4 pounds turkey cutlets, cut into strips
Finely grated peel of 1 lemon
2 teaspoons all-purpose flour
2 tablespoons whipping cream
Fresh sage leaves and lemon slices, to garnish
Orzo pasta, to serve

In a small bowl, combine Marsala and raisins. Let stand 20 minutes. Heat a wok until hot. Add 1 tablespoon of the butter and swirl to melt and coat wok. Add leeks and stir-fry 1 minute. Add 1/3 cup of the chicken stock, the bay leaf, thyme and sage and cook, covered, 4 to 6 minutes or until leeks are tender and liquid has evaporated. Discard bay leaf. Remove to a bowl and cover to keep warm. Wipe wok dry. Add remaining butter to wok and swirl to coat.

Add turkey, in 2 batches, and stir-fry for 2 minutes. Remove to a plate. Stir lemon peel and flour into remaining butter; cook 1 minute. Stir in remaining stock; bring to a boil. Add Marsala, raisins and cream; simmer 2 minutes. Spoon leek mixture onto plates, top with turkey and sauce. Garnish with sage and lemon. Serve with rice.

Makes 4 servings.

CREAMY TURKEY & PEAR

2 tablespoons olive oil
1-1/2 pounds turkey cutlets
1 garlic clove, finely chopped
4 green onions, thinly sliced
1 tablespoon green peppercorns
1/4 cup brandy or white wine
1/2 cup whipping cream
1/2 teaspoon salt
1 pear or apple, cored and cut lengthwise into thin slices
Toasted sliced almonds and fresh chives, to garnish
Cooked snow peas, to serve

Heat a wok until hot. Add oil; swirl to coat wok. Arrange cutlets on bottom and up side of wok in a single layer, working in 2 batches.

Cook 3 to 5 minutes, turning once. Remove to a serving plate and keep warm. Add garlic, green onions and green peppercorns to wok and stir-fry 1 minute or until onions begin to soften. Add brandy and stir to deglaze. Cook 1 or 2 minutes to reduce slightly.

Stir in whipping cream and salt and bring to a boil. Reduce heat and add pear slices. Cook, covered, 1 or 2 minutes or until fruit slices are heated through, then arrange them over turkey cutlets. Pour sauce over and sprinkle with toasted almonds and chives. Serve with snow peas.

Makes 4 servings.

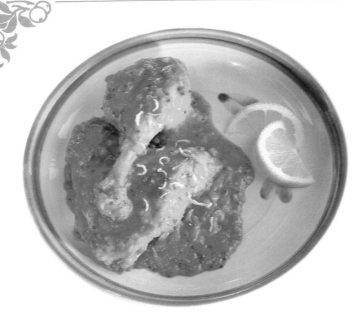

—DUCK & COCONUT CURRY—

4 (8-oz.) duck quarters, skinned
2 tablespoons vegetable oil
1 teaspoon mustard seeds
1 onion, finely chopped
3 garlic cloves, crushed
1 (2-inch) piece fresh gingerroot, grated
2 green chiles, seeded, chopped
1 teaspoon ground cumin
1 tablespoon ground coriander
1 teaspoon ground turmeric
1 tablespoon white wine vinegar
Salt and red (cayenne) pepper to taste
1-1/4 cups coconut milk
2 tablespoons shredded coconut, toasted, and lemon
   wedges to garnish

Rinse duck; pat dry with paper towels. Heat oil in a large skillet, add duck and cook, turning often over high heat 8 to 10 minutes, until browned all over, then remove from pan. Pour off all but 2 tablespoons fat from pan, add mustard seeds and fry 1 minute, or until they begin to pop.

Add onion to pan and cook, stirring, over medium heat 8 minutes, or until soft and golden. Stir in garlic, gingerroot, chiles, cumin, coriander and turmeric; cook 2 minutes. Stir in vinegar, return duck to pan and turn pieces to coat them in spice mixture. Stir in coconut milk and bring to a boil. Cover and cook over low heat about 40 minutes, or until duck is tender and sauce has thickened. Season with salt and cayenne. Serve hot, garnished with shredded coconut and lemon wedges.

Makes 4 servings.

—DUCK IN GINGER SAUCE—

3 tablespoons olive oil
1 onion, chopped, and 5 garlic cloves, chopped
2-inch piece of gingerroot, peeled and sliced
1 tablespoon all-purpose flour
1/2 cup red wine
1 cup port
3 or 4 sprigs each thyme and rosemary
2 bay leaves
1 tablespoon black peppercorns
3 cups veal, duck or chicken stock
1-1/2 pounds duck breast fillets, skinned and excess fat
   removed, cut crosswise into thin strips
1 pound shiitake mushrooms, sliced
1/2 cup raisins
6 green onions, cut into 2-inch pieces
1 pound pappardelle or wide egg noodles

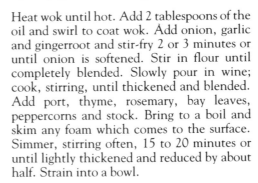

Heat wok until hot. Add 2 tablespoons of the oil and swirl to coat wok. Add onion, garlic and gingerroot and stir-fry 2 or 3 minutes or until onion is softened. Stir in flour until completely blended. Slowly pour in wine; cook, stirring, until thickened and blended. Add port, thyme, rosemary, bay leaves, peppercorns and stock. Bring to a boil and skim any foam which comes to the surface. Simmer, stirring often, 15 to 20 minutes or until lightly thickened and reduced by about half. Strain into a bowl.

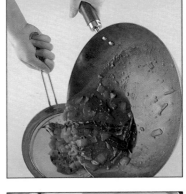

Wipe wok and heat until very hot, but not smoking. Add remaining oil and swirl to coat wok. Add duck strips and cook 2 or 3 minutes or until browned. Remove to a bowl. Stir in mushrooms, raisins and green onions and stir-fry 2 or 3 minutes. Add strained sauce and bring to a simmer. Add cooked duck. Cook pappardelle according to package directions. Drain and place in a large serving dish. Toss with sauce and duck.

Makes 4 servings.

RABBIT STIFADO

2 tablespoons all-purpose flour
Salt and pepper
1-1/2 to 2 pounds rabbit pieces
1/3 cup extra-virgin olive oil
1 pound tiny pearl onions
1 garlic clove, crushed
1 tablespoon tomato paste
1-1/4 cups red wine
1-1/4 cups chicken stock
1 bay leaf
2 fresh thyme sprigs
2 bread slices, crusts removed
2 tablespoons chopped fresh parsley

On a plate, mix together flour, salt and pepper. Toss rabbit pieces in seasoned flour. In a skillet, heat half the oil. Fry rabbit pieces until brown on both sides. Transfer to a flameproof casserole dish. Add onions to skillet and cook until they begin to brown. Add garlic and tomato paste to pan, then stir in wine and stock. Add bay leaf, thyme, salt and pepper. Add to casserole dish, cover and cook over low heat 1-1/2 to 2 hours or until rabbit is tender.

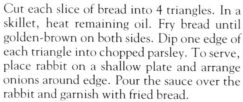

Cut each slice of bread into 4 triangles. In a skillet, heat remaining oil. Fry bread until golden-brown on both sides. Dip one edge of each triangle into chopped parsley. To serve, place rabbit on a shallow plate and arrange onions around edge. Pour the sauce over the rabbit and garnish with fried bread.

Makes 6 servings.

SOY-ROASTED DUCKLING

1 (5-lb.) duckling, giblets removed
1/4 cup dark soy sauce
2 tablespoons brown sugar
2 garlic cloves, finely chopped
DIP:
1 tablespoon sunflower oil
4 green onions, finely chopped
1 garlic clove, finely chopped
3 tablespoons dark soy sauce
2 teaspoons brown sugar
2 tablespoons dry sherry

Preheat oven to 375F (190C). Rinse duckling and pat dry. Place on a wire rack in a roasting pan. Prick all over with a fork.

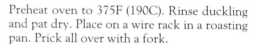

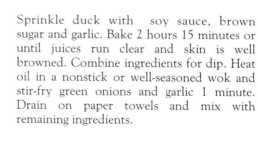

Sprinkle duck with soy sauce, brown sugar and garlic. Bake 2 hours 15 minutes or until juices run clear and skin is well browned. Combine ingredients for dip. Heat oil in a nonstick or well-seasoned wok and stir-fry green onions and garlic 1 minute. Drain on paper towels and mix with remaining ingredients.

To serve, remove all skin and fat from duckling and shred flesh away from bone. Serve with the dip, soft pancakes and shredded green onions and cucumber.

Makes 4 servings.

Note: Soft pancakes can be bought ready-made from Chinese supermarkets.

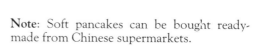

GUINEA FOWL CASSEROLE

1/4 cup extra-virgin olive oil
1 guinea fowl, cut into 4 pieces
1 large onion, finely sliced
1 garlic clove, crushed
1 (14-oz.) can chopped tomatoes
1-1/4 cups water
1 tablespoon chopped fresh oregano
Salt and pepper
1 pound small okra
Halved ripe olives, to garnish

In a flameproof casserole dish, heat oil. Add guinea fowl pieces and cook on both sides until brown. Transfer to a plate.

Add onion and garlic to casserole dish and cook until soft. Add tomatoes, water, oregano, salt and pepper. Bring to a boil, then add guinea fowl and coat well with sauce. Cover pan and simmer 40 minutes.

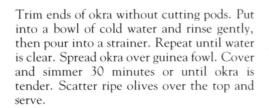

Trim ends of okra without cutting pods. Put into a bowl of cold water and rinse gently, then pour into a strainer. Repeat until water is clear. Spread okra over guinea fowl. Cover and simmer 30 minutes or until okra is tender. Scatter ripe olives over the top and serve.

Makes 4 servings.

QUAIL WITH GRAPES

3 tablespoons olive oil
1 Spanish onion, finely chopped
2 small carrots, finely chopped
Salt and pepper
8 bacon slices
8 quail
4 black peppercorns
2 garlic cloves
9 ounces muscatel grapes, peeled and seeded
Pinch of freshly grated nutmeg
1 cup medium-bodied dry white wine
1/4 cup Spanish brandy

Preheat oven to 375F (190C). In a heavy roasting pan that will hold the quail in a single layer, heat oil. Add onion and carrots and cook, stirring occasionally, 4 to 5 minutes. Season quail inside and out, lay a slice of bacon over each one and tie in place with string. Place on the vegetables, then roast 30 minutes.

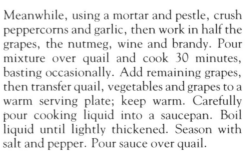

Meanwhile, using a mortar and pestle, crush peppercorns and garlic, then work in half the grapes, the nutmeg, wine and brandy. Pour mixture over quail and cook 30 minutes, basting occasionally. Add remaining grapes, then transfer quail, vegetables and grapes to a warm serving plate; keep warm. Carefully pour cooking liquid into a saucepan. Boil liquid until lightly thickened. Season with salt and pepper. Pour sauce over quail.

Makes 4 to 6 servings.

MEAT

MINTY MINCED LAMB PATTIES

LAMB STEAKS WITH PASTA

1/3 cup whole brown lentils
1-1/4 cups boiling water
3 onions, finely chopped
1 pound ground lamb
2 tablespoons Garam Masala
2 dried red chiles, seeded, crushed
1 egg, beaten
1/4 cup plain yogurt
2 tablespoons chopped fresh mint
2 green chiles, seeded, chopped
1/4 cup vegetable oil
Lettuce and fresh mint leaves, to garnish

Put lentils in a bowl, add water and leave to soak 2 hours.

Put lentils, their soaking water, 2 onions, lamb, Garam Masala and red chiles in a large heavy saucepan and bring to a boil. Cook over medium heat until all the liquid has evaporated and mixture is very dry, stirring constantly. Remove from heat; cool. Put mixture in a blender or food processor fitted with the metal blade; process to a smooth paste. Add egg and yogurt and blend again. Cover and refrigerate 2 to 3 hours, then form into 16 balls.

Mix together remaining onion, mint and green chiles. Make an indentation in each lamb ball and stuff with a little mint mixture, then cover up with meat. Flatten balls into 2-inch rounds. Heat oil in a skillet; add patties a few at a time. Cook 4 to 6 minutes, until well browned, turning over after 2 to 3 minutes. Serve, garnished with lettuce and mint.

Makes 4 servings.

4 thick lamb leg steaks
Salt and pepper
2 garlic cloves, sliced
2/3 cup water
1 (14-oz.) can chopped tomatoes
1/3 cup extra-virgin olive oil
1 tablespoon chopped fresh marjoram
1 tablespoon chopped fresh parsley
1-1/4 cups boiling water
10 ounces orzo (rice-shaped pasta)
Salad leaves, to serve

Preheat oven to 400F (205C). Season meat with salt and pepper. Place in a large roasting pan.

Scatter garlic over meat. Add the 2/3 cup water, tomatoes, olive oil, marjoram and parsley. Cook 40 minutes, basting occasionally and turning lamb over.

Add 1-1/4 cups boiling water and the pasta. Stir in more salt and pepper. Cook about 40 minutes or until pasta is cooked. If necessary, add more hot water. Serve with salad greens.

Makes 6 servings.

LAMB WITH SPINACH

LAMB WITH LEMON & GARLIC

3 tablespoons soy sauce
1/4 teaspoon five-spice powder
1-inch piece gingerroot, peeled and cut into julienne strips
2 garlic cloves, finely chopped
1-1/2 pounds lean lamb, cut into thin strips
1 tablespoon sesame oil
1 fresh hot red chile, seeded and thinly sliced
8 green onions, cut into 2-inch pieces
1 mango, peeled and cut into 1/2-inch-thick pieces
6 ounces fresh spinach leaves, washed and dried
3 tablespoons dry sherry or rice wine
1 teaspoon cornstarch dissolved in 1 tablespoon water

3 tablespoons olive oil
2 pounds lean, boneless lamb, cut into 1-inch pieces
1 Spanish onion, finely chopped
3 garlic cloves, crushed
1 tablespoon paprika
3 tablespoons finely chopped fresh parsley
3 tablespoons fresh lemon juice
Salt and pepper
3 tablespoons dry white wine (optional)

In a shallow baking dish, combine soy sauce, five-spice powder, gingerroot and garlic. Add lamb strips and toss to coat well. Marinate 1 hour, covered, stirring occasionally. Heat a wok until very hot. Add sesame oil and swirl to coat. With a slotted spoon and working in 2 batches, add lamb to wok, draining off and reserving as much marinade as possible. Stir-fry lamb 2 or 3 minutes or until browned on all sides. Remove to a bowl. Add chile to oil remaining in wok and stir-fry 1 minute.

In a heavy large pan, heat oil. Add lamb and cook, stirring occasionally, until lightly browned. Do this in batches if necessary so the pieces are not crowded. Using a slotted spoon, transfer meat to a plate or bowl and reserve.

Add green onions and mango and stir-fry 1 minute. Stir in spinach leaves, reserved lamb, sherry and reserved marinade. Stir cornstarch mixture and stir into wok. Stir-fry 1 minute, tossing all ingredients until spinach wilts and lamb is lightly glazed with sauce. Serve with noodles.

Makes 4 servings.

Stir onion into pan and cook about 5 minutes, stirring occasionally, until softened. Stir in garlic and cook 2 minutes, then stir in paprika. When well blended, stir in lamb and any juices on plate or in bowl, the parsley, lemon juice, salt and pepper. Cover tightly and cook over very low heat 1-1/4 to 1-1/2 hours, shaking pan occasionally, until lamb is very tender. If necessary, add wine or 3 tablespoons water.

Makes 4 to 6 servings.

BRAISED LAMB & VEGETABLES

ORANGE-GLAZED LAMB

1 pound firm, yellow potatoes, cut into 1/4-inch slices
2 garlic cloves, pounded to a paste
6 to 8 green onions, thinly sliced
2 medium or large artichoke bottoms sliced
3 cups chopped brown mushrooms
Handful of parsley, finely chopped
1 tablespoon chopped mixed herbs
Salt and pepper
3 tablespoons olive oil
4 lamb shoulder or loin chops
3/4 cup full-bodied dry white wine
Fresh parsley sprigs, to garnish

1 tablespoon vegetable oil
8 (1-inch-thick) boneless lean lamb chops about 1-1/2
   pounds total
2/3 cup dry white wine
2/3 cup freshly squeezed orange juice
1 teaspoon ground coriander
1/2 teaspoon dry mustard powder
Salt and freshly ground pepper
1 tablespoon cornstarch dissolved in 2 tablespoons
   water
1 large orange, peel removed and cut into julienne
   strips, and divided into segments
Fresh green beans, to serve

Heat a wok until very hot. Add vegetable oil
and swirl to coat wok.

Preheat oven to 375F (190C). In a bowl,
combine potatoes, garlic, green onions, artichoke bottoms, mushrooms, parsley, mixed
herbs, salt and pepper. In a heavy large pan,
heat half the mixture. In a skillet, heat oil.
Add lamb and brown on both sides. Drain on
paper towels, then season with salt and
pepper and place in pan.

Add lamb strips and stir-fry 4 or 5 minutes.
Remove to a plate and keep warm. Pour off all
the fat from the wok and add wine, stirring to
deglaze. Add orange juice, coriander,
mustard powder, salt and pepper and bring to
a boil. Stir the cornstarch mixture and slowly
pour into the wok, stirring constantly until
sauce thickens.

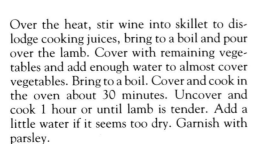

Over the heat, stir wine into skillet to dis-
lodge cooking juices, bring to a boil and pour
over the lamb. Cover with remaining vegetables and add enough water to almost cover
vegetables. Bring to a boil. Cover and cook in
the oven about 30 minutes. Uncover and
cook 1 hour or until lamb is tender. Add a
little water if it seems too dry. Garnish with
parsley.

Makes 4 servings.

Return the lamb strips to the sauce and,
turning to coat, cook 1 or 2 minutes or until
sauce has glazed the lamb strips and they are
heated through. Add orange peel and orange
segments and cook 1 minute to heat through.
Arrange lamb mixture on 4 dinner plates.
Serve with green beans.

Makes 4 servings.

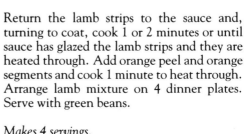

SPICED RACK OF LAMB

LAMB CHILINDRON

1 tablespoon all-purpose flour
Salt and pepper
2 racks of lamb
1 garlic clove, finely chopped
2 tablespoons extra-virgin olive oil
1 pound tomatoes, coarsely chopped
1/2 lemon, chopped
1 cinnamon stick
3 whole cloves
1 small red chile, seeded and chopped
1/2 cup dry white wine
2 tablespoons tomato paste
Lemon slices, to garnish

1/4 cup olive oil
1-1/2 pounds lean lamb, cubed
Salt and black pepper
1 Spanish onion, chopped
2 garlic cloves, chopped
3 red bell peppers, cut into strips
4 beefsteak tomatoes, peeled, seeded and chopped
1 dried red chile, chopped
Chopped fresh herbs, to garnish

In a large pan, heat oil. Season lamb with salt and black pepper and add to pan.

Preheat oven to 350F (175C). Mix together flour, salt and pepper. Rub over lamb. Press garlic into gaps between bones. In a roasting pan, heat oil. Put lamb, skin-side down, in oil to brown. Remove lamb. Add tomatoes, lemon, cinnamon, cloves and chile to roasting pan. Return lamb, skin-side up, to pan.

Cook, stirring, until evenly browned, then using a slotted spoon, transfer to a bowl. Add onion to pan and cook about 4 minutes, stirring occasionally, until softened but not colored. Stir in garlic, cook 1 to 2 minutes, then stir in peppers, tomatoes and chile. Simmer 5 minutes.

In a bowl, mix together wine, 1/2 cup water and tomato paste. Pour over lamb. Cover pan loosely with foil. Roast 1 hour. Remove foil and roast 30 minutes or until lamb is cooked to desired doneness. Cut lamb into individual chops and keep warm. Place roasting pan on heat and boil liquid to reduce to a thick sauce. Pour over meat. Garnish with lemon.

Makes 6 servings.

Return lamb and any juices that have collected in bowl to pan. Cover tightly and simmer about 1-1/2 hours, or until lamb is tender. Taste for seasoning and adjust if necessary. Serve garnished with chopped herbs.

Makes 6 servings.

PORK & BAMBOO SHOOTS

2 tablespoons vegetable oil
4 garlic cloves, very finely chopped
12 ounces lean pork, very finely chopped
4 ounces whole bamboo shoots, sliced crosswise
1/4 cup peanuts, coarsely chopped
2 teaspoons fish sauce
Freshly ground pepper
4 large green onions, thinly sliced
Thai basil leaves to garnish

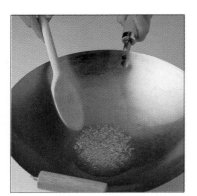

In a wok, heat oil, add garlic and fry, stirring occasionally, about 3 minutes until lightly colored.

Add pork and stir-fry 2 minutes. Add bamboo shoots and cook 1 minute.

Stir in peanuts, fish sauce, plenty of pepper and half of the green onions. Transfer to a warmed serving plate and sprinkle with remaining green onions and the basil leaves.

Makes 4 servings.

PORK WITH PEARS

2 tablespoons extra-virgin olive oil
2 onions, chopped
2 pounds boned lean pork, cut into cubes
1 cup red wine
Grated zest of 1/2 orange
1/2 cinnamon stick
Salt and pepper
1-1/4 cups water
2 pears
2 teaspoons honey
Chopped fresh cilantro leaves, orange peel strips and
  pita bread, to garnish

In a flameproof casserole dish, heat oil. Add onions and cook until soft. Push to side of pan, turn up heat and brown meat in batches.

Add wine, orange zest, cinnamon stick, salt, pepper and water. Bring to a simmer, then cover casserole and cook 1 hour.

Peel, core and slice pears and place on top of meat. Drizzle honey over pears. Cover pan and simmer 30 to 40 minutes or until meat is tender. Garnish with chopped cilantro leaves, strips of orange peel and pita bread.

Makes 6 servings.

Note: This recipe is traditionally made with quinces. If quinces are available, use them instead of pears.

PORK WITH HERB SAUCE

PORK KABOBS

1/2 cup fresh white bread crumbs
2 tablespoons white-wine vinegar
2 garlic cloves
2 canned anchovy fillets, drained
1/4 cup chopped fresh parsley
2 teaspoons capers, drained
1 hard-cooked egg yolk
1 cup extra-virgin olive oil
Salt and pepper
4 boneless pork loin chops, about 1 inch thick

In a small bowl, soak bread crumbs in vinegar.

Meanwhile, using a mortar and pestle, crush garlic with anchovy fillets, parsley, capers and egg yolk. Squeeze vinegar from bread crumbs, then mix bread crumbs into mortar. Slowly stir in oil to make a creamy sauce. Add salt and pepper to taste. Set aside.

Preheat broiler. Broil chops about 12 minutes on each side until lightly browned and cooked through but still juicy in center. Season chops with salt and pepper and top with some of sauce. Serve remaining sauce separately.

Makes 4 servings.

1 pound lean pork
1 onion
1 green bell pepper
8 cherry tomatoes
MARINADE:
Juice of 1/2 orange
2 tablespoons extra-virgin olive oil
1 garlic clove, crushed
1 teaspoon chopped fresh thyme
1 teaspoon coriander seeds, crushed
Salt and pepper
Shredded lettuce, orange slices and fresh thyme sprigs, to garnish

To make the marinade, in a bowl, mix together orange juice, oil, garlic, thyme, coriander seeds, salt and pepper. Cut pork into 3/4-inch cubes and add to marinade. Mix thoroughly, cover and refrigerate 2 hours. Cut onion into quarters and separate the layers. Cut bell pepper into small squares, removing core and seeds.

Thread pork, onion, pepper and tomatoes onto 8 bamboo skewers. Preheat grill or broiler. Cook, turning occasionally, 10 to 15 minutes or until pork is cooked through. Serve on a bed of shredded lettuce, garnished with orange slices and fresh thyme.

Makes 8.

PORK & BEAN STIR-FRY

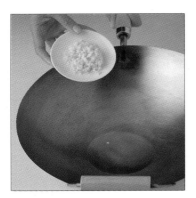

2 tablespoons vegetable oil
6 garlic cloves, chopped
12 ounces lean pork, finely chopped
12 ounces long beans or small green beans
12 water chestnuts, sliced
4 ounces cooked peeled shrimp
1 tablespoon fish sauce
1/2 teaspoon crushed palm sugar
Freshly ground pepper
About 3 tablespoons water

In a wok, heat oil, add garlic and fry, stirring occasionally, until golden.

Add pork and beans and stir-fry 2 minutes, then add water chestnuts.

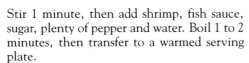

Stir 1 minute, then add shrimp, fish sauce, sugar, plenty of pepper and water. Boil 1 to 2 minutes, then transfer to a warmed serving plate.

Makes 4 servings.

VEGETABLES & PORK

8 ounces lean pork, very finely chopped
Freshly ground pepper
2 tablespoons vegetable oil
3 garlic cloves, finely chopped
1 pound prepared mixed vegetables, such as snow peas, broccoli, red bell pepper and zucchini
1 tablespoon fish sauce
1/2 teaspoon crushed palm sugar
1 cup water
3 green onions, finely chopped

In a bowl, mix together pork and plenty of pepper. Set aside 30 minutes.

In a wok or skillet, heat oil, add garlic, cook, stirring occasionally, 2 to 3 minutes, then stir in pork.

Stir briefly until pork changes color. Stir in vegetables, then fish sauce, sugar and water. Stir 3 to 4 minutes until snow peas are bright green and vegetables are crisp-tender. Stir in green onions.

Makes 4 servings.

PORK & PRUNE MEDLEY

1 pound pork tenderloin, cut into thin slices
2 tablespoons soy sauce
2 tablespoons balsamic vinegar or cider vinegar
2 tablespoons olive oil
2 zucchini, sliced
1 onion, cut lengthwise into thin wedges
1 red bell pepper, cut into thin strips
4 ounces mushrooms, sliced
4 ounces snow peas
4 ounces asparagus, cut into 2-inch pieces
1/2 cup walnut halves
6 ounces pitted prunes
Salt and freshly ground black pepper

In a shallow baking dish, sprinkle pork slices with soy sauce and vinegar and toss to coat well. Let stand 30 minutes. Heat a wok until hot. Add olive oil and swirl to coat wok. Add pork slices and stir-fry 3 to 5 minutes, or until golden on all sides. With a slotted spoon, remove to a bowl.

Add zucchini, onion, bell pepper, mushrooms, snow peas, asparagus, walnut halves and prunes and stir-fry 2 or 3 minutes until coated with oil. Add 2 tablespoons water to wok and cover wok quickly. Steam 1 or 2 minutes or until vegetables just begin to soften. Uncover wok, return pork to wok and toss to mix. Season with salt and pepper. Stir-fry 1 or 2 minutes or until pork is heated through.

Makes 4 servings.

COCONUT PORK WITH LIME

6 pork cutlets, about 4 ounces each
1/2-inch piece gingerroot, peeled and grated
2 teaspoons ground cumin
1 teaspoon ground coriander
1 teaspoon chili powder to taste
1 teaspoon paprika
1/2 teaspoon salt
2 tablespoons vegetable oil
1 onion, cut lengthwise into thin wedges
3 or 4 garlic cloves, finely chopped
1-1/4 cups unsweetened coconut milk
Grated peel and juice of 1 large lime
1 small bok choy, shredded
Lime slices and cilantro leaves, to garnish
Noodles, to serve

Place cutlets between 2 sheets of waxed paper. Pound to 1/4 inch thickness. Cut pork into strips. In a large shallow dish, combine gingerroot, cumin, coriander, chili powder, paprika and salt. Stir in pork strips and let stand 15 minutes. Heat a wok until very hot. Add oil and swirl to coat wok. Add pork and stir-fry 2 or 3 minutes or until cooked through. Remove to a plate and keep warm. Pour off all but 1 tablespoon oil from the wok.

Add onion and garlic to wok and stir-fry 2 or 3 minutes or until onion is softened. Slowly add coconut milk. Bring to a simmer but do not boil. Stir in lime peel, lime juice and bok choy cabbage. Simmer 5 to 7 minutes, stirring frequently, or until bok choy is tender and sauce slightly thickened. Add pork and cook, covered, 1 or 2 minutes or until heated through. Arrange pork mixture on plates and garnish with lime slices and cilantro. Serve with noodles.

Makes 6 servings.

RATATOUILLE-STYLE PORK

1 tablespoon olive oil
4 (1-inch-thick) boneless loin pork chops, about 1-1/4
   pounds total, trimmed of fat
1 onion, coarsely chopped
2 garlic cloves, chopped
1 small eggplant, cut into 1-inch cubes
1 red or green bell pepper, diced
2 zucchini, thickly sliced
1 (8-oz.) can chopped tomatoes
1 teaspoon chopped fresh oregano or basil or 1/2
   teaspoon dried leaf oregano or basil
1/2 teaspoon dried thyme leaves
Salt and freshly ground black pepper
Flat leaf parsley, to garnish
Fresh noodles, to serve

Heat a wok until very hot. Add olive oil and swirl to coat wok. Arrange pork chops on bottom and side of wok, in a single layer. Fry 4 or 5 minutes or until well browned on both sides, turning once and rotating during cooking. Remove to a plate. Add onion and garlic to remaining oil in wok and stir-fry 1 minute or until onion begins to soften. Add eggplant and bell pepper and stir-fry 3 to 5 minutes to brown and soften.

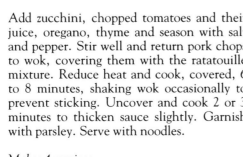

Add zucchini, chopped tomatoes and their juice, oregano, thyme and season with salt and pepper. Stir well and return pork chops to wok, covering them with the ratatouille mixture. Reduce heat and cook, covered, 6 to 8 minutes, shaking wok occasionally to prevent sticking. Uncover and cook 2 or 3 minutes to thicken sauce slightly. Garnish with parsley. Serve with noodles.

Makes 4 servings.

PORK WITH WALNUTS

1 lb. lean pork fillet
1 tablespoon rice wine
1 tablespoon light soy sauce
1 teaspoon cornstarch
1 bunch green onions
2 teaspoons sunflower oil
1 teaspoon sugar
Salt and freshly ground pepper
1 oz. walnut pieces

Trim any fat and silver skin from pork and cut fillet into 1/4-inch strips. Place in a bowl and add rice wine, soy sauce and cornstarch. Mix well, cover and chill 30 minutes.

Trim green onions, discarding any damaged outer leaves. Cut green onions into 2-inch pieces.

Heat oil in a nonstick or well-seasoned wok and stir-fry pork mixture 2 or 3 minutes or until browned. Add green onions, sugar, salt and pepper and stir-fry 3 minutes. Sprinkle with walnut pieces and serve with noodles.

Makes 4 servings.

— PORK CUTLETS NORMANDY —

4 (1/2-inch-thick) pork cutlets, about 1-1/4 pounds
   total
2 tablespoons vegetable oil
2 tablespoons butter
1 garlic clove, chopped
2 Golden Delicious apples, cored and thinly sliced
1/2 teaspoon dried leaf thyme
3 tablespoons Calvados or brandy
1/2 cup whipping cream
Salt and freshly ground pepper
Flat-leaf parsley, to garnish

Place pork cutlets between 2 sheets of waxed
paper and pound to 1/4 inch thickness. Cut
into thin strips.

Heat a wok until very hot. Add oil and swirl
to coat wok. Add pork strips and stir-fry 3 or
4 minutes or until cooked through. Remove
to a plate and keep warm. Pour off any oil
from the wok. Add butter to the wok and
melt. Add garlic, apple slices and thyme and
stir-fry 1 or 2 minutes or until apple slices are
golden.

Add Calvados to the wok and stir to deglaze.
Add cream and bring to a boil. Add salt and
pepper to taste. Cook 1 minute, stirring
constantly, until sauce thickens slightly and
apples are tender. Arrange pork on a serving
dish. Garnish with parsley sprigs. Serve with
buttered egg noodles.

Makes 4 servings.

— SPICY PORK WITH PEAS —

1 pound pork tenderloin, cut crosswise into thin slices
1-1/2 tablespoons soy sauce
2 tablespoons cider vinegar
1 tablespoon vegetable oil
1-inch piece gingerroot, peeled and finely chopped
2 garlic cloves, finely chopped
1 fresh hot red chile, seeded and thinly sliced
1/2 pound fresh or frozen green peas or sugar snap peas
1 head radicchio or 1/2 head small red cabbage, thinly
   shredded
Rice pilaf, to serve

In a small baking dish, sprinkle pork slices
with soy sauce and vinegar. Toss to coat well.
Let stand 15 to 20 minutes.

Heat a wok until hot. Add oil and swirl to
coat wok. Add pork slices and stir-fry 2
minutes. Push to one side and add gingerroot,
garlic and chile and stir-fry 1 minute to mix.

Add peas and radicchio and stir-fry 2 or 3
minutes or until vegetables are tender but still
crisp. Serve with rice pilaf.

Makes 4 servings.

SPICED PORK LOIN

PORK WITH BASIL

1 tablespoon paprika
3 garlic cloves, finely crushed
1 teaspoon chopped fresh oregano
1/2 teaspoon finely crushed cumin seeds
1 bay leaf, crushed
Salt
3 tablespoons extra-virgin olive oil
1 (1-1/2-lb.) boned and rolled pork loin roast
2 tablespoons olive oil
1/4 cup full-bodied dry white wine
Pitted green olives, to serve

In a small bowl, mix together paprika, garlic, oregano, cumin seeds, bay leaf and salt. Stir in olive oil.

9 ounces thin egg noodles
4 tablespoons olive oil
1-1/4 pounds pork tenderloin, cut into shreds
1 red onion, cut lengthwise in half, and thinly sliced
1/4 cup shredded fresh basil leaves
2 tablespoons balsamic vinegar
3 tablespoons pine nuts, toasted
Salt and freshly ground pepper
Basil leaves, to garnish

In a large saucepan of boiling water, cook egg noodles according to package directions. Drain, turn into a large bowl and toss with 2 tablespoons of the olive oil. Keep warm.

Rub spice mixture well into pork. Place in a non-metallic dish, cover and refrigerate 2 to 5 days. Bring pork to room temperature 30 minutes before cooking.

Heat a wok until very hot. Add remaining olive oil and swirl to coat wok. Add shredded pork and stir-fry 2 or 3 minutes or until pork is golden. Add onion and toss with the pork, then stir-fry 1 minute.

Cut pork into 4 slices. In a skillet over medium-high heat, heat oil. Add pork and brown quickly on both sides, then reduce heat and cook 4 to 5 minutes on each side until cooked through. Transfer slices to a warm serving plate. Stir wine into cooking juices, boil 2 to 3 minutes, then pour over pork. Scatter green olives over the top.

Makes 4 servings.

Stir in shredded basil, the balsamic vinegar and pine nuts and toss to mix well. Add noodles to the wok, season to taste and toss with pork mixture. Turn into shallow a serving dish and garnish with basil leaves.

Makes 4 servings.

SPICED HONEY HAM

1 (3-lb.) smoked ham
Finely shredded peel and juice 2 oranges
2 tablespoons honey
1 teaspoon ground mace
1 teaspoon freshly grated ginger
4 oz. kumquats, sliced
2 tablespoons whole cloves
1 tablespoon cornstarch

Soak ham in a bowl of cold water overnight. Drain and transfer to a large saucepan. Cover with fresh cold water. Bring to a boil, cover and cook 30 minutes. Drain and cool. Remove skin from ham, leaving a layer of fat on surface of ham.

Score fat in a lattice pattern with a sharp knife. Preheat oven to 375F (190C). Place ham in a roasting pan. In a bowl, mix orange peel and juice, honey, mace and ginger until evenly blended. Brush surface of ham and bake in oven 30 minutes. Remove ham from oven and brush surface with more orange mixture. Stud surface of ham with kumquat slices; hold in position with whole cloves. Return to oven another 30 to 40 minutes or until ham is golden brown and tender. Remove and place on a serving dish. Keep warm.

To prepare sauce, add 3/4 cup water to roasting pan. Stir to mix juices, then strain into a saucepan. Blend cornstarch with remaining orange juice and honey mixture. Add to pan, bring to a boil and cook 1 minute. Serve ham with sauce.

Makes 8 servings.

HAM & PLUM STIR-FRY

2 tablespoons vegetable oil
1 red bell pepper, cut lengthwise in half, thinly sliced
12 ounces plums or nectarines, thinly sliced
1/2 pound oyster mushrooms, sliced
2 leeks, trimmed, washed and cut diagonally into 1/2-inch pieces
6 green onions, thinly sliced
1 pound ham steaks, cut into thin strips
1 cup orange juice
2 tablespoons peach or apricot preserve
2 tablespoons soy sauce
2 tablespoons white-wine vinegar
2 tablespoons cornstarch dissolved in 2 tablespoons water
Noodles or rice, to serve

Heat a wok until hot. Add oil and swirl to coat wok. Add bell pepper, and plums and stir-fry 1 or 2 minutes. Add oyster mushrooms and leeks and stir-fry 1 or 2 minutes or until vegetables begin to soften. Push vegetables to one side and add green onions and ham strips. Stir-fry 2 or 3 minutes, tossing ingredients to mix, or until ham is heated through.

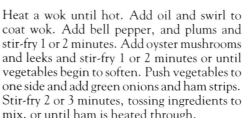

Stir in orange juice, peach preserve, soy sauce and vinegar. Stir cornstarch mixture, then stir into wok. Bring to a boil and stir-fry 1 or 2 minutes or until sauce thickens and coats ingredients. Serve with noodles or rice.

Makes 4 to 6 servings.

SAUSAGE & PEPPERS

2 tablespoons olive oil
1-1/2 pounds hot, sweet or mixed Italian sausages
2 onions, halved lengthwise, then cut lengthwise into
   thin wedges
4 to 6 garlic cloves, finely chopped
1 each large red, green and yellow bell peppers, cut in
   half lengthwise, then into strips
1 (8-oz.) can peeled tomatoes
1 tablespoon shredded fresh oregano or basil or
   1 teaspoon dried leaf oregano or basil
1/2 teaspoon crushed dried chiles
1/2 teaspoon dried leaf thyme
1/2 teaspoon rubbed sage
Salt and freshly ground black pepper
Oregano or basil leaves, to garnish
Parmesan cheese, to garnish

Heat a wok until hot. Add olive oil and swirl to coat wok. Add sausages and cook over medium heat 8 to 10 minutes or until sausages are brown on all sides, turning and rotating sausages frequently during cooking. Remove sausages to a plate and pour off all but 2 tablespoons oil from the wok. Add onions and garlic and stir-fry 2 minutes or until golden. Add bell pepper strips and stir-fry 1 or 2 minutes or until just beginning to soften.

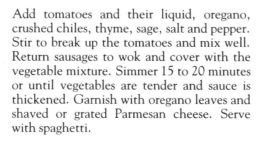

Add tomatoes and their liquid, oregano, crushed chiles, thyme, sage, salt and pepper. Stir to break up the tomatoes and mix well. Return sausages to wok and cover with the vegetable mixture. Simmer 15 to 20 minutes or until vegetables are tender and sauce is thickened. Garnish with oregano leaves and shaved or grated Parmesan cheese. Serve with spaghetti.

Makes 6 servings.

SPICY BRAISED BEEF

1 (3-lb.) beef round roast
2 garlic cloves, crushed
1/2 teaspoon ground cinnamon
1/4 teaspoon ground cloves
Salt and pepper
3 tablespoons extra-virgin olive oil
4 onions, thinly sliced
1/2 cup red wine
2 tablespoons tomato paste
1 pound spaghetti
1 tablespoon balsamic vinegar
Fresh herbs, to garnish

With a sharp knife, make slits in the beef.

In a bowl, mix garlic, cinnamon, cloves, salt and pepper. Press mixture into slits and let beef stand in a cool place 1 hour. In a flame-proof casserole dish into which meat will just fit, heat oil. Turn meat in hot oil until brown all over. Remove from casserole dish. Add onions and cook gently until soft and lightly browned. Replace meat. Add the wine and enough hot water to barely cover it. Mix tomato paste with a little water; stir into casserole. Season with salt and pepper.

Cover pan and simmer about 1-1/2 hours, turning meat frequently, or until it is tender. Bring a large pan of salted water to a boil and cook spaghetti until al dente. Remove meat and keep hot. Add vinegar to sauce. Boil briskly until reduced to a smooth glossy sauce. Slice beef. Garnish with herbs and serve with some sauce poured over beef and remainder stirred into spaghetti.

Makes 6 servings.

BEEF-STUFFED CABBAGE

2 onions
5 tablespoons vegetable oil
3 garlic cloves, crushed
2 green chiles, seeded, chopped
1 (3-inch) piece fresh gingerroot, grated
1 pound ground beef
1/4 teaspoon ground turmeric
2 teaspoons Garam Masala
1 savoy cabbage
1 (14-oz.) can chopped tomatoes
2 tablespoons lemon juice
Salt and pepper to taste
2/3 cup water
Lemon slices, to garnish

Chop 1 onion and slice the other. Heat 2 tablespoons oil in a heavy saucepan, add chopped onion and cook, stirring, over medium heat about 8 minutes, until soft and golden brown. Add garlic, chiles and one-third of the gingerroot; cook 1 minute, then remove with a slotted spoon and set aside.

Add beef to pan and cook, stirring, until browned and well broken up. Stir in turmeric and Garam Masala, cook 1 minute, then add onion mixture.

Cover and cook 20 to 30 minutes, stirring occasionally, until cooking liquid is absorbed; cool. Remove core from cabbage with a sharp knife. Cook whole cabbage in boiling salted water 8 minutes, then drain and rinse in cold water. Leave until cool enough to handle, then carefully peel off 12 to 16 outside leaves, keeping them whole. Finely shred rest of cabbage.

Make sauce, heat remaining oil in a heavy saucepan, add sliced onion and cook, stirring frequently, 5 minutes, or until soft, but not brown. Add shredded cabbage, tomatoes, remaining gingerroot, lemon juice, salt, pepper and water. Bring to a boil and simmer 5 minutes

Preheat oven to 375F (190C). Put about 2 tablespoons beef mixture on each cabbage leaf, fold sides in and roll up neatly. Pour a little sauce into bottom of a casserole dish, add cabbage rolls and pour over rest of sauce. Cover and bake 40 to 50 minutes, until cabbage is tender. Serve hot, garnished with lemon slices.

Makes 4 servings.

BEEF WITH TOMATO SAUCE

GARLIC BEEF

2 garlic cloves, thinly sliced
1 tablespoon finely chopped fresh thyme
1 tablespoon finely chopped fresh marjoram
1 (1-1/2-lb.) beef chuck steak
2 tablespoons olive oil
TOMATO SAUCE:
2 tablespoons olive oil
8 garlic cloves, chopped
1 fresh thyme sprig
2 fresh marjoram sprigs
3 fresh parsley sprigs
1 (14-oz) can chopped tomatoes
8 canned anchovy fillets, drained and chopped
3/4 cup dry white wine
24 small ripe olives, pitted
Salt and pepper

2 tablespoons olive oil
1 (4-oz) piece slab bacon, cut into 2-inch cubes
1 (2-lb.) beef chuck steak, cut into 1-1/2-inch cubes
1 Spanish onion, chopped
1 head garlic, divided into cloves
1 cup red wine
2 whole cloves
Bouquet garni of 1 fresh marjoram sprig, 1 fresh thyme
   sprig, 2 fresh parsley sprigs and 1 bay leaf
Salt and pepper

To make the sauce, in a saucepan, heat oil. Add garlic and herbs and simmer 5 minutes. Add tomatoes with their juice, then stir in anchovies, wine and olives. Simmer 15 minutes. Season to taste with salt and pepper.

In a large pan, heat oil. Add bacon and cook over low heat until bacon is almost crisp. Increase heat, add beef and cook about 5 minutes, stirring occasionally, until browned all over. Using a slotted spoon, transfer beef and bacon to a bowl.

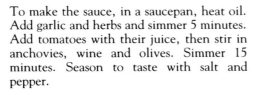

Meanwhile, mix garlic with chopped herbs. Using the point of a sharp knife, cut small slits in beef and push the herb-covered slices of garlic deep into slits. In a large pan, heat oil. Add beef and cook 10 minutes until evenly browned. Add sauce, cover tightly and simmer about 1-1/2 hours, turning beef occasionally, until beef is tender.

Makes 4 servings.

Stir onion and garlic into pan and cook 6 minutes, stirring occasionally. Stir in wine, cloves, bouquet garni, salt and pepper. Return meat to pan, cover tightly and simmer 2 hours, stirring occasionally, until meat is very tender. Add a little water if mixture gets too dry. Discard bouquet garni.

Makes 6 servings.

TERIYAKA STEAKS

1/4 cup mirin or dry sherry sweetened with
  1 teaspoon sugar
1/4 cup light soy sauce
1/2-inch piece gingerroot, peeled and minced
1 garlic clove, finely chopped
1 teaspoon sugar
1/2 teaspoon red pepper sauce or to taste
4 beef sirloin or tenderloin steaks, cut into strips
2 tablespoons sesame oil
4 green onions, thinly sliced
Cilantro leaves, to garnish
Marinated cucumbers and rice, to serve

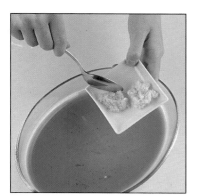

In a shallow baking dish, combine mirin, soy sauce, gingerroot, garlic, sugar and red pepper sauce to taste.

Add the meat and turn to coat well. Let stand 1 hour, turning strips once or twice.

Heat a wok until very hot. Add sesame oil and swirl to coat wok. Drain meat, reserving marinade, and add to wok. Stir-fry 2 or 3 minutes or until browned on all sides. Add marinade and green onions. Cook 3 to 5 minutes or until meat is cooked to desired doneness and most of marinade has evaporated, glazing the meat. Garnish with cilantro and serve with marinated cucumbers and rice.

Makes 4 servings.

SPICY SESAME BEEF

1 tablespoon cornstarch
3 tablespoons light soy sauce
1 pound beef sirloin steak, cut crosswise into thin strips
12 ounces broccoli
2 tablespoons sesame oil
1-inch piece gingerroot, peeled and cut into julienne
  strips
2 garlic cloves, finely chopped
1 fresh hot red chile, seeded and thinly sliced
1 red bell pepper, thinly sliced
1 (14-oz.) can baby corn on-the-cob, drained
1/2 cup beef stock, chicken stock or water
4 to 6 green onions, cut into 2-inch pieces
Toasted sesame seeds, to garnish
Noodles or rice, to serve

In a bowl, combine cornstarch and soy sauce. Add beef strips and toss to coat well. Let stand 20 minutes. Cut large flowerets from the broccoli and divide into small flowerets. With a vegetable peeler, peel the stalk and cut diagonally into 1-inch pieces. Heat a wok until very hot. Add sesame oil and swirl to coat. Add beef strips and marinade and stir-fry 2 or 3 minutes or until browned.

With a slotted spoon, remove beef strips to a bowl. Add gingerroot, garlic and chile to the wok and stir-fry 1 minute. Add broccoli, bell pepper and baby corn and stir-fry 2 or 3 minutes or until broccoli is tender but still crisp. Add the stock and stir 1 minute or until sauce bubbles and thickens. Add green onions and reserved beef strips and stir-fry 1 or 2 minutes or until beef strips are heated through. Sprinkle with sesame seeds and serve with noodles or rice.

Makes 4 servings.

BEEF IN OYSTER SAUCE

1 tablespoon cornstarch
1-1/2 tablespoons soy sauce
1-1/2 tablespoons rice wine or dry sherry
1 pound beef round, sirloin or tenderloin steak, cut crosswise into thin strips
2 tablespoons sesame oil
1/2-inch piece gingerroot, peeled and chopped
2 garlic cloves, finely chopped
4 stalks celery, sliced
1 red bell pepper sliced
4 ounces mushrooms, sliced
4 green onions, sliced
2 tablespoons oyster sauce
1/2 cup chicken stock or water
White and wild rice mixture, to serve

In a bowl, combine 2 teaspoons of the cornstarch with soy sauce and sherry. Add beef strips and toss to coat well. Let stand 25 minutes. Heat a wok until very hot. Add oil and swirl to coat wok. Add beef strips and stir-fry 2 or 3 minutes or until browned. With a slotted spoon, remove to a bowl. Add gingerroot and garlic to oil remaining in wok and stir-fry 1 minute. Add celery, bell pepper, mushrooms and green onions and stir-fry 2 or 3 minutes or until vegetables begin to soften.

Stir in oyster sauce and combine remaining cornstarch with the stock, then stir into mixture in wok and bring to a boil. Add reserved beef strips and cook, stirring, 1 minute or until sauce bubbles and thickens and beef is heated through. Serve with rice.

Makes 4 servings.

SPICY BEEF WITH PEPPERS

1 tablespoon cornstarch
1/4 cup water
1/4 cup light soy sauce
1 tablespoon honey or brown sugar
1 teaspoon Chinese chili sauce
2 tablespoons vegetable oil
1 pound beef round or sirloin steak, cut crosswise into thin strips
1 tablespoon sesame oil
2 garlic cloves, finely chopped
1 fresh hot red chile, seeded and thinly sliced
1 onion, thinly sliced
1 each red, green and yellow bell pepper, cut into thin strips
Rice, to serve

In a small bowl, dissolve cornstarch in the water. Stir in soy sauce, honey and chili sauce until blended. Set aside. Heat a wok until very hot. Add vegetable oil and swirl to coat wok. Add beef strips and stir-fry 2 or 3 minutes or until beef is browned. With a slotted spoon, remove beef to a bowl.

Add sesame oil to the wok and add garlic and chile. Stir-fry 1 minute or until fragrant. Add onion and bell pepper strips and stir-fry 2 or 3 minutes or until beginning to soften. Stir cornstarch mixture, then stir into mixture in wok and stir until sauce bubbles and begins to thicken. Add beef strips and any juices and stir-fry 1 minute or until beef is heated through. Serve with rice.

Makes 4 servings.

MEXICAN BEEF WITH BEANS

1 pound ground beef
1 onion, chopped
3 or 4 garlic cloves, finely chopped
1 green or red bell pepper, diced
1 (4-oz.) can chopped green chiles, drained
1 (14-oz.) can red kidney beans, drained
1 (11-1/2-oz.) can whole-kernel corn, drained
2 tablespoons chili powder or to taste
2 teaspoons ground cumin
1 teaspoon dried leaf oregano
1 (28-oz.) can peeled tomatoes
Salt and freshly ground black pepper
3 tablespoons chopped fresh parsley
1 cup shredded sharp Cheddar cheese

In a wok, place beef and heat until it begins to release juices. Increase heat and stir to break up meat and stir-fry 5 or 6 minutes or until meat is browned. Add onion, garlic, bell pepper, chopped chiles, kidney beans and corn and bring to a boil.

Stir in chili powder, cumin, oregano and peeled tomatoes with their juice. Stir to break up tomatoes. Season with salt and pepper, reduce heat and cook, covered, 20 to 30 minutes or until slightly thickened. Remove from heat, stir in parsley and half of the cheese. Sprinkle with remaining cheese.

Makes 6 to 8 servings.

BEEF STROGANOFF

2 tablespoons peanut oil and 1 tablespoon butter
1 pound beef tenderloin or boneless sirloin steak, cut crosswise into 1/2-inch strips
1 onion, thinly sliced
1/2 pound mushrooms, thinly sliced
Salt and freshly ground black pepper
1 tablespoon all-purpose flour
1/2 cup beef stock or veal stock
1 tablespoon Dijon-style mustard (optional)
1 cup dairy sour cream
2 tablespoons chopped dill
Pinch of red (cayenne) pepper
Rice, to serve

Heat a wok until very hot. Add oil and swirl to coat wok. Add half of the beef strips.

Stir-fry 1 minute or until just browned and still pink in center. With a slotted spoon, remove beef to a bowl. Reheat wok and add remaining beef strips. Stir-fry 1 minute and turn beef and any juices into bowl. Add butter to wok, then add onion. Reduce heat to medium and stir-fry onion 3 or 4 minutes or until softened and beginning to color. Add mushrooms and increase heat; stir-fry 2 minutes or until mushrooms and onions are softened and golden. Add salt and pepper and stir in flour until well-blended.

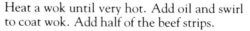

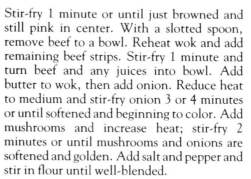

Add beef broth and bring to a boil, then simmer 1 minute or until sauce thickens. Stir in mustard, if using, and gradually add the sour cream. (Do not allow sour cream to boil.) Return beef strips and any juices to sauce, stir in chopped dill and simmer 1 minute or until beef is heated through. Sprinkle a little cayenne. Serve with rice.

Makes 6 servings.

STEAK AU POIVRE

1-1/2 teaspoons green peppercorns
1 teaspoon black peppercorns
1 teaspoon white peppercorns
4 (6-oz.) boneless strip beef steaks
3 tablespoons unsalted butter
Few drops hot-pepper sauce
Few drops Worcestershire sauce
2 tablespoons brandy
3 tablespoons whipping cream
Salt to taste

Coarsely crush all peppercorns in a pestle and mortar.

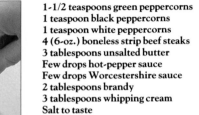

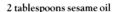

Sprinkle crushed pepper over both sides of steaks, pressing in well with palm of hand. Let stand 30 minutes. Melt 1 tablespoon of butter in a skillet and heat until foaming. Add steaks and cook 2 to 3 minutes, then turn and cook other sides 2 to 3 minutes. (This timing gives medium-rare steaks, so adjust cooking time to suit personal preference.) Turn steaks again and top each one with remaining butter and sprinkle with a few drops hot-pepper sauce and Worcestershire sauce.

Pour brandy over steaks and allow to heat through a few seconds. Flame and remove from heat. When flames subside, remove steaks to a warm serving plate and keep warm. Add whipping cream to skillet and stir well. Heat through 1 minute, scraping up sediment from bottom of skillet. Season with salt and spoon mixture over steaks. Serve at once with fried potatoes and a green salad.

Makes 4 servings.

DRY-FRIED BEEF STRIPS

2 tablespoons sesame oil
1 pound beef round or sirloin steak, cut crosswise into
    julienne strips
2 tablespoons rice wine or dry sherry
1 tablespoon light soy sauce
2 garlic cloves, finely chopped
1/2-inch piece gingerroot, peeled and finely chopped
1 tablespoon Chinese hot bean sauce
2 teaspoons sugar
1 carrot, cut into julienne strips
2 celery stalks, cut into julienne strips
2 or 3 green onions, thinly sliced
1/4 teaspoon ground Szechuan pepper
White and wild rice mixture, to serve

Heat a wok until very hot. Add oil and swirl to coat wok. Add beef and stir-fry 15 seconds to quickly seal meat. Add 1 tablespoon of the rice wine and stir-fry 1 or 2 minutes or until beef is browned. Pour off and reserve any excess liquid and continue stir-frying until beef is dry.

Stir in soy sauce, garlic, gingerroot, bean sauce, sugar, remaining rice wine and any reserved cooking juices and stir to blend well. Add carrot, celery, green onions and ground Szechuan pepper and stir-fry until the vegetables begin to soften and all the liquid is absorbed. Serve with rice.

Makes 4 servings.

GINGER BEEF WITH PINEAPPLE

BEEF IN SPINACH SAUCE

1 lb. lean beef round or sirloin steak
Salt and freshly ground pepper
1 tablespoon sweet sherry
1-inch piece fresh ginger root, peeled and finely
  chopped
1 garlic clove, finely chopped
1 teaspoon cornstarch
8 oz. fresh pineapple
1 tablespoon sunflower oil
2 red bell peppers, thinly sliced
4 green onions, chopped
2 tablespoons light soy sauce
1 piece stem ginger in syrup, drained and thinly
  sliced

2 tablespoons olive oil
1-1/2 pounds beef chuck steak, cut into 1-1/2-inch
  cubes
8 pearl onions
1 tablespoon red-wine vinegar
8 ounces fresh spinach, trimmed
1 tablespoon fresh bread crumbs
3 garlic cloves
About 2 cups veal stock or water
Salt and pepper
1 tablespoon ripe olive paste

Trim any visible fat from the beef and cut into 1/4-inch strips. Place in a bowl and season. Add sherry, chopped ginger, garlic and cornstarch and mix well. Cover and chill 30 minutes. Meanwhile, peel and core the pineapple and cut into 1-inch cubes.

In a large pan, heat oil. Add beef and brown on all sides. Remove with a slotted spoon and set aside. Add onions to pan and cook, stirring frequently, until evenly browned. Stir in vinegar and boil 1 minute.

Heat oil in a nonstick or well-seasoned wok, add beef mixture and stir-fry 1 or 2 minutes or until beef is browned all over. Add bell peppers and stir-fry for another minute. Add green onions, pineapple and soy sauce and simmer 2 or 3 minutes, to heat through. Sprinkle with stem ginger and serve on a bed of noodles.

Makes 4 servings.

Into a blender or food processor with the metal blade, put spinach, bread crumbs, garlic and half the stock or water. Process until smooth. Return beef to pan, add spinach mixture and remaining stock or water. Season with salt and pepper. Heat to a simmer, then cover and simmer over very low heat 1-1/2 to 2 hours until beef is tender. Stir in olive paste and serve.

Makes 4 to 6 servings.

CALVES LIVER WITH BACON

VEAL WITH ANCHOVIES

4 slices bacon, cut into pieces
1 onion, thinly sliced lengthwise into 'petals'
1 Granny Smith apple, cored and thinly sliced
Salt and freshly ground pepper
1 tablespoon vegetable oil
12 ounces calves liver, cut into thin strips
2 tablespoons cider vinegar
1/4 cup dry white wine or apple juice
2 teaspoons cornstarch, dissolved in 1/4 cup chicken
    stock or water
1/2 teaspoon dried leaf thyme
Thyme sprigs or lemon wedges, to garnish

1/2 cup olive oil
Flour for coating
Salt and pepper
4 veal loin chops, 3/4 inch thick
2 small garlic cloves, coarsely chopped
2 canned anchovy fillets, drained and chopped
2 tablespoons chopped fresh parsley
1-1/2 tablespoons coarsely chopped capers
Squeeze of lemon juice
Parsley and lemon slices, to garnish

Place bacon in a cold wok and heat over medium heat until bacon begins to cook.

In a skillet large enough to hold chops in a single layer, heat 1/4 cup of the oil. Season chops with salt and pepper, then coat with flour.

Increase heat and stir-fry 1 or 2 minutes or until bacon is crisp. Remove to a bowl. Add onion to dripping in wok and stir-fry 1 or 2 minutes or until just beginning to soften. Add apple slices and stir-fry 1 or 2 minutes or until apple begins to soften. Season with salt and pepper and remove to bowl. Add oil to wok and increase heat. Add liver strips and stir-fry 1 or 2 minutes or until just browned. The liver should be pink inside. Remove to bowl.

Add chops to pan and cook about 10 minutes, turning occasionally, until light brown and crisp on outsides and just cooked in centers.

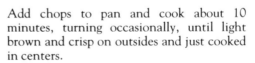

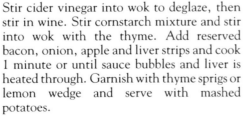

Stir cider vinegar into wok to deglaze, then stir in wine. Stir cornstarch mixture and stir into wok with the thyme. Add reserved bacon, onion, apple and liver strips and cook 1 minute or until sauce bubbles and liver is heated through. Garnish with thyme sprigs or lemon wedge and serve with mashed potatoes.

Makes 2 servings.

Meanwhile, in a small saucepan, heat remaining oil. Add garlic and cook until garlic is pale gold. Stir in anchovies and parsley. Cook 20 to 30 seconds, mashing and stirring anchovies with a wooden spoon. Add capers, and pepper and lemon juice to taste. Transfer chops to a warmed plate and top with sauce. Serve garnished with parsley and lemon slices.

Makes 4 servings.

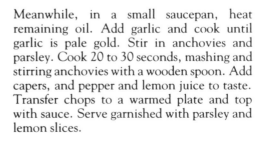

VEGETARIAN MAIN COURSES

—BRAISED FENNEL PROVENÇAL—

3 fennel bulbs
3 tablespoons olive oil
4 garlic cloves, peeled
1 pound plum tomatoes, peeled and diced
2/3 cup dry white wine
12 Niçoise olives
4 fresh thyme sprigs
2 bay leaves
Pinch of sugar
Salt and pepper
Thyme sprigs, to garnish

Cut fennel bulbs lengthwise into 1/2-inch slices.

In a large skillet, heat oil. Add fennel slices and garlic; cook 4 to 5 minutes on each side or until golden. Remove from pan with a slotted spoon and set aside.

Add tomatoes and wine to pan and boil rapidly 5 minutes. Stir in olives, herbs and sugar. Arrange fennel slices over tomatoes, in a single layer, if possible. Cover and simmer 20 minutes. Season with salt and pepper and serve hot or at room temperature, garnished with thyme.

Makes 4 servings.

— BROCCOLI CAPONATA —

2 tablespoons olive oil
1 red onion, chopped
1 red bell pepper, chopped
1 garlic clove, chopped
1 teaspoon chopped fresh thyme
1/3 cup dry red wine
1 pound tomatoes, peeled and chopped
2/3 cup vegetable stock
1 tablespoon red-wine vinegar
1 tablespoon brown sugar
2-2/3 cups chopped broccoli
2 tablespoons tomato paste
1/2 cup pitted green olives
1/4 cup capers, drained
1 tablespoon shredded fresh basil

In a large pan, heat oil. Add onion, bell pepper, garlic and thyme; cook 6 to 8 minutes or until lightly browned. Add wine and boil rapidly 3 minutes. Add tomatoes, stock, vinegar and sugar. Stir well, then cover and simmer 20 minutes.

Steam broccoli over boiling water 5 minutes or until crisp-tender. Add tomato mixture, tomato paste, olives, capers and basil. Cook 3 to 4 minutes. Cool to room temperature and serve.

Makes 4 servings.

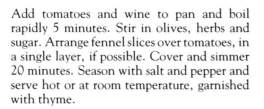

VEGETABLE GRATIN

2/3 cup long-grain rice
3 zucchini
1 red bell pepper
1 onion
6 ripe tomatoes
2 tablespoons olive oil
2 fresh thyme sprigs, chopped
2 fresh rosemary sprigs, chopped
2 bay leaves
1 teaspoon dried leaf oregano
1 teaspoon fennel seeds, toasted
2/3 cup vegetable stock
3/4 cup shredded vegetarian Cheddar cheese

Preheat oven to 400F (205C). Into a small pan, put rice. Cover with cold water. Bring to a boil and cook 3 minutes. Drain well and transfer to a casserole dish. Cut zucchini into thick slices, cut bell pepper and onion into 1/2-inch pieces and chop tomatoes.

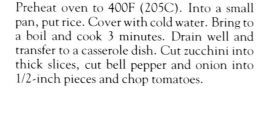

Into a large bowl, place prepared vegetables. Add oil and stir to coat vegetables with oil. Add thyme, rosemary, bay leaves, oregano and fennel seeds. Stir and spoon over rice. Pour stock over vegetables, cover with foil and bake 40 minutes. Remove foil, sprinkle with cheese and bake 10 to 15 minutes or until cheese is melted and all liquid is absorbed. Brown under a hot broiler, if desired, and serve hot.

Makes 6 servings.

TOMATO & BEAN TIAN

3 tablespoons olive oil
1 red onion, chopped
1 garlic clove, crushed
1 large red bell pepper, chopped
1 tablespoon chopped fresh thyme
2 teaspoons chopped fresh rosemary
1 (14-oz.) can chopped tomatoes
1 (15-oz.) can cannellino beans, drained
1/2 cup each fresh bread crumbs, chopped pine nuts
    and grated Parmesan cheese or shredded vegetarian
    Cheddar cheese
2 large zucchini, thinly sliced
2 beefsteak tomatoes, thinly sliced
Rosemary sprigs, to garnish

Preheat oven to 375F (190C). In a saucepan, heat 2 tablespoons of the oil. Add onion, garlic, bell pepper, 2 teaspoons of the thyme and 1 teaspoon of the rosemary; cook 5 minutes. Add tomatoes. Cover and cook 20 minutes. Stir in beans and transfer to a shallow baking dish.

In a small bowl, mix bread crumbs, pine nuts and cheese together. Sprinkle half of the mixture over tomato layer. Arrange zucchini and beefsteak tomatoes in rows over the top. Sprinkle with remaining crumb mixture. Drizzle a little remaining oil and herbs over top, if desired. Cover with foil. Bake 30 minutes. Remove foil and bake 15 to 20 minutes or until golden. Garnish with rosemary sprigs and serve hot.

Makes 4 to 6 servings.

PARSNIP, PEAR & ALMOND SAUTÉ

MUSHROOM & BEAN CHILI

12 pearl onions
3 tablespoons olive oil
1-1/4 pounds baby parsnips, halved or quartered
1 garlic clove, chopped
2 teaspoons chopped fresh thyme
1/2 cup cider
2/3 cup vegetable stock
1 tablespoon brown sugar
2 teaspoons whole-grain mustard
2 small pears, cored and thickly sliced
1/2 cup blanched almonds, toasted
Salt and pepper

4 tablespoons olive oil
1 large eggplant, diced
6 ounces button mushrooms, wiped
1 large onion, chopped
1 garlic clove, chopped
1-1/2 teaspoons paprika
1 teaspoon chili powder
1 teaspoon ground coriander
1/2 teaspoon ground cumin
2 pounds tomatoes, peeled and chopped
2/3 cup vegetable stock
10 tortilla chips
1 tablespoon tomato paste
1 (14-oz.) can red kidney beans
1 tablespoon chopped fresh cilantro
Salt and pepper

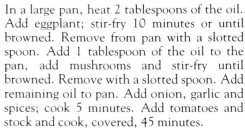

In a small pan, place onions. Cover with cold water and bring to a boil. Drain and refresh under cold water. Peel parsnips and cut in half. In a large skillet, heat 2 tablespoons of the oil. Add onions, parsnips, garlic and thyme; stir-fry 10 minutes or until browned. Add cider and boil rapidly 5 minutes. In a small bowl, blend stock, sugar and mustard together. Stir into pan. Cover and cook 10 to 12 minutes or until parsnips are tender.

In a large pan, heat 2 tablespoons of the oil. Add eggplant; stir-fry 10 minutes or until browned. Remove from pan with a slotted spoon. Add 1 tablespoon of the oil to the pan, add mushrooms and stir-fry until browned. Remove with a slotted spoon. Add remaining oil to pan. Add onion, garlic and spices; cook 5 minutes. Add tomatoes and stock and cook, covered, 45 minutes.

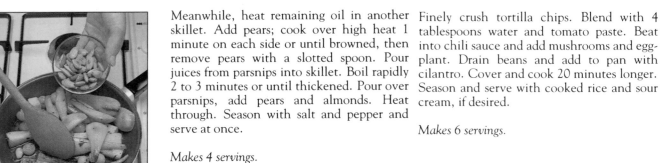

Meanwhile, heat remaining oil in another skillet. Add pears; cook over high heat 1 minute on each side or until browned, then remove pears with a slotted spoon. Pour juices from parsnips into skillet. Boil rapidly 2 to 3 minutes or until thickened. Pour over parsnips, add pears and almonds. Heat through. Season with salt and pepper and serve at once.

Finely crush tortilla chips. Blend with 4 tablespoons water and tomato paste. Beat into chili sauce and add mushrooms and eggplant. Drain beans and add to pan with cilantro. Cover and cook 20 minutes longer. Season and serve with cooked rice and sour cream, if desired.

Makes 4 servings.

Makes 6 servings.

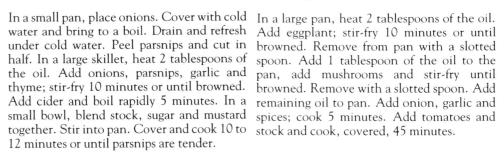

— VEGETABLE & FRUIT CURRY —

BUTTERNUT SQUASH CRUMBLE

1-1/2 teaspoons each coriander seeds and cumin seeds
4 tablespoons vegetable oil
1 large onion, chopped
2 carrots, chopped
2 potatoes, diced
3 garlic cloves, crushed, or 1 tablespoon garlic paste
2 teaspoons grated gingerroot
1 teaspoon each curry powder and turmeric
1 pound tomatoes, peeled and chopped
2 cups vegetable stock
1 cup frozen green peas, thawed
1 apple, chopped
1 mango, chopped
2/3 cup cashews, toasted
1 ounce creamed coconut
1 tablespoon chopped fresh cilantro

1-1/2 pounds butternut squash (about 3 small squash)
1 small fennel bulb, trimmed
1 garlic clove, crushed
1 tablespoon chopped fresh sage
1 (14-oz.) can chopped tomatoes
2/3 cup whipping cream
Salt and pepper
1 cup whole-wheat flour
1/4 cup butter or margarine, diced
1/3 cup macadamia nuts, chopped
1/4 cup grated Parmesan cheese or vegetarian Cheddar
   cheese

In a small pan, roast coriander seeds and cumin seeds until browned. In a blender or spice grinder, grind seeds. In a large pan, heat 2 tablespoons of the oil. Add onion, carrots and potatoes; cook 10 minutes or until browned. In a medium-size pan, heat remaining oil. Add garlic, gingerroot, ground spices, curry powder and turmeric; cook 5 minutes. Add tomatoes. Cover and cook 10 minutes. Stir tomato mixture and stock into carrot mixture; simmer 20 minutes.

Preheat oven to 400F (205C). Peel squash, cut in half and scrape out and discard squash seeds. Cut flesh into 1/2-inch pieces. In a large baking dish, place squash pieces. Cut fennel crosswise into very thin slices. Scatter over squash with garlic and sage. Pour in tomatoes and cream and add a little salt and pepper.

Add peas, apple and mango. Cook 5 minutes longer. Grind half the cashews and mix with creamed coconut in a small bowl. Stir in enough pan juices to form a paste. Carefully stir into curry until evenly combined. Heat through and serve at once, sprinkled with the whole cashews and cilantro.

Makes 4 to 6 servings.

In a bowl, put flour. Cut in butter until the mixture resembles fine bread crumbs. Stir in nuts and cheese. Sprinkle topping over squash. Cover with foil. Bake 40 minutes. Remove foil and bake 15 to 20 minutes longer or until topping is golden and squash is tender.

Makes 6 servings.

LENTIL-STUFFED PEPPERS

2/3 cup red split lentils
4 tablespoons vegetable oil
4 medium green or red bell peppers
1 teaspoon cumin seeds
2 onions, finely chopped
2 green chiles, seeded, chopped
1 (1-inch) piece fresh gingerroot, grated
1 tablespoon ground coriander
1-1/4 cups water
Salt and pepper to taste
2 tablespoons chopped cilantro (fresh coriander)
Cilantro leaves, to garnish

Rinse lentils, then soak in cold water 30 minutes.

Heat half the oil in a skillet. Add peppers and cook 3 to 5 minutes, until golden brown. Drain on paper towels; cool. Add remaining oil to pan, add cumin seeds; cook until just beginning to pop. Add onions and chiles and cook, stirring, 8 minutes, until onions are soft and golden brown. Stir in gingerroot and ground coriander. Drain lentils; add to pan with 1-1/4 cups water. Stir well, then cover.

Cook over low heat 15 to 20 minutes, until tender and liquid has evaporated. Stir in salt, pepper and cilantro. Preheat oven to 350F (175C). Cut tops from peppers and remove seeds. Stuff peppers with lentil mixture and replace tops. Stand in a baking dish. Bake 15 to 20 minutes until peppers are soft. Serve hot, garnished with cilantro leaves.

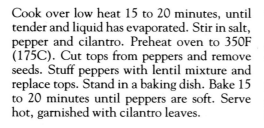

Makes 4 servings.

DHAL BALLS WITH YOGURT

2/3 cup whole green lentils
1 cup plain yogurt
6 tablespoons chopped cilantro
1/4 teaspoon chile powder
4 tablespoons shredded fresh coconut
1 cup fresh bread crumbs
2 green chiles, seeded, chopped
1 (1-inch) piece fresh gingerroot, grated
1 egg, beaten
Salt and pepper to taste
1/2 cup whole-wheat flour
Vegetable oil for deep-frying
Cilantro (fresh coriander) leaves, to garnish

Put lentils in a sieve and rinse thoroughly.

Pick over lentils and remove any grit. Put in a bowl, cover with cold water and soak 2 hours. Meanwhile, mix yogurt with 2 tablespoons of the cilantro and the chile powder. Cover and refrigerate. Drain lentils, cover with fresh water and simmer 30 minutes, or until tender. Puree in a vegetable mill or food processor, or mash well. Transfer to a bowl, add 2 tablespoons of the coconut, the bread crumbs, remaining cilantro, chiles, gingerroot, egg, salt and pepper; mix well. Refrigerate 30 minutes.

With damp hands, carefully roll mixture into 1-inch balls, then roll balls in flour to coat completely. Half-fill a deep pan or deep-fryer with oil and heat to 375F (190C), or until a 1-inch cube of bread browns in 50 seconds. Fry about 6 balls at a time 2 to 3 minutes, until golden brown. Drain on paper towels. Serve hot with yogurt sauce, sprinkled with remaining coconut and garnished with cilantro leaves.

Makes 4 servings.

TAMIL NADU VEGETABLES

MIXED VEGETABLE CURRY

2/3 cup red split lentils
1/2 teaspoon ground turmeric
2-1/2 cups water
1 small eggplant
1/4 cup vegetable oil
1/3 cup shredded coconut
1 teaspoon cumin seeds
1/2 teaspoon mustard seeds
2 dried red chiles, crushed
1 red bell pepper, seeded, sliced
4 ounces zucchini, thickly sliced
3 ounces green beans, cut into 3/4-inch pieces
2/3 cup vegetable stock
Salt to taste
Red bell pepper strips, to garnish

3 tablespoons vegetable oil
1 onion, sliced
1 teaspoon ground cumin
1 teaspoon chile powder
2 teaspoons ground coriander
1 teaspoon ground turmeric
8 ounces potatoes, diced
6 ounces cauliflower, broken into flowerets
6 ounces green beans, sliced
6 ounces carrots, diced
4 tomatoes, peeled, chopped
1-1/4 cups hot vegetable stock
Onion rings, to garnish

Rinse lentils and put in a large pan with turmeric and water. Boil 10 minutes, then reduce heat and cover. Simmer 15 to 20 minutes until lentils are soft. Meanwhile, cut eggplant into 1/2-inch cubes. Heat oil in a large shallow pan, add coconut, cumin seeds, mustard seeds and chiles.

Heat oil in a large saucepan, add onion and cook 5 minutes until softened. Stir in cumin, chile power, coriander and turmeric; cook 2 minutes. Add potatoes, cauliflower, green beans and carrots, tossing them in the spices until coated.

Cook 1 minute, then add eggplant, bell pepper, zucchini, green beans, stock and salt. Bring to a boil, reduce heat, cover and simmer 10 to 15 minutes, until vegetables are just tender. Stir in lentils and any cooking liquid and cook another 5 minutes. Serve hot, garnished with bell pepper strips.

Makes 4 servings.

Add tomatoes and stock and cover. Bring to a boil, then reduce heat and simmer 10 to 12 minutes or until vegetables are just tender. Serve hot, garnished with onion rings.

Makes 4 servings.

Variations: Use any mixture of vegetables to make a total of 1-1/2 pounds – turnips, zucchini, eggplant, parsnips and leeks are all suitable.

CHICKPEA & PEPPER OMELET

FRESH HERB FRITTATA

2 tablespoons olive oil
1 red onion, chopped
1 red bell pepper, chopped
2 garlic cloves, crushed
1 cup cooked chickpeas
1 teaspoon ground turmeric
2 tablespoons chopped fresh parsley
4 large eggs
Salt and pepper
Parsley sprigs and tomato wedges, to garnish

6 eggs
2 egg whites
2 green onions, chopped
1/2 cup cottage cheese
1/2 cup fresh chopped mixed herbs
1 cup arugula leaves
Salt and pepper
1/4 cup olive oil

In a bowl, beat eggs and egg whites together
until thoroughly mixed. Stir in green onions,
cheese and herbs. Roughly chop arugula
leaves and add to mixture with salt and
pepper.

In a nonstick skillet, heat oil. Add onion,
bell pepper and garlic; cook 10 minutes or
until light golden and softened. Add chickpeas, mashing them lightly. Stir in turmeric
and parsley. Stir-fry 2 minutes. Lightly beat
eggs with salt and pepper and stir into pan
until evenly mixed.

Preheat broiler. In a nonstick skillet, heat
oil. Pour in egg mixture, swirling to reach
edges of pan. Cook, stirring, over medium-
low heat about 3 minutes or until eggs are
beginning to set.

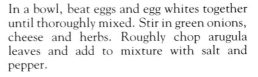

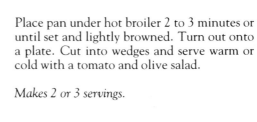

Cook over medium heat 5 to 6 minutes or
until cooked and browned underneath.
Loosen around edges with a spatula. Carefully slip omelet out onto a plate. Invert pan
over omelet and flip over so top is now on
bottom. Cook 3 to 4 minutes longer or until
golden on bottom. Turn out onto a plate.
Cool to room temperature. Garnish with
parsley and tomato wedges.

Makes 6 servings.

Place pan under hot broiler 2 to 3 minutes or
until set and lightly browned. Turn out onto
a plate. Cut into wedges and serve warm or
cold with a tomato and olive salad.

Makes 2 or 3 servings.

POTATO & ONION TART

CHEESE & EGG STRATA

3/4 cup all-purpose flour
Pinch of salt
1/2 cup unsalted butter, chilled
1 egg yolk
2 tablespoons iced water
FILLING:
1 pound waxy potatoes
2 tablespoons butter or margarine
2 large onions, thinly sliced
1 teaspoon chopped fresh rosemary
1/2 teaspoon caraway seeds
3/4 cup half and half
1/4 cup shredded vegetarian Cheddar cheese
Freshly grated nutmeg

2-1/2 cups milk
1 bay leaf
2 cardamom pods, bruised
1 tablespoon butter
1 onion, thinly sliced
1/2 teaspoon chopped fresh thyme
1/2 cup sun-dried tomatoes in oil, drained and chopped
1/4 cup Mascarpone cheese
2 cups shredded vegetarian Cheddar cheese
12 whole-wheat bread slices
3 eggs
Pinch of grated nutmeg
Salt and pepper

Preheat oven to 400F (205C). Into a large bowl, sift flour and salt. Cut in butter until mixture resembles fine bread crumbs. Make a well in center. Work in egg yolk and water to form a soft dough. On a lightly floured surface, knead dough. Wrap and refrigerate 30 minutes. Roll out thinly and use to line a deep 9-inch fluted tart pan. Prick bottom. Refrigerate 20 minutes. Line with foil and pie weights. Bake blind 10 minutes. Remove weights and foil and bake 10 to 12 minutes or until crisp.

Preheat oven to 400F (205C). Lightly oil a 9-cup deep, oval baking dish. Into a small pan, put milk, bay leaf and cardamom pods. Heat until almost boiling. Remove from heat and leave to infuse 10 minutes. Strain into a bowl. In a skillet, melt butter. Add onion and thyme; cook 10 minutes or until softened. Add tomatoes. Remove from heat, cool slightly and stir in Mascarpone cheese and 1/2 cup Cheddar cheese.

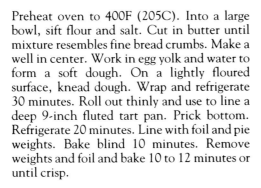

Increase oven temperature to 450F (230C). Boil potatoes 15 minutes or until just tender. Let cool, carefully peel and cut into very thin slices. Melt butter in a skillet. Add onions, rosemary and caraway seeds; cook 10 minutes or until golden. Spread onion mixture over pastry shell and top with potato slices. Beat remaining ingredients together. Pour over potatoes; bake on top rack 15 minutes or until golden.

Makes 6 to 8 servings.

Spread half of onion mixture over bottom of dish. Top with half of the bread and remaining onion mixture. Sprinkle with half of the remaining cheese. Top with remaining bread. Beat eggs, nutmeg, salt and pepper into milk. Pour into baking dish. Sprinkle remaining cheese over top. Place dish in a roasting pan. Pour in boiling water to come two-thirds of the way up side of dish. Cover with foil and bake 30 minutes. Remove foil and bake 20 minutes longer.

Makes 6 to 8 servings.

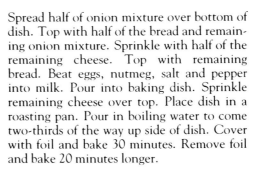

BROCCOLI & OLIVE TART

BAKED EGGS WITH MOZZARELLA

Whole-wheat pastry dough for a 9-inch pie
1 yellow bell pepper
1 red bell pepper
4 ounces broccoli flowerets
1/2 cup pitted ripe olives, halved
2 eggs, beaten
1/2 cup half and half
1/2 cup soft goat cheese
2 tablespoons chopped fresh parsley
Salt and pepper

1 large ripe tomato
1 green onion, chopped
1/3 cup shredded mozzarella cheese
4 pitted ripe olives, sliced
1 tablespoon shredded fresh basil
Salt and pepper
1/3 cup whipping cream
4 eggs
Parsley sprigs, to garnish
Bread slices, toasted, or Melba toast, to serve

Preheat oven to 375F (190C); lightly butter 4 ramekins. Peel and seed tomato and finely dice flesh.

On a lightly floured surface, roll out dough. Use to line a deep 9-inch fluted tart pan. Prick bottom and refrigerate 20 minutes. Preheat oven to 400F (205C). Quarter and seed bell peppers. Broil 4 to 5 minutes or until lightly charred. Let cool slightly, then peel and thinly slice flesh. Steam broccoli 3 minutes.

In a small bowl, combine tomato, green onion, cheese, olives, basil, salt and pepper. Divide among ramekins.

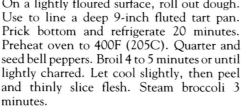

Line the tart shell with foil and pie weights. Bake blind 10 minutes. Remove weights and foil and bake 10 to 12 minutes longer until pastry is crisp and golden. Cool slightly and arrange bell peppers, broccoli and olives over bottom. Beat remaining ingredients together until smooth. Pour over vegetables. Bake 35 minutes or until set in center. Cool and serve warm or cold.

Makes 6 to 8 servings.

In a small pan, heat cream until almost boiling. Pour over tomato mixture and break an egg into each dish. Place in a roasting pan and pour in enough boiling water to come two-thirds up sides of ramekins. Bake 10 to 15 minutes until eggs are just set. Cool slightly, garnish with parsley and serve with toasted bread or Melba toast.

Makes 4 servings.

— VEGETABLE FILO PACKAGES —

— POLENTA WITH MUSHROOMS —

4 small new potatoes, halved
8 baby carrots
8 baby zucchini, halved
8 asparagus tips
1 baby leek, sliced into 8 pieces
1/4 cup butter or margarine, softened
1 tablespoon chopped fresh mint
1/4 teaspoon ground cumin
Pinch red (cayenne) pepper
Salt and pepper
4 large sheets filo pastry
1/3 cup olive oil

Preheat oven to 375F (190C); place a baking sheet on middle shelf.

3-3/4 cups vegetable stock
1/2 teaspoon salt
1 cup polenta
1 teaspoon chopped fresh thyme
1/2 cup freshly grated Parmesan cheese
2 tablespoons butter
1/2 ounce dried cep mushrooms
1/3 cup boiling water
1/4 cup port wine
3 tablespoons virgin olive oil
1 garlic clove, crushed
1 shallot, finely chopped
5 cups sliced mixed fresh mushrooms, sliced
1 tablespoon chopped fresh parsley

In a large pan of boiling water, cook potatoes 6 to 8 minutes or until almost cooked. Blanch remaining vegetables 2 to 3 minutes, depending on size, until almost tender. Drain all vegetables. Cool in cold water. Drain and dry thoroughly. Cream together butter, mint, spices, salt and pepper. Take 1 large sheet of dough and, using a 10-inch plate or a pan lid as a template, carefully cut out a circle. Repeat to make 4 circles. Brush liberally with oil.

In a large pan, bring 3-1/4 cups of the stock and the salt to a boil. Stir in polenta. Stir, cover and simmer 25 minutes, stirring frequently. Add thyme and cook 5 minutes. Stir in cheese and butter. Spoon polenta mixture into a lightly oiled, shallow pan. Smooth surface and let cool. Soak ceps in the boiling water 20 minutes. Into a pan, strain soaking liquid. Chop ceps. Add port and remaining 1/2 cup stock to pan. Boil rapidly until reduced to about 1/2 cup. Set aside.

Place one-quarter of vegetables in a small pile on one side of dough circle. Dot with mint butter. Fold other side of dough over filling, pressing edges together to seal. Brush a little oil along edge and turn over a bit at a time to ensure filling is totally enclosed. Repeat to make 4 packages and transfer to heated cookie sheet. Carefully brush with remaining oil. Bake 12 to 15 minutes or until pastry is golden. Serve immediately.

Makes 4 servings.

Turn out polenta. Cut into 12 triangles. Brush with oil and broil 8 to 10 minutes on each side until golden. Meanwhile, in a large pan, heat oil. Add garlic, shallot and ceps; cook 5 minutes. Add sliced fresh mushrooms and stir-fry 3 to 4 minutes or until browned. Add reduced liquid, cover and cook 5 minutes. Add parsley. Serve broiled polenta triangles with mushroom sauce.

Makes 6 servings.

TOFU, LEEK & MUSHROOM SATE

3/4 pound plain tofu
3 leeks, trimmed
12 shiitake or button mushrooms
2 tablespoons dark soy sauce
1 garlic clove, crushed
1/2 teaspoon grated fresh gingerroot
1 small red chile, seeded and chopped
Grated peel and juice of 1 lime
3 tablespoons sweet sherry
2 teaspoons honey
1/4 cup crunchy peanut butter
1 ounce creamed coconut

With a sharp knife, cut tofu into 12 cubes and leeks into 12 thick slices. Place in a shallow dish with mushrooms. Mix together soy sauce, garlic, gingerroot, chile, lime peel, lime juice, sherry, honey and 3 tablespoons water. Pour over tofu mixture. Cover and refrigerate several hours, stirring from time to time.

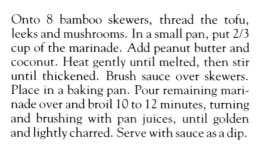

Onto 8 bamboo skewers, thread the tofu, leeks and mushrooms. In a small pan, put 2/3 cup of the marinade. Add peanut butter and coconut. Heat gently until melted, then stir until thickened. Brush sauce over skewers. Place in a baking pan. Pour remaining marinade over and broil 10 to 12 minutes, turning and brushing with pan juices, until golden and lightly charred. Serve with sauce as a dip.

Makes 4 servings.

OLIVE & MOZZARELLA PUFFS

1/2 cup pitted green olives
1 ounce mozzarella cheese
2 teaspoons chopped fresh parsley
1/2 teaspoon chopped fresh sage
Pinch of chili powder
1 sheet prepared puff pastry dough from a 17-oz. pkg., thawed if frozen
1 egg
Salt
Parsley leaves and extra olives, to garnish

Preheat oven to 425F (220C); lightly oil a baking sheet. Very finely chop olives and cheese. Mix with herbs and chili powder to form a paste. Set aside.

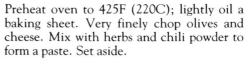
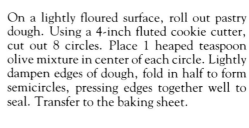

On a lightly floured surface, roll out pastry dough. Using a 4-inch fluted cookie cutter, cut out 8 circles. Place 1 heaped teaspoon olive mixture in center of each circle. Lightly dampen edges of dough, fold in half to form semicircles, pressing edges together well to seal. Transfer to the baking sheet.

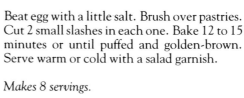

Beat egg with a little salt. Brush over pastries. Cut 2 small slashes in each one. Bake 12 to 15 minutes or until puffed and golden-brown. Serve warm or cold with a salad garnish.

Makes 8 servings.

Note: These make ideal buffet party nibbles. Make up double quantity of filling, cut dough into smaller circles to make bite-sized appetizers.

WINTER VEGETABLE PIE

1-1/4 cups self-rising flour
Salt
8 tablespoons vegetable shortening
2 tablespoons chopped fresh mixed herbs
4 to 5 tablespoons iced water
2 tablespoons olive oil
6 ounces pearl onions, halved
1 garlic clove, chopped
1-1/4 pounds prepared mixed winter vegetables
    (carrots, turnips, parsnips, cauliflower flowerets)
4 ounces button mushrooms
2/3 cup dry red wine
1-1/2 cups vegetable stock (see opposite)
2 tablespoons tomato paste

Roll out dough to a 1/4-inch rectangle. Cut out a pie top a little larger than dish. Cut remaining dough into strips, dampen and press around edge of dish. Dampen edge of dough. Place dough lid over pie and press edges to seal. Bake 30 minutes.

Makes 6 servings.

Into a large bowl, sift flour with 1 teaspoon salt. Cut in 2 tablespoons of the shortening. Stir in half the herbs and work in enough iced water to form a soft dough. Knead lightly. Wrap and refrigerate 30 minutes. Roll out dough to a rectangle about 1/2 inch thick. Dot top two-thirds with 2 tablespoons of the shortening. Bring the bottom third of dough up into middle and top third over this. Press edges to seal. Wrap and refrigerate 30 minutes. Repeat process twice and refrigerate a final 30 minutes.

Note: To make vegetable stock, cook 1 coarsely chopped onion and 1 trimmed and sliced leek in 2 teaspoons olive oil until softened. Add 2 chopped carrots, 1 diced large potato and 2 sliced celery stalks. Cook 5 minutes longer.

Preheat oven to 400F (205C). In a skillet, heat oil. Add onions, garlic and vegetables; cook 10 minutes. Add wine and boil 5 minutes. Add stock and tomato paste. Simmer 20 minutes. Transfer to a 5-cup deep oval baking dish.

Add 4 coarsely chopped ripe tomatoes, 1-1/2 cups quartered mushrooms, 1/3 cup rice, 2 parsley sprigs, 2 thyme sprigs, 1 bay leaf, 1 teaspoon salt, 6 white peppercorns and 5 cups water. Bring to a boil. Cover and simmer 30 minutes. Strain through a fine strainer.

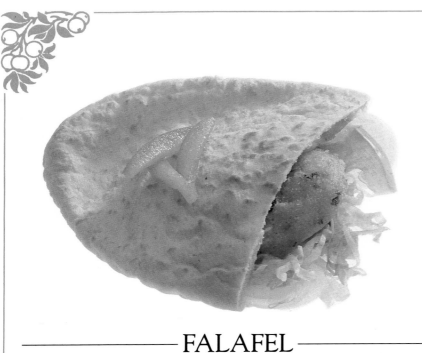

FALAFEL

1 (13-oz.) can garbanzo beans, drained
1 onion, cut in fourths
2 cloves garlic
4 slices fresh white bread, cubed
1/4 teaspoon cumin seeds
4 small dried red chilies, crushed
1 tablespoon chopped fresh parsley
Salt and freshly ground pepper to taste
1 egg, beaten
1/3 cup dry fine bread crumbs
Vegetable oil for deep frying
4 pieces pita bread, warmed
Shredded lettuce
Onion slices
Tomato slices

TOFU & PEPPERS

8 oz. fresh tofu, drained and cut into 3/4-inch cubes
1 tablespoon dark soy sauce
1 tablespoon sweet sherry
1-inch piece fresh ginger root, peeled and finely
  chopped
Salt and freshly ground pepper
1 tablespoon sunflower oil
1 fresh red chile, seeded and finely chopped
2 garlic cloves, thinly sliced
1 red bell pepper, thinly sliced
1 green bell pepper, thinly sliced
1 yellow bell pepper, thinly sliced
3 tablespoons chopped fresh basil

Process garbanzo beans, onion, garlic, bread, cumin and chilies in a blender or food processor until smooth, then spoon mixture into a bowl. Add parsley, salt, pepper and egg; mix well. Form in 8 balls and coat in bread crumbs. Flatten balls slightly to form oval shapes.

Place tofu on a plate or in a shallow dish. Mix together soy sauce, sherry, ginger, salt and pepper. Spoon over tofu, cover and chill 30 minutes.

Half fill a deep fay fryer or saucepan with oil; heat to 375F (190C) or until a 1/2-inch cube of day-old bread browns in 40 seconds. Fry Falafel, a few at a time, 3 minutes or until golden brown. Drain on paper towels. Cut pita bread in half and open to form pockets. Put 1 Falafel into each pocket with lettuce, onion and tomato slices and serve hot.

Makes 8 servings.

Heat oil in a nonstick or well-seasoned wok and stir-fry tofu mixture, chile and garlic 2 minutes. Add bell peppers and stir-fry 4 minutes. Stir in basil and serve immediately with noodles.

Makes 4 servings.

PIZZAS, PASTA & RICE

BLUE CHEESE PIZZAS

1/2 cup pitted ripe olives
1 garlic clove, chopped
1 teaspoon chopped fresh thyme
1 tablespoon olive oil
1 recipe Pizza Dough (see opposite)
3 tablespoons butter
2 red onions, thinly sliced
1/2 teaspoon fennel seeds
1 teaspoon chopped fresh rosemary
3 oz. vegetarian blue cheese, crumbled
Grated peel of 1 lemon
Rosemary sprigs, to garnish

In a blender or food processor, puree olives, garlic, thyme and oil to form a smooth paste.

Make Pizza Dough. Cover and let rise in a warm place 30 minutes. In a skillet, melt butter. Add onions; cook over low heat 20 to 25 minutes or until golden. Let cool. Preheat oven to 450F (230C); place a baking sheet or pizza stone on top shelf.

Divide pizza dough into 4 pieces. Roll out each piece on a lightly floured surface to a 5-inch circle. Spread olive paste and onion mixture over each circle. Sprinkle with fennel seeds and rosemary, then cheese. Sprinkle with lemon peel and transfer pizzas to hot baking sheet. Bake 10 to 12 minutes or until bubbly and golden. Serve hot, garnished with rosemary.

Makes 4 servings.

BROILED VEGETABLE PIZZA

1 red bell pepper, quartered
1 small zucchini, sliced
1 small eggplant, sliced
1 small onion, thinly sliced
6 large tomatoes, quartered and seeded
2 tablespoons prepared pesto sauce
Salt and pepper
1-1/4 cups shredded vegetarian mozzarella cheese
PIZZA DOUGH:
1-2/3 cups all-purpose flour
1/2 teaspoon quick-rise dried yeast
1/2 teaspoon salt
1/2 cup warm water
1 tablespoon olive oil

To prepare dough: In a bowl, mix flour, yeast and salt together. Make a well in center; stir in water and oil to form a stiff dough. Knead 5 minutes. Place in a greased bowl, cover and let rise in a warm place 30 minutes or until doubled in size. Preheat oven to 450F (230C) and place a baking sheet or pizza stone on top shelf. Place pepper, zucchini, eggplant and onion on a rack in a baking sheet; brush with a little oil. Broil until charred on all sides.

Broil tomato quarters, skin-sides up, until blistered. Peel and discard skin and mash flesh with pesto sauce, salt and pepper. Roll out dough to a 9-inch circle. Spread tomato mixture over dough; arrange broiled vegetables over top. Sprinkle with cheese. Transfer to hot baking sheet or pizza stone. Bake 25 to 30 minutes until bubbly and golden.

Makes 4 servings.

BELL PEPPER PIZZETTES

PIZZA DOUGH:
4 cups bread flour or all-purpose flour
Pinch of salt
1 (1/4-oz.) package active dry yeast (about 1 tablespoon)
1 teaspoon sugar
Scant 1 cup warm water (110F, 45C)
2 tablespoons extra-virgin olive oil
Oregano sprigs to garnish
TOPPING:
2 red or yellow bell peppers
3 tablespoons sun-dried tomato paste
1/4 cup capers in wine vinegar, drained
2 tablespoons chopped fresh oregano or 2 teaspoons dried leaf oregano
Salt and freshly ground pepper

Preheat oven to 450F (230C). Oil 2 baking sheets. Turn out dough onto a lightly floured surface. Knead gently and cut into 16 equal pieces. Roll each piece into a small oval about 1/4 inch thick.

Sift flour and salt into a large bowl. In a small bowl, dissolve yeast and sugar in water. Let stand 5 to 10 minutes until frothy. Stir in olive oil. Using a wooden spoon, gradually stir yeast mixture into flour to give a soft, but not sticky, dough. Knead on a floured surface 5 minutes until smooth and elastic. Place in an oiled medium-size bowl, cover and let rise in a warm place 35 to 40 minutes until doubled in size.

Transfer to the baking sheets and prick dough with a fork. Divide sun-dried tomato paste, reserved peppers, capers and oregano among dough ovals. Season with salt and freshly ground pepper. Bake in preheated oven 8 to 10 minutes until golden. Serve hot or warm garnished with oregano sprigs.

Makes 16 pizzettes.

Meanwhile, preheat broiler. Cook bell peppers under hot broiler about 10 minutes, turning occasionally, until skins are evenly blistered and charred. Transfer peppers to a plastic bag a few minutes, then peel away and discard skins. Cut peppers into strips. Set aside.

Red Onion & Gorgonzola Pizzettes In place of above topping, use 1-1/2 cups (4 ounces) crumbled Gorgonzola cheese, 1/2 chopped red onion and 2 tablespoons chopped thyme.

Shrimp & Fennel Pizzettes Replace bell peppers, capers and herbs with 1 small roasted fennel bulb, 4 ounces cooked shrimp and 2 teaspoons fennel seeds. To roast fennel, brush with olive oil and place in a preheated 350F (175C) oven 35 to 40 minutes. Cool and chop.

PENNE WITH LEEKS & RICOTTA

1 pound leeks, rinsed
2 to 3 tablespoons hazelnut oil
1 garlic clove, sliced
4 cups dried penne or other pasta shape
Olive oil
1 cup ricotta cheese
1/4 cup milk
1/3 cup freshly grated Pecorino cheese or Parmesan
   cheese
2 tablespoons mixed chopped fresh herbs
1/2 teaspoon grated lemon peel
1/2 teaspoon lemon juice
Salt and pepper
Parsley sprigs, to garnish

Preheat oven to 425F (220C). Cut leeks into thick slices. Into a roasting pan, place leeks with 2 tablespoons of the oil and the garlic. Roast 25 minutes or until lightly browned. After 10 minutes, bring a large pan of water to a boil. Add pasta, a little olive oil and return to a boil. Reduce heat and simmer 10 minutes or until pasta is cooked but still firm to the bite.

Meanwhile, in a small pan, place all remaining ingredients. Stir over low heat until melted. Heat through 5 minutes without boiling. Drain pasta. Stir in a little more hazelnut oil and toss with cooked leeks. Stir in hot cheese mixture, season with salt and pepper and serve at once, garnished with parsley.

Makes 4 servings.

RATATOUILLE PASTA SAUCE

1 onion
2 garlic cloves
1 tablespoon olive oil
1 eggplant
3 zucchini
1 green bell pepper
1 red bell pepper
1 (14-1/2-oz.) can crushed tomatoes
1 (8-oz.) can crushed tomatoes
1 tablespoon tomato paste
1 teaspoon dried basil
1 teaspoon dried oregano
Salt and pepper

Slice onion and crush both garlic cloves.

In a large saucepan, heat oil 1 minute. Cook onion and garlic 3 minutes, stirring. Dice eggplant, slice zucchini, and slice bell peppers, then add to saucepan.

Stir in tomatoes, tomato paste, herbs, salt, and pepper and mix together well. Bring slowly to a boil, then cover and simmer 30 minutes, stirring occasionally. Adjust seasoning before serving. Serve with freshly cooked pasta.

Makes 4 servings.

TUNA, TOMATO & PENNE

2 tablespoons olive oil
1 onion, chopped
2 garlic cloves, finely chopped
1 (28-oz.) can peeled tomatoes
1 tablespoon tomato paste
1 tablespoon chopped fresh oregano or 1 teaspoon dried
    leaf oregano
1/3 cup sun-dried tomatoes in oil, drained and chopped
Salt and freshly ground pepper
12 ounces penne or rigatoni
1/3 cup ripe olives, coarsely chopped
2 tablespoons capers, drained
1 (7-oz.) can light tuna, drained
2 tablespoons chopped fresh parsley
Parmesan cheese, to garnish

Heat a wok until hot. Add the oil and swirl to coat wok. Add onion and garlic and stir-fry 1 to 2 minutes or until beginning to soften. Add the tomatoes, stirring to break up the large pieces. Stir in the tomato paste, oregano and sun-dried tomatoes. Bring to a boil and simmer 10 to 12 minutes or until sauce is slightly thickened. Season with salt and pepper. Meanwhile, in a large saucepan of boiling water, cook penne according to package directions.

Stir olives, capers and tuna into sauce. Drain pasta and add to tomato sauce, stirring gently to mix well. Stir in chopped parsley and serve immediately from the wok, or spoon into 4 pasta bowls. Using a vegetable peeler, shave flakes of Parmesan cheese over each serving. Or, grate Parmesan cheese over each serving.

Makes 4 servings.

BOLOGNESE PASTA SAUCE

1 onion
1 garlic clove
1 tablespoon sunflower oil
2 carrots
2 stalks celery
8 ounces mushrooms
2 ounces lean bacon, diced
1 pound extra-lean ground beef
1 (14-1/2-oz.) can crushed tomatoes
1 tablespoon tomato paste
2/3 cup beef stock
2/3 cup dry white wine
1 teaspoon Italian seasoning
1/4 teaspoon ground bay leaves or fresh bay leaves
Salt and pepper

Chop onion and crush garlic. In a large saucepan, heat oil 1 minute. Add onion and garlic and cook 3 minutes, stirring. Using a sharp knife, finely chop carrots and celery and slice mushrooms. Add to saucepan and cook 5 minutes, stirring. Add bacon and ground beef to saucepan, mixing together well. Cook until meat is browned all over, stirring.

Stir in tomatoes, tomato paste, stock, wine, herbs, salt, and pepper and mix together well. Bring slowly to a boil, then cover and simmer 1-1/2 to 2 hours, stirring occasionally. Uncover last 30 minutes of cooking time. Adjust seasoning before serving. Serve with freshly cooked spaghetti or pasta shapes.

Makes 6 servings.

—MACARONI WITH EGGPLANT—

1 pound eggplant, cut into 1/4-inch strips
1 pound macaroni
3 tablespoons olive oil
3 garlic cloves, finely chopped
1 pound tomatoes, peeled, seeded and chopped
1 fresh hot red chile, seeded and chopped
4 ounces Italian salami, cut into julienne strips
1/2 cup Italian-style ripe olives
2 tablespoons capers, drained and rinsed
1/4 cup shredded fresh basil or oregano
1 cup crumbled feta cheese (4 oz.)
1/4 cup grated Parmesan cheese

Place eggplant strips into a colander and sprinkle with salt. Toss to mix and let stand, on a plate, 1 hour. Rinse with cold water and pat dry with paper towels.

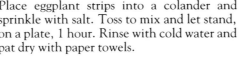

In a large saucepan of boiling water, cook pasta according to package directions. Drain pasta and set aside. Heat a wok until very hot. Add oil and swirl to coat wok. Add eggplant and stir-fry 4 minutes or until browned. Drain on paper towels. Add garlic, tomatoes and chile and stir-fry 2 minutes or until juices are absorbed. Add salami, olives, capers, basil, eggplant and pasta and toss to coat well. Heat through. Stir in feta cheese and remove from heat. Serve with Parmesan cheese.

Makes 6 servings.

—NOODLES, PORK & SHRIMP—

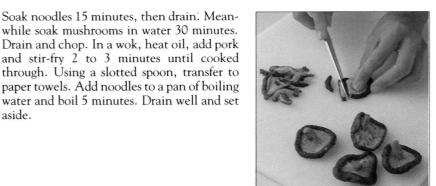

7 ounces bean thread noodles
6 dried Chinese black mushrooms
2 tablespoons vegetable oil
12 ounces lean pork, very finely chopped
4 ounces peeled cooked large shrimp
3 shallots, finely chopped
4 green onions, including some green tops, sliced
3 small inner celery stalks, thinly sliced
2 ounces dried shrimp
2 tablespoons fish sauce
5 tablespoons lime juice
1-1/2 teaspoons crushed palm sugar
2 fresh red chiles, seeded, chopped
1/4 cup cilantro leaves, chopped
Whole cooked shrimp and cilantro leaves to garnish

Soak noodles 15 minutes, then drain. Meanwhile soak mushrooms in water 30 minutes. Drain and chop. In a wok, heat oil, add pork and stir-fry 2 to 3 minutes until cooked through. Using a slotted spoon, transfer to paper towels. Add noodles to a pan of boiling water and boil 5 minutes. Drain well and set aside.

Cut each large shrimp into 3 pieces, place in a bowl and add shallots, green onions, celery, mushrooms, noodles, pork and dried shrimp. Toss together. In a small bowl, mix together fish sauce, lime juice, sugar and chiles. Add cilantro leaves and toss ingredients together. Serve garnished with shrimp and cilantro leaves.

Makes 4 servings.

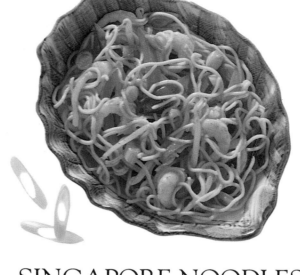

PASTA WITH PEANUT SAUCE

SINGAPORE NOODLES

1 pound thin spaghetti
2 tablespoons sesame oil
8 ounces lean ground pork
1 red bell pepper, thinly sliced
4 ounces snow peas, cut diagonally in half
1 tablespoon sugar
1-inch piece gingerroot, grated
1/2 teaspoon crushed dried chiles
1/4 cup soy sauce
3 tablespoons cider vinegar
2/3 cup peanut butter
8 green onions, thinly sliced
2 tablespoons chopped cilantro

8 ounces thin round noodles
1/4 cup vegetable oil
2 garlic cloves, chopped
1-inch piece gingerroot, peeled and finely chopped
1 fresh hot red chile, seeded and chopped
1 red bell pepper, thinly sliced
4 ounces snow peas, sliced if large
4 to 6 green onions, thinly sliced
6 ounces peeled cooked shrimp
4 ounces bean sprouts
1/3 cup ketchup
1 teaspoon chili powder
1 teaspoon Chinese chili sauce

In a large saucepan of boiling water, cook pasta according to package directions. Drain pasta, turn into a large bowl and toss with 1 tablespoon of the oil. Place pork into a cold wok and cook over medium heat, stirring and breaking up meat, until pork is no longer pink. Add bell pepper, snow peas and sugar and stir-fry 1 minute. Add gingerroot, crushed chiles, soy sauce, vinegar, peanut butter and 2/3 cup hot water; cook, stirring, until sauce bubbles and peanut butter thins out. Add more water if needed.

In a large saucepan of boiling water, cook noodles according to package directions. Drain noodles, turn into a large bowl and toss with 1 tablespoon of the oil. Heat a wok until hot. Add remaining oil and swirl to coat wok. Add garlic, gingerroot and chile and stir-fry 1 minute. Add bell pepper and snow peas and stir-fry 1 minute.

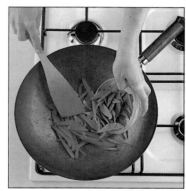

Stir in green onions and reserved pasta. Toss and stir-fry 2 or 3 minutes until pasta is coated evenly with sauce and is heated through. Toss with cilantro.

Makes 4 to 6 servings.

Add green onions, shrimp and bean sprouts. Stir in ketchup, chili powder, chili sauce and 1/2 cup water. Bring to a boil. Add noodles and stir-fry 2 minutes or until coated with sauce and heated through. Serve hot.

Makes 4 servings.

CARAMELIZED CABBAGE & PASTA

1 red bell pepper
1/4 cup butter or margarine
1 large onion, thinly sliced
1 garlic clove, chopped
1 small green cabbage (about 1-1/4 lbs.)
1 tablespoon brown sugar
1 cup dried shell pasta
Salt and black pepper
Chopped fresh parsley, to garnish

Preheat oven to 400F (205C). Under hot broiler, roast bell pepper 20 minutes. Place in a plastic bag and leave until cool enough to handle. Peel, seed and cut flesh into thin strips.

In a large nonstick skillet, melt butter. Add onion and garlic; cook 10 minutes or until lightly browned. Trim outer leaves off cabbage. Cut cabbage into quarters and discard central core. Roughly shred cabbage; stir into onion mixture with sugar. Stir well, cover and cook over very low heat 15 minutes, stirring occasionally, or until cabbage is golden and just tender.

In a pan of lightly salted, boiling water, cook pasta 10 minutes or until tender but still firm to the bite. Drain well. Stir into cabbage with roasted pepper, salt and black pepper. Serve at once, garnished with chopped parsley.

Makes 6 servings.

PASTA PRIMAVERA

1 pound tagliatelle, linguine or thin spaghetti
2 to 4 tablespoons olive oil
8 ounces asparagus, cut into 2-inch pieces
8 ounces broccoli flowerets
2 yellow or green zucchini, sliced
4 ounces snow peas, cut in half if large
2 to 4 garlic cloves, finely chopped
1 (14-oz.) can chopped tomatoes
2 tablespoons butter
4 ounces fresh or frozen green peas
4 to 6 tablespoons shredded fresh basil
Shaved Parmesan cheese, to serve

In a large saucepan of boiling water, cook pasta according to package directions.

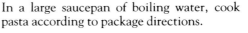

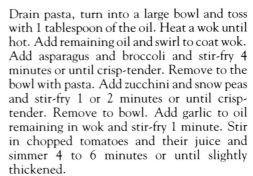

Drain pasta, turn into a large bowl and toss with 1 tablespoon of the oil. Heat a wok until hot. Add remaining oil and swirl to coat wok. Add asparagus and broccoli and stir-fry 4 minutes or until crisp-tender. Remove to the bowl with pasta. Add zucchini and snow peas and stir-fry 1 or 2 minutes or until crisp-tender. Remove to bowl. Add garlic to oil remaining in wok and stir-fry 1 minute. Stir in chopped tomatoes and their juice and simmer 4 to 6 minutes or until slightly thickened.

Stir butter into tomato sauce and add reserved pasta and vegetables and basil. Toss to coat well. Stir and toss 1 minute to heat through. Serve with Parmesan cheese.

Makes 6 servings.

SPINACH GNOCCHI

3/4 pound trimmed spinach leaves
3/4 cup ricotta cheese
Pinch of freshly grated nutmeg
1/3 cup all-purpose flour
1 large egg, lightly beaten
1/4 cup grated Parmesan cheese or vegetarian Cheddar
   cheese
2 tablespoons olive oil
Salt and pepper
1 (14-oz.) can chopped tomatoes
1 garlic clove, crushed
1 tablespoon chopped fresh basil
Pinch of sugar
4 ounces vegetarian blue cheese
2 tablespoons milk

In a large pan, cook spinach with the water clinging to leaves until wilted. Drain, squeeze out excess liquid and chop finely. Cool and beat in the ricotta cheese, nutmeg, flour, egg, Parmesan cheese, half of the oil, salt and pepper. Refrigerate 2 hours.

In a small pan, put tomatoes, remaining oil, garlic, basil and sugar. Simmer 30 minutes. In a blender or food processor, process mixture until pureed. Keep warm.

Shape ricotta mixture into walnut-size balls to make 32 small gnocchi. Flatten out and place on a floured tray.

Into a large pan of simmering water, drop gnocchi, in batches. Cook 6 minutes. Drain on paper towels and keep warm while cooking remaining gnocchi in same way.

Preheat broiler. In a small pan, gently heat milk and blue cheese, stirring until smooth. Pour tomato sauce over bottom of 4 gratin dishes or flameproof plates. Arrange gnocchi on top and drizzle cheese sauce over top. Broil 3 to 4 minutes until bubbling and golden.

Makes 4 servings.

GREEN RICE

ORIENTAL FRIED RICE

1-1/4 cups long grain white rice, rinsed
3-1/2 cups vegetable stock
8 oz. small broccoli flowerets
8 oz. fresh spinach, tough ribs removed
1 tablespoon peanut oil
2 garlic cloves, finely chopped
1 fresh green chile, seeded and chopped
1 bunch green onions, finely chopped
1 (8-oz.) package frozen green peas
2 tablespoons light soy sauce
Salt and freshly ground black pepper
1/4 cup chopped fresh chives
Fresh chives, to garnish

1-1/4 cups long-grain rice
1-1/4 cups chicken stock
2 tablespoons sesame oil
1 (1/2-inch) piece gingerroot, grated
1 garlic clove, crushed
6 ounces raw chicken, thinly sliced
6 green onions, sliced
1 small red bell pepper, sliced
4 ounces shelled shrimp
2 large eggs
2 tablespoons light soy sauce
1 tablespoon chopped fresh cilantro
1/3 cup cashew nuts, toasted

Place rice and stock in a large saucepan, bring to a boil, reduce heat and simmer 25 minutes or until rice is cooked and liquid has been absorbed. Cook broccoli in a saucepan of boiling water 2 minutes. Drain and set aside. Blanch spinach in a saucepan of boiling water a few seconds or until just wilted. Drain well, shred and set aside.

Into a saucepan, put rice and stock. Bring to a boil. Cover and simmer 10 minutes. Remove pan from heat and let stand 10 minutes longer. Drain off any excess liquid and cool slightly. In a large skillet or wok, heat sesame oil. Add gingerroot, garlic and chicken; stir-fry 4 to 5 minutes or until chicken is cooked.

Heat oil in a nonstick or well-seasoned wok and stir-fry garlic, chile, green onions and broccoli 1 minute. Add cooked rice, spinach, frozen peas and soy sauce. Season with salt and pepper and simmer 5 minutes. Stir in chopped chives. Garnish with chives and serve with a mixed salad.

Makes 4 servings.

Add onions, bell pepper and shrimp; stir-fry 1 minute longer. In a bowl, beat together eggs and soy sauce. Stir in rice. Continue to cook over high heat 1 minute, stirring. Remove from heat and stir in cilantro. Garnish with cashew nuts.

Makes 4 servings.

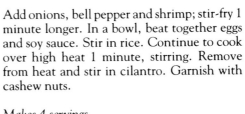

SWEET SAFFRON RICE

1-1/2 cups basmati rice
2-1/2 cups water
1 teaspoon saffron threads
3 tablespoons boiling water
3 tablespoons vegetable oil
6 whole cloves
6 green cardamom pods, bruised
1 (3-inch) cinnamon stick
1/2 cup raisins
3 tablespoons sugar
Salt to taste
Flat-leaf parsley sprigs

Place rice in a sieve and rinse under cold running water until water runs clear.

Put rice in a bowl with 2-1/2 cups water and soak 30 minutes. Put saffron in a small bowl, add boiling water and soak. Heat oil in a heavy saucepan, add cloves, cardamom pods and cinnamon and cook 1 minute. Drain rice and reserve the soaking water. Add rice to the pan and cook 2 to 3 minutes until opaque and light golden.

Stir in reserved water, saffron and its soaking water, raisins, sugar and salt. Bring to a boil, then reduce heat and cover. Simmer 12 to 15 minutes, stirring once or twice until liquid is absorbed and rice is very tender. Remove spices before serving. Serve hot, garnished with parsley.

Makes 4 servings.

Note: The whole spices in the rice are not meant to be eaten.

FRAGRANT FRIED RICE

1-1/4 cups basmati rice
2-1/2 cups water
3 tablespoons vegetable oil
8 whole cloves
4 black cardamom pods, bruised
1 bay leaf
1 (3-inch) cinnamon stick
1 teaspoon black peppercorns
1 teaspoon cumin seeds
1 teaspoon coriander seeds
Salt to taste
1 small cauliflower, cut into tiny flowerets
1 onion, sliced into rings
Onion rings and bay leaves, to garnish

Place rice in a sieve and rinse under cold running water until water runs clear. Put in a bowl with 2-1/2 cups water and soak 30 minutes. Heat oil in a heavy saucepan, add cloves, cardamom pods, bay leaf, cinnamon, peppercorns, cumin seeds, coriander seeds and cook 1 minute. Add onion and cook 5 minutes, until softened. Drain rice and reserve the soaking water.

Add rice to the pan and cook 2 to 3 minutes until opaque and light golden. Stir in reserved water, salt and cauliflower. Bring to a boil, reduce heat and cover. Simmer 12 to 15 minutes, stirring once or twice, until liquid is absorbed and rice and cauliflower are tender. Remove whole spices before serving. Serve hot.

Makes 4 servings.

Note: The whole spices in the rice are not meant to be eaten.

RADICCHIO RISOTTO

2 tablespoons olive oil
1 large onion, chopped
1 large garlic clove, chopped
1 teaspoon chopped fresh thyme
2 cups risotto rice
1 large head radicchio, shredded
2/3 cup dry red wine
2-1/2 cups vegetable stock
2 tablespoons sun-dried tomato paste
Salt and pepper
Chopped fresh parsley, to garnish
Freshly grated Parmesan cheese, to serve

In a large, heavy nonstick skillet, heat oil. Add onion, garlic and thyme; cook 5 minutes or until softened. Add rice. Stir over medium heat 1 minute or until rice is transparent. Stir in radicchio and immediately add wine. Boil rapidly until all liquid has evaporated.

Gradually stir in stock in 3 to 4 batches, cooking over low heat, stirring constantly, 25 minutes or until all stock is absorbed and rice is tender. Stir in tomato paste, salt and pepper. Garnish with chopped parsley. Serve hot with Parmesan cheese.

Makes 6 to 8 servings.

LEEK & MUSHROOM PILAF

1/4 cup dried cep mushrooms
Pinch of saffron strands
2/3 cup boiling water
1-1/4 cups basmati rice
2 cups vegetable stock
2 tablespoons olive oil
3 large leeks
4 ounces fresh mushrooms
Salt and pepper
Chives, to garnish

In a small bowl, place ceps and saffron. Add boiling water. Let soak 10 minutes.

Rinse rice under cold running water several minutes until the water runs clear; drain well. In a saucepan, place rice. Add stock and cep mixture. Bring to a boil, stir once, cover and simmer 12 minutes.

Meanwhile, in a skillet, heat oil. Add leeks; cook 3 minutes. Add fresh mushrooms and stir-fry 3 minutes. Keep warm. As soon as rice is tender, stir it into mushroom mixture. Heat through 1 to 2 minutes. Season, garnish with chives and serve at once.

Makes 6 servings.

LEMON VEGETABLE RICE

Juice of 2 lemons
2 tablespoons sugar
About 4 cups vegetable stock
1-1/2 cups long-grain rice
1/2 teaspoon salt
1 cinnamon stick
5 whole cloves
2 tablespoons butter or margarine
1 teaspoon cumin seeds
1 small onion, thinly sliced
2 small zucchini
1/3 cup cashews, toasted
2 tablespoons chopped fresh mint
Lime wedges, to garnish

SPICED RICE & PEPPERS

1/4 cup olive oil
1-1/3 cups long-grain white rice
2 garlic cloves
Salt
1 teaspoon each cumin seeds and coriander seeds
3 tablespoons tomato paste
2 teaspoons paprika
1 teaspoon chili powder
Pinch of saffron threads, crushed and dissolved in 2
    tablespoons boiling water
2-1/2 cups boiling chicken stock, vegetable stock or
    water
3 or 4 red bell peppers, roasted, peeled and halved
    (page 42)
Extra-virgin olive oil to serve, if desired
Fresh herbs, to garnish

In a 4-cup measure, mix lemon juice and sugar together. Make up to 2-1/2 cups with vegetable stock. Pour mixture into a saucepan. Add rice, salt, cinnamon and cloves. Bring to a boil, stir once and simmer 10 minutes or until all liquid is absorbed. Remove from heat, cover with a tight-fitting lid, let sit undisturbed 10 minutes.

In a paella pan or a wide, shallow saucepan, heat oil. Stir in rice and stir-fry 2 to 3 minutes. Meanwhile, using a mortar and pestle, grind together garlic, salt, cumin seeds and coriander seeds. Stir in tomato paste, paprika, chili powder and saffron liquid. Stir into rice. Stir in stock or water. Bring to a boil, then reduce heat, cover and simmer about 7 minutes.

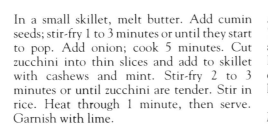

In a small skillet, melt butter. Add cumin seeds; stir-fry 1 to 3 minutes or until they start to pop. Add onion; cook 5 minutes. Cut zucchini into thin slices and add to skillet with cashews and mint. Stir-fry 2 to 3 minutes or until zucchini are tender. Stir in rice. Heat through 1 minute, then serve. Garnish with lime.

Makes 4 to 6 servings.

Arrange peppers around sides of pan. Simmer 7 to 10 minutes until rice is tender and plump and liquid is absorbed. Remove from heat and let stand 5 minutes. Drizzle extra-virgin oil over pepper, if desired, and garnish with herbs.

Makes 4 servings.

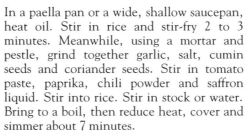

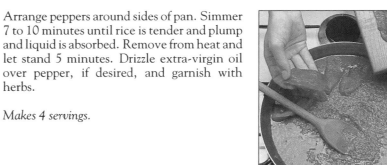

RICE & CHICKEN

3 tablespoons olive oil
1 (3-lb.) chicken, cut into 8 pieces, or 4 large chicken
   pieces, halved
1 Spanish onion, finely chopped
2 garlic cloves, chopped
1 large red bell pepper, cut into strips
1 tablespoon paprika
1-1/2 cups peeled, seeded and chopped beefsteak
   tomatoes
2 cups short-grain white rice
1/4 teaspoon saffron threads, finely crushed
3-3/4 cups boiling chicken stock or water
1 cup small shelled fresh or frozen green peas
2 tablespoons chopped fresh parsley
Lime wedges, to serve

In a paella pan or large skillet, heat oil. Add chicken and cook about 10 minutes or until a light golden color all over. Remove and set aside. Add onion, garlic and bell pepper to pan and simmer 8 to 10 minutes until vegetables are soft. Stir in paprika and heat 30 to 60 seconds, then add tomatoes and cook about 10 minutes or until mixture is thick.

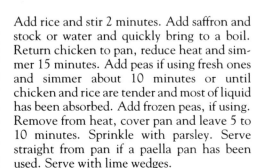

Add rice and stir 2 minutes. Add saffron and stock or water and quickly bring to a boil. Return chicken to pan, reduce heat and simmer 15 minutes. Add peas if using fresh ones and simmer about 10 minutes or until chicken and rice are tender and most of liquid has been absorbed. Add frozen peas, if using. Remove from heat, cover pan and leave 5 to 10 minutes. Sprinkle with parsley. Serve straight from pan if a paella pan has been used. Serve with lime wedges.

Makes 4 servings.

RICE, CHICKEN & MUSHROOMS

3/4 cup long-grain white rice
2 tablespoons vegetable oil
1 small onion, finely chopped
2 garlic cloves, finely chopped
2 fresh red chiles, seeded, cut into slivers
8 ounces boneless skinless chicken breasts, finely
   chopped
3 ounces bamboo shoots, chopped
8 pieces dried Chinese black mushrooms, soaked 30
   minutes, drained and chopped
2 tablespoons dried shrimp
1 tablespoon fish sauce
About 25 Thai basil leaves
Thai basil leaves to garnish

Cook rice, see page 144. Heat oil in a wok, add onion and garlic and cook, stirring occasionally, until golden. Add chiles and chicken and stir-fry 2 minutes.

Stir in bamboo shoots, mushrooms, dried shrimp and fish sauce. Stir-fry 2 minutes, then stir in rice and the 25 basil leaves. Garnish with additional basil leaves.

Makes 4 servings.

SIDE ORDERS

BROCCOLI CAULIFLOWER CRUMBLE

8 oz. each of cauliflower and broccoli florets
TOPPING
2 tablespoons butter
1 cup soft white bread crumbs
1 tablespoon chopped fresh parsley
1 hard-cooked egg, sieved
SAUCE
2 tablespoons butter
1/4 cup all-purpose flour
1-1/4 cups milk
Salt and ground black pepper

To prepare topping, heat butter in a skillet. Add bread crumbs and fry until golden. In a bowl, combine crumbs, parsley and egg.

To prepare sauce, place butter, flour, milk, salt and pepper in a saucepan. Whisk over moderate heat until thick. Cook 1 to 2 minutes. Keep warm.

In a saucepan, cook cauliflower and broccoli in boiling salted water 3 to 4 minutes or until just tender. Drain and place in a warmed serving dish. Pour over sauce and sprinkle with topping.

Makes 4 to 6 servings.

BRUSSEL SPROUTS WITH ALMONDS

1 lb. small Brussel sprouts
2 tablespoons butter
1/4 cup flaked almonds
1 clove garlic, crushed
1 teaspoon grated lemon peel
1 teaspoon fresh lemon juice
1/2 teaspoon salt
1/2 teaspoon ground black pepper
Lemon twists and herb sprigs to garnish

Trim tops off sprouts and cut across top of each. In a saucepan, cook sprouts in boiling salted water 4 to 5 minutes or until just tender. Drain well and place in a warmed serving dish.

Meanwhile, melt butter in a skillet. Add flaked almonds and garlic. Fry until almonds are golden brown. Stir in lemon peel, juice, salt and pepper and mix well.

Sprinkle almonds over sprouts; stir gently to mix. Garnish with lemon twist and herb sprigs.

Makes 4 servings.

SPICY OKRA

12 ounces okra
2 tablespoons vegetable oil
1 (1-inch) piece fresh gingerroot, grated
1 teaspoon ground turmeric
1/2 teaspoon chile powder
Salt to taste
1 teaspoon garbanzo bean flour
3 tablespoons water
1-1/4 cups plain yogurt
2 tablespoons chopped cilantro (fresh coriander),
    to garnish

Rinse okra and pat dry with paper towels, then cut into thick slices.

Heat oil in a medium saucepan, add okra and cook 4 minutes, stirring occasionally. Stir in gingerroot, turmeric, chile powder, salt and flour; cook 1 minute more.

Stir in water, then cover and simmer 10 minutes, or until okra is tender. Stir in yogurt and reheat gently. Serve hot, sprinkled with cilantro.

Makes 4 servings.

Note: Choose okra pods that are about 4 inches long – larger pods are tough and stringy to eat.

PEPPERS WITH CAULIFLOWER

1/4 cup vegetable oil
1 large onion, sliced
2 garlic cloves, crushed
2 green chiles, seeded, chopped
1 cauliflower, cut into small flowerets
1/2 teaspoon ground turmeric
1 teaspoon Garam Masala
1/4 cup water
1 green bell pepper
1 red bell pepper
1 orange or yellow bell pepper
Salt and pepper to taste
1 tablespoon chopped cilantro (fresh coriander),
    to garnish

Heat oil in a large saucepan, add onion and cook over medium heat 8 minutes, or until soft and golden brown. Stir in garlic, chiles and cauliflowerets and cook 5 minutes, stirring occasionally. Stir in turmeric and Garam Masala; cook 1 minute.

Reduce heat and add water. Cover and cook 10 to 15 minutes, until cauliflower is almost tender. Meanwhile, cut peppers in half lengthwise, remove stalks and seeds and thinly slice peppers. Add to pan and cook another 3 to 5 minutes, until softened. Season with salt and pepper. Serve hot, garnished with chopped cilantro.

Makes 4 servings.

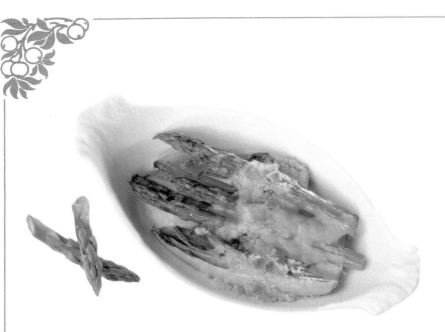

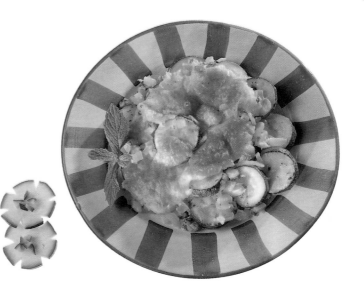

—ENDIVE ASPARAGUS GRATIN—

20 asparagus spears
4 small heads Belgian endive
1/2 cup virgin olive oil
1 garlic clove, crushed
Grated peel and juice of 1/2 lemon
1 tablespoon chopped fresh basil
1/3 cup freshly grated Parmesan cheese
Salt and pepper

Trim asparagus spears, removing woody ends. Peel almost to tips. Steam spears 2 minutes or until bright green.

Lightly oil 4 small gratin dishes. Preheat broiler. Halve and trim endives. Place 2 halves into each dish. Arrange asparagus between endive halves.

In a bowl, mix together oil, garlic, lemon peel, lemon juice and basil. Pour over vegetables. Broil 3 to 4 minutes. Sprinkle with cheese and return to broiler 2 to 3 minutes or until cheese is lightly browned.

Makes 4 servings.

—ZUCCHINI WITH CHEESE—

1-1/2 pounds zucchini
2 tablespoons extra-virgin olive oil
1 large onion, chopped
1 teaspoon chopped fresh mint
2 eggs
1-1/2 cups grated kefalotiri cheese (6 ounces)
1/4 teaspoon grated nutmeg
Salt and pepper

Preheat oven to 350F (175C). Trim zucchini ends, then cut into 1/2-inch slices. Put zucchini slices into a steamer above boiling water and steam a few minutes or until crisp-tender. Cook in batches, if necessary.

In a skillet, heat oil, add onion and cook until soft. Mix zucchini and mint with onion, then put in a baking dish.

In a bowl, beat eggs with cheese, nutmeg, salt and pepper, then pour over the zucchini. Bake 20 minutes, or until top is lightly browned.

Makes 4 servings.

Variation: This dish may also be made with summer squash.

—SWEET & SOUR VEGETABLES—

5 teaspoons cornstarch
1 (15-1/2-oz.) can pineapple chunks in juice, drained, juice reserved
3 or 4 tablespoons light brown sugar
1/3 cup cider vinegar
2 tablespoons soy sauce
2 tablespoons dry sherry or rice wine
1/4 cup ketchup
2 tablespoons vegetable oil
2 carrots, thinly sliced
1 fennel bulb, thinly sliced
1 red bell pepper, cut lengthwise in half and thinly sliced
6 ounces canned baby corn, rinsed
6 ounces snow peas
1 zucchini, thinly sliced

In a small bowl, dissolve cornstarch in reserved pineapple juice. Stir in sugar, vinegar, soy sauce, sherry and ketchup until combined; set aside.

Heat a wok until very hot. Add oil and swirl to coat wok. Add carrots, fennel and bell pepper and stir-fry 3 or 4 minutes or until carrots just begin to soften. Stir cornstarch mixture and stir into wok. Bring to a boil and stir until sauce bubbles and thickens. Add baby corn, snow peas and zucchini and simmer 1 or 2 minutes. Stir in reserved pineapple chunks and stir-fry 30 minutes.

Makes 4 servings.

—SPINACH WITH RAISINS—

1/3 cup raisins
2 pounds fresh spinach
3 tablespoons olive oil
1 garlic clove, finely chopped
3 tablespoons pine nuts
Salt and pepper
Croutons, to serve

Into a small bowl, put raisins. Cover with boiling water and let soak.

Rinse spinach well, then shake off surplus water but do not dry the leaves. Into a large saucepan, put spinach. Cover and cook until spinach wilts. Uncover and cook until excess moisture has evaporated. Chop coarsely. Drain raisins.

In a skillet, heat oil. Add garlic and pine nuts and fry, stirring occasionally, until beginning to color. Stir in spinach and raisins, season with salt and pepper and cook over low heat 5 minutes. Serve with croutons sprinkled over the top.

Makes 4 servings.

SESAME GARLIC VEGETABLES

BROCCOLI WITH CHILES

8 oz. broccoli
1 large green bell pepper
2 small zucchini
8 oz. asparagus
2 garlic cloves, thinly sliced
2 teaspoons sesame oil
1 tablespoon sesame seeds

Slice broccoli into small flowerets. Slice zucchini into 1-inch pieces and halve. Cut bell pepper into 8. Trim away tough ends from asparagus and slice into 2-inch pieces. Place vegetables in a colander and rinse well.

1 pound broccoli
Olive oil
2 garlic cloves, sliced
2 dried red chiles, seeded and crushed
Salt

With a sharp knife, cut thick broccoli stems in half or thirds lengthwise. Add all of broccoli to a saucepan of boiling salted water and boil 2 minutes, then drain and rinse under cold running water.

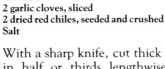

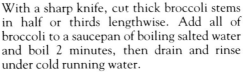

Bring a wok or large saucepan of water to a boil. Arrange vegetables on a layer of parchment paper in a steamer and place over water. Sprinkle with garlic and sesame oil. Cover and steam 10 minutes.

In a heavy skillet large enough to hold broccoli in a single layer, heat oil. Add garlic and chiles to pan. Cook over medium heat 3 to 4 minutes or until sizzling.

Remove vegetables from steamer and place on warmed serving plates. Sprinkle with sesame seeds and serve with soy sauce, for dipping.

Makes 4 servings.

Add broccoli and turn to coat in oil and then reduce heat to very low. Pour in 1/2 cup water, add salt and cover tightly. Simmer about 20 minutes, turning broccoli carefully 2 or 3 times or until broccoli is tender. If necessary, uncover and boil off excess liquid. Serve hot or warm.

Makes 4 servings.

SZECHUAN EGGPLANT

1 pound small eggplants, cut into 1-inch cubes or
    thin slices
Salt
2 tablespoons peanut oil
2 garlic cloves, finely chopped
1-inch piece gingerroot, peeled and finely chopped
3 or 4 green onions, finely sliced
2 tablespoons dark soy sauce
1 or 2 tablespoons hot bean sauce or 1 teaspoon crushed
    dried chiles
1 tablespoon yellow bean paste (optional)
2 tablespoons dry sherry or rice wine
1 tablespoon cider vinegar
1 tablespoon sugar
Chopped parsley, to garnish

Place eggplant cubes in a plastic or stainless steel colander or sieve, placed on a plate or baking sheet. Sprinkle with salt and let stand 30 minutes. Rinse eggplant under cold running water and turn out onto layers of paper towels; pat dry thoroughly. Heat wok until very hot. Add oil and swirl to coat wok. Add garlic, gingerroot and green onions and stir-fry 1 or 2 minutes or until green onions begin to soften. Add eggplant and stir-fry 2 or 3 minutes or until softened and beginning to brown.

Stir in remaining ingredients and 2/3 cup water and bring to a boil. Reduce heat and simmer 5 to 7 minutes or until eggplant is very tender, stirring frequently. Increase heat to high and stir-fry mixture until the liquid is almost completely reduced. Spoon into a serving dish and garnish with parsley.

Makes 4 to 6 servings.

SPICY STIR-FRIED CABBAGE

1 lb. bok choy
1/2 head napa cabbage
1 tablespoon peanut oil
2 garlic cloves, finely chopped
1 tablespooon light soy sauce
1 teaspoon five-spice powder
1 teaspoon chile sauce
Salt and freshly ground pepper
Sliced fresh red chile, to garnish

Discard damaged outer leaves from boy choy and cabbage. Break bok choy leaves from stem, rinse well and dry on paper towels. Discard coarse stem at base of leaves then shred finely.

Bring a large saucepan of water to a boil and cook the bok choy for a few seconds until just wilted. Drain well and rinse in cold water. Drain thoroughly and pat dry with paper towels. Remove core from napa cabbage, and shred finely.

Heat oil in a nonstick or well-seasoned wok and stir-fry bok choy and garlic 2 minutes. Add the napa cabbage and all the remaining ingredients except the garnish and stir-fry 2 minutes. Garnish with sliced red chile and serve immediately. Ideal accompaniment for Beef with Oyster Sauce, page 116.

Makes 4 servings.

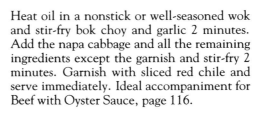

CHILE ROAST PEPPERS

1 large red bell pepper
1 large orange bell pepper
1 large green bell pepper
1 large yellow bell pepper
1 tablespoon dark soy sauce
1 teaspoon chile sauce
1 tablespoon sunflower oil
Freshly ground pepper
2 tablespoons chopped fresh chives

Halve bell peppers lengthwise, remove core and seeds then halve again. Place in a nonstick roasting pan.

Preheat oven to 375F (190C). In a small bowl, mix together the remaining ingredients except the chives and spoon over the bell peppers, turning to make sure they are well coated. Roast 30 minutes, basting occasionally, or until softened.

Transfer roast bell peppers to warmed serving plates, sprinkle with chives and serve.

Makes 4 servings.

FAVA BEANS IN TOMATO SAUCE

6 tablespoons olive oil
2 garlic cloves, chopped
1 small onion, finely chopped
2 sage sprigs
2 pounds fresh fava beans, shelled
1 (14-oz.) can chopped plum tomatoes
1 tablespoon sun-dried tomato paste
Salt and freshly ground pepper
Sage leaves to garnish

Heat oil in a large heavy saucepan. Add garlic, onion and sage sprigs and cook 4 to 5 minutes to soften.

Stir in beans, tomatoes and tomato paste and bring to a boil. Reduce heat, cover and cook 20 minutes, stirring frequently, until beans are tender. Discard sage sprigs and season with salt and freshly ground pepper. Serve hot garnished with sage leaves.

Makes 4 to 6 servings.

BUTTERY COUSCOUS

2 cups couscous
1-1/3 cups green lima beans
1 (8-oz.) can whole-kernel corn, drained
1 cup green peas
1/2 cup butter or margarine
1 teaspoon ground cumin
1 teaspoon ground paprika
1 tablespoon chopped fresh cilantro
1/4 cup chopped mixed nuts, toasted
Juice of 1/2 lime
Salt and pepper
Lime slices and parsley, to garnish

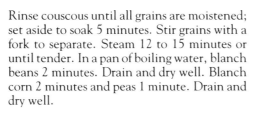

Rinse couscous until all grains are moistened; set aside to soak 5 minutes. Stir grains with a fork to separate. Steam 12 to 15 minutes or until tender. In a pan of boiling water, blanch beans 2 minutes. Drain and dry well. Blanch corn 2 minutes and peas 1 minute. Drain and dry well.

In a large pan, melt butter. Stir in spices and cook over low heat 2 minutes. Add blanched vegetables and cook 2 minutes longer. Fluff cooked couscous with a fork to break up any lumps. Stir into pan until well coated with butter. Stir in cilantro, nuts, lime juice, salt and pepper. Serve hot. Garnish with lime slices and parsley.

Makes 4 to 6 servings.

SPICED BROWN LENTILS

1-1/4 cups whole brown lentils
1-1/4 cups coconut milk
1/4 teaspoon chile powder
1/2 teaspoon ground turmeric
2 tablespoons vegetable oil
1 onion, finely chopped
4 curry leaves, optional
1/2 stalk lemon grass
1 (3-inch) cinnamon stick
Lemon thyme sprigs, to garnish

Rinse lentils, put in a bowl, cover with cold water and leave to soak 6 hours or overnight.

Drain lentils and put them in a large saucepan with coconut milk, chile powder and turmeric. Bring to a boil, cover and simmer 30 minutes, or until just tender. Heat oil in a separate pan, add onion, curry leaves, lemon grass and cinnamon and fry, stirring, over a medium heat 8 minutes, or until onion is soft and golden brown.

Stir into lentil mixture and simmer another 10 minutes, or until liquid has evaporated and lentils are soft but not broken up. Remove whole spices and serve hot, garnished with thyme sprigs.

Makes 4 servings.

Note: Substitute a few sprigs of lemon thyme if lemon grass is unavailable.

SWEET POTATO WEDGES

GARLIC-ROASTED POTATOES

About 2 tablespoons olive oil
4 small sweet potatoes (1-1/2 pounds)
2 teaspoons paprika
1/2 teaspoon chili powder
Salt and pepper
Thyme sprigs, to garnish

Preheat oven to 450F (230C). Pour enough olive oil into a large roasting pan to just cover bottom. Place in the oven 2 to 3 minutes or until hot.

Rinse and dry potatoes. Cut each one into 8 wedges. Carefully spoon into hot oil, avoiding splashing. Bake on top rack 10 minutes, then turn potatoes over and bake 10 minutes longer until golden on outside and cooked through.

Mix spices together. Using a slotted spoon, transfer potatoes to a serving dish. Sprinkle with spices, salt and pepper and stir well to coat evenly. Serve hot, garnished with thyme.

Makes 6 servings.

2-1/4 pounds new potatoes
12 unpeeled shallots
12 unpeeled garlic cloves
1 tablespoon chopped fresh sage
1 tablespoon chopped fresh thyme or rosemary
1/4 cup hazelnut oil or olive oil
Salt and pepper

Preheat oven to 400F (205C). Rinse and dry potatoes and halve any large ones. Trim shallots, removing root ends. Combine with potatoes, garlic and herbs.

Into a roasting pan, place oil. Place in the oven 5 minutes until hot and starting to smoke. Add potato and shallot mixture, taking care not to splash the hot oil. Stir until potatoes, shallots, garlic and herbs are well coated.

Return to the oven and roast 50 to 60 minutes or until potatoes are tender, turning occasionally to brown evenly. Transfer to a hot serving dish and serve at once.

Makes 6 servings.

POTATOES WITH GARLIC SAUCE

—— DRY POTATO CURRY ——

1 pound small potatoes, preferably new, unpeeled
Sea salt
1 tablespoon finely chopped fresh parsley
GARLIC SAUCE:
6 to 9 garlic cloves
Salt and pepper
About 2/3 cup olive oil

Add potatoes to a saucepan of boiling salted water and boil until tender.

1 pound red potatoes
Salt to taste
2 tablespoons vegetable oil
1 teaspoon mustard seeds
1 onion, finely sliced
2 garlic cloves
1 (1-inch) piece fresh gingerroot, grated
1 green chile, seeded, chopped
1 teaspoon ground turmeric
1/2 teaspoon red (cayenne) pepper
1 teaspoon ground cumin
Green bell pepper strips, to garnish, if desired

Cut potatoes into 3/4-inch chunks.

Meanwhile, to make the sauce, using a mortar and pestle, crush garlic with a little salt. Work in oil a drop at a time; as the sauce thickens the oil can be added more quickly. Season with salt and pepper.

Cook potatoes in boiling salted water 6 to 8 minutes, until just tender. Drain and set aside. Heat oil in a large saucepan, add mustard seeds and cook 5 minutes, until soft, but not brown. Stir in garlic and gingerroot; cook 1 minute more.

Drain potatoes well. As soon as potatoes are cool enough to handle, cut into bite-size chunks and toss with sea salt and the sauce. Sprinkle with parsley and serve warm.

Makes 4 to 6 servings.

Add cooked potatoes, chile, turmeric, cayenne and cumin and stir well. Cover and cook 3 to 5 minutes, stirring occasionally, until potatoes are very tender and coated with spices. Serve hot, garnished with bell pepper strips.

Makes 4 servings.

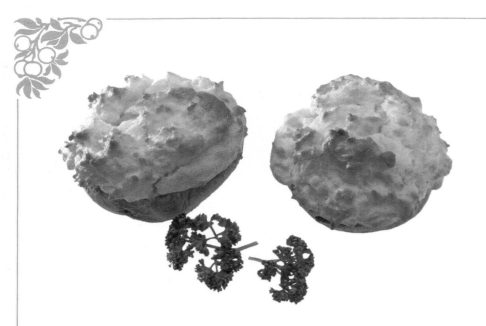

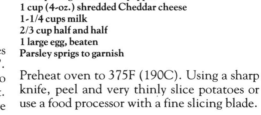

SOUFFLÉ POTATOES

4 large potatoes
2 tablespoons butter
2 tablespoons half and half
1 teaspoon salt
1/2 teaspoon ground black pepper
1/2 teaspoon grated nutmeg
2 eggs, separated
Parsley sprigs to garnish

Preheat oven to 425F (220C). Scrub potatoes until skins are clean and remove any 'eyes'. Using a small sharp knife, pierce each potato several times and arrange on a baking sheet. Bake in oven 1 hour or until potatoes are tender.

Cut each potato in half. Carefully scoop out potato flesh and place in a bowl. Replace potato skins on baking sheet and bake 10 to 15 minutes or until crisp and golden. Meanwhile, mash or beat potato flesh until smooth. Add butter, half and half, salt, pepper, nutmeg and egg yolks. Mash or beat until thoroughly blended.

In a small bowl, stiffly whisk egg whites until stiff. Using a spatula, gently fold egg whites into potato mixture until evenly mixed. Fill each potato skin with mixture and bake 10 to 15 minutes or until risen and lightly browned. Garnish with parsley sprigs and serve immediately.

Makes 8 servings.

Variations: Add 1/2 cup chopped crispy bacon, shredded cheese or chopped mixed fresh herbs to potato mixture.

BAKED POTATO LAYER

2 lb. medium-size potatoes
2 tablespoons butter
1 clove garlic, crushed
1 teaspoon salt
1 teaspoon ground black pepper
1 cup (4-oz.) shredded Cheddar cheese
1-1/4 cups milk
2/3 cup half and half
1 large egg, beaten
Parsley sprigs to garnish

Preheat oven to 375F (190C). Using a sharp knife, peel and very thinly slice potatoes or use a food processor with a fine slicing blade.

Lightly butter a 9-inch shallow oven-proof dish using 1/2 of butter. Arrange a layer of potato slices over bottom and up sides of dish. Sprinkle with some of garlic, salt, pepper and cheese. Continue to layer until all these ingredients have been used, finishing with a layer of potatoes and a sprinkling of cheese.

In a bowl, whisk milk, half and half and egg until smooth. Pour over potato layer and dot with remaining butter. Bake 1 hour or until golden brown and potatoes are tender. Garnish with parsley sprigs and serve hot.

Makes 4 servings.

DESSERTS

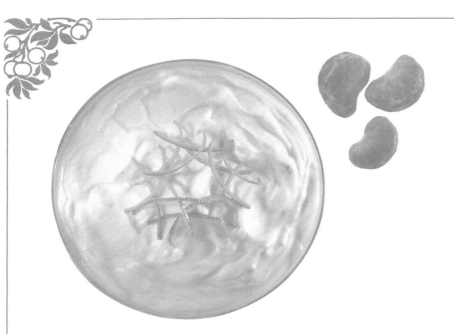

TANGERINE SYLLABUB — — TROPICAL FLUMMERY

Grated peel and juice of 3 tangerines
Grated peel and juice of 1 lemon
1/3 cup superfine sugar
1/3 cup cream sherry
1-1/4 cups whipping cream
Additional grated peel to decorate, if desired

In a bowl, combine tangerine and lemon peels and juices, sugar and sherry. Chill at least 1 hour to infuse.

1-1/4 cups whipping cream
1/3 cup thawed frozen concentrated tropical fruit juice
1 egg white
1 tablespoon plus 2 teaspoons superfine sugar
Orange wedges and passion fruit to decorate, if desired
Langue de chats cookies to serve

In a bowl, whip cream to soft peaks.

In a large bowl, whip cream while gradually pouring in tangerine mixture. Whip until mixture is thick enough to form soft peaks.

Add fruit juice gradually, continuing to whip cream until fairly thick.

Pour mixture into a glass serving bowl or individual dessert dishes and chill at least 2 hours before serving. Decorate with additional grated peel, if desired.

Makes 4 to 6 servings.

Note: Use a sharp grater to grate tangerine peel, otherwise peel tends to tear. Warm citrus fruits slightly before squeezing and they will yield more juice.

In a separate bowl, whisk egg white until stiff. Whisk in sugar, then fold into creamy mixture. Spoon into individual dessert dishes and chill 1 hour. Decorate with orange wedges and passion fruit, if desired. Serve with cookies.

Makes 4 to 6 servings.

Note: To flavor sugar for desserts and cakes, keep it in a container with a vanilla bean. This will give it a strong vanilla flavor.

COEURS À LA CRÈME

1 cup ricotta or cottage cheese
1 tablespoon plus 2 teaspoons superfine sugar
1 teaspoon lemon juice
1-1/4 cups whipping cream
2 egg whites
Fresh fruit or 1 recipe Blackcurrant Sauce, page 231,
    and whipping cream, to serve, if desired

Line 4 heart-shaped molds with muslin. Press cheese through sieve into a bowl. Stir in sugar and lemon juice.

In a separate bowl, whip cream until stiff. Stir into cheese mixture. Whisk egg whites until stiff, then fold into the cheese mixture.

Spoon cheese mixture into the molds, place on a plate overnight to drain. To serve, unmold onto individual plates and gently remove the muslin. Serve hearts with fresh fruit or Blackcurrant Sauce and whipped cream, if desired.

Makes 4 servings.

CHARLOTTE RUSSE

16 ladyfingers
1 (1/4-oz.) envelope unflavored gelatin (1 tablespoon)
4 egg yolks
1/3 cup superfine sugar
2-1/2 cups whipping cream
1 vanilla bean, split open
1-1/4 cups dairy sour cream
Additional whipped cream and 1-1/4 cups fresh
    raspberries to decorate

Line bottom of a 4-1/4-cup charlotte mold with waxed paper. Stand ladyfingers, pressing against each other, around sides of mold and trim to fit.

In a small bowl, sprinkle gelatin over 3 tablespoons water and let stand 2 to 3 minutes, until softened. In a bowl, whisk egg yolks and sugar until thick and mousse-like. In a saucepan, place 1-1/2 cups of whipping cream and vanilla bean and bring almost to a boil. Strain over egg mixture, stirring well. Pour back into saucepan and stir over low heat until mixture has thickened slightly; do not boil.

Strain into a clean bowl and add gelatin. Stir until dissolved. Cool, then set bowl in a larger bowl of iced water and stir until mixture thickens. Whip remaining cream with sour cream and fold into mixture. Pour into prepared mold, cover with plastic wrap and chill overnight. To serve, turn out onto a serving plate. Remove waxed paper and decorate with additional whipped cream and raspberries. Tie ribbon around pudding.

Makes 6 to 8 servings.

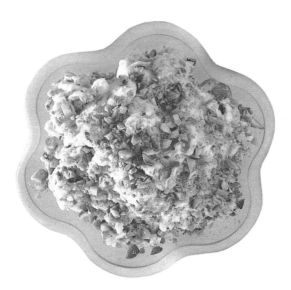

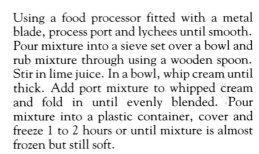

ATHOLL BROSE

3 tablespoons regular rolled oats
1/3 cup whole blanched almonds
1-1/4 cups whipping cream
1/4 cup whiskey
1/4 cup orange flower honey
1 tablespoon lemon juice

Toast oats under broiler until brown. Toast almonds under broiler to brown evenly and chop finely.

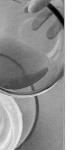

In a large bowl, whip cream to soft peaks, then gradually whisk in whiskey, honey and lemon juice.

Fold oats and 1/2 of chopped almonds into creamy mixture and spoon into 4 dessert dishes. Chill. To serve, sprinkle remaining almonds on top of each pudding.

Makes 4 servings.

Note: This is a traditional Scottish dessert – delicious and very rich.

LYCHEE & PORT ICE CREAM

1/2 superfine sugar
2/3 cup ruby port
20 fresh lychees or 1 (15-oz.) can lychees
1 tablespoon plus 1 teaspoon lime juice
1-1/4 cups whipping cream
Fresh or canned lychees and lime peel twists to decorate

In a saucepan, combine sugar and port. Heat gently, stirring occasionally, until sugar has dissolved. Peel lychees and remove pits or drain canned lychees. Add lychees to port mixture. Bring to a boil, cover and cook very gently 2 minutes. Let stand until completely cold.

Using a food processor fitted with a metal blade, process port and lychees until smooth. Pour mixture into a sieve set over a bowl and rub mixture through using a wooden spoon. Stir in lime juice. In a bowl, whip cream until thick. Add port mixture to whipped cream and fold in until evenly blended. Pour mixture into a plastic container, cover and freeze 1 to 2 hours or until mixture is almost frozen but still soft.

Return mixture to food processor. Process until smooth and creamy. Return mixture to plastic container and freeze until firm. Scoop ice cream to serve. Decorate with lychees and lime peel.

Makes 6 servings.

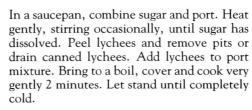

MAPLE BAVARIAN CREAM

1-1/2 tablespoons lemon juice
1-1/2 tablespoons water
1/2 (1/4-oz.) envelope unflavored gelatin
** (1-1/2 teaspoons)**
1-1/4 cups whipping cream
1/4 cup plus 1 tablespoon maple syrup
1/3 cup crème fraîche
Additional maple syrup and langues de chat cookies to
** serve**

In a small bowl, combine lemon juice and water. Sprinkle gelatin over lemon-water and let stand 2 to 3 minutes, until softened. In a bowl, whip cream lightly, adding 2-1/2 table-spoons of maple syrup.

Set bowl of gelatin in a saucepan of hot water and stir until dissolved. Stir in remaining maple syrup, then pour into whipped cream. Whisk again until cream stands in soft peaks.

Fold crème fraîche into maple-cream mixture. Spoon into individual dessert dishes and chill until set. Spoon additional maple syrup over top and serve with cookies.

Makes 4 servings.

Note: Real maple syrup, as opposed to maple-flavored syrup, is very expensive and not always easy to obtain. It is worth seeking out for this dessert, as it greatly improves the flavor.

NUTTY-CRUMB CREAM

1/2 cup hazelnuts
1-1/4 cups fresh whole-wheat bread crumbs
2 tablespoons light-brown sugar
2 egg whites
1/3 cup superfine sugar
1-1/4 cups whipping cream
1 to 2 drops vanilla extract
Fresh flower buds or leaves to decorate, if desired

Toast hazelnuts under broiler evenly. Cool, then grind coarsely in a coffee grinder or a food processor fitted with the metal blade. In a bowl, mix ground nuts with bread crumbs and brown sugar.

Spread crumb mixture evenly on a baking sheet. Broil, turning and shaking, until brown; cool. Whisk egg whites in a large bowl, until stiff. Sprinkle in sugar and whisk 2 minutes more. Whip cream and vanilla to soft peaks, then fold into egg whites with all but 1 tablespoon of browned crumb mixture.

Spoon mixture into 6 dessert dishes and chill until ready to serve. Sprinkle with reserved crumb mixture just before serving. Decorate with fresh flower buds or leaves, if desired.

Makes 6 servings.

Note: This mixture makes a delicious ice cream. Pour finished cream into a plastic container and freeze.

—CREAM & SUGAR PARFAITS—

1-1/4 cups whipping cream
1 cup plain yogurt
1-1/2 cups packed light-brown sugar
Fresh strawberries or raspberries to serve, if desired

In a large bowl, whip cream to stiff peaks. Fold in yogurt.

Half fill 4 glasses with creamy mixture. Sprinkle with about 1/3 of brown sugar. Spoon remaining creamy mixture into glasses, then pile on remaining brown sugar.

Refrigerate overnight. Serve puddings with fresh strawberries or raspberries, if desired.

Makes 4 servings.

Note: The brown sugar melts and forms a fudgy layer in these parfaits. They must be prepared a day in advance to allow for this.

PINK GRAPEFRUIT CHEESECAKE

8 ounces graham crackers
8 tablespoons butter, melted
2 pink grapefruits
1 (1/4-oz.) envelope unflavored gelatin (1 tablespoon)
1 (8-oz.) package cream cheese, softened
2/3 cup half and half
2 tablespoons superfine sugar
Grated peel and juice of 1 lemon
4 egg whites

Crush crackers to crumbs and mix with melted butter.

Press 2/3 of crumb mixture over bottom of a 9-inch loose-bottomed or springform pan and chill. Cut off peel and pith from grapefruits, holding over a bowl to catch juice. Cut out sections from between membranes and set aside. Squeeze membranes into bowl to extract juice. Sprinkle gelatin over juice and let stand 2 to 3 minutes, until softened. Set bowl of gelatin in a pan of hot water and stir until dissolved. In a bowl, beat cream cheese, half and half and sugar. Stir in gelatin and lemon peel and juice.

In a large bowl, whisk egg whites until stiff. Fold into creamy mixture. Pour over crust and refrigerate until set. To serve, remove cheesecake from pan and decorate with reserved grapefruit sections. Press remaining crumbs evenly into sides of cheesecake.

Makes 6 to 8 servings.

AMARETTI & ALMOND MOUSSE

BANANA BRÛLÉE

1/2 cup whole blanched almonds
2 ounces amaretti cookies (macaroons)
3 eggs plus 2 egg yolks
1/3 cup superfine sugar
1 (1/4-oz.) envelope unflavored gelatin (1 tablespoon)
2 tablespoons lemon juice
1 to 2 tablespoons lemon juice
1 to 2 tablespoons amaretto or kirsch
1-1/4 cups whipping cream

Toast nuts under broiler until brown. In a food processor fitted with the metal blade, process nuts and cookies to crumbs.

In a bowl, whisk eggs, extra yolks and sugar until thick and mousse-like. In a small bowl, sprinkle gelatin over lemon juice and let stand 2 to 3 minutes, until softened. Set bowl of gelatin in a saucepan of hot water and stir until dissolved. Reserve 1/4 of crumbs. Add gelatin, amaretto or kirsch and remaining crumbs to egg mixture. Whip cream stiffly. Reserve 1/3 of whipped cream and fold remaining into egg mixture.

Pour creamy mixture into a 4-cup soufflé dish and chill until set. Just before serving, using a pastry bag fitted with a star nozzle, pipe rosettes of reserved whipping cream on mousses and sprinkle with reserved crumbs.

Makes 6 to 8 servings.

Note: Amaretto is a very sweet liqueur made from almonds. Using kirsch instead gives a subtler flavor and makes the dessert less sweet.

Few crumbled Meringues, page 169, if desired
2-1/2 cups whipping cream
3 large bananas
Juice of 1 small lemon
1/4 cup superfine sugar
1/2 cup granulated sugar
1 tablespoon water

Prepare meringues, if desired, according to directions. In a large bowl, whip cream until thick. Slice bananas thinly into a separate bowl and toss in lemon juice.

Fold crumbled meringues, if desired, bananas and superfine sugar into whipped cream. Spoon mixture into a serving dish and chill.

In a small saucepan, combine granulated sugar and water. Cook over low heat until sugar dissolves; do not stir. When sugar has dissolved, increase heat and boil syrup to a rich brown caramel. Immediately pour caramel in a thin stream over banana cream mixture and chill until caramel hardens. Serve within 1 to 2 hours.

Makes 6 servings.

BREAD & FRUIT PUDDING

3/4 cup raisins and currants, mixed
8 thin slices white bread, buttered
2 tablespoons candied fruit, chopped
Superfine sugar
CUSTARD
1 egg yolk
1-1/4 cups milk
2/3 cup half and half
1 vanilla bean
1 teaspoon superfine sugar

In a bowl, cover raisins and currants with water; let stand to swell. Preheat oven to 350F (175C). Grease an oval baking dish.

Cut crusts from bread and sandwich 4 slices together. Cut in 4 squares and place in greased dish. Drain fruit and sprinkle fruit and chopped candied fruit over bread. Top with remaining bread, buttered side up.

To prepare custard, place egg yolk in a large glass measure. In a saucepan, combine milk, half and half, vanilla bean and sugar and bring almost to boiling point. Pour over egg, stir, then strain into dish, pouring down sides so top slices of bread are not soaked. Let stand 30 minutes. Sprinkle with sugar and place in a roasting pan. Pour in enough boiling water to come halfway up sides of dish and bake 45 to 50 minutes, until top is golden-brown. Serve immediately.

Makes 4 servings.

QUEEN OF PUDDINGS

2 cups milk
2/3 cup half and half
Grated peel of 1 small lemon
1-1/2 cups fresh white bread crumbs
3 tablespoons butter
1-1/4 cups superfine sugar
3 small eggs, separated
3 tablespoons raspberry jam
Orange slices, fresh raspberries and fresh herbs to garnish, if desired

Preheat oven to 350F (175C). Butter an oval flameproof dish. In a saucepan, combine milk, half and half and lemon peel.

Heat milk mixture gently 5 minutes, then remove from heat and let stand 5 minutes to infuse. Place bread crumbs, butter and 1/4 of sugar in a bowl; pour warm milk on top. Stir until butter and sugar are dissolved. In a small bowl, beat egg yolks, then stir into bread crumb mixture. Pour into buttered dish and bake 45 to 50 minutes, until set. Remove from oven and cool slightly. Warm raspberry jam and spread over pudding.

Reduce oven temperature to 325F (165C). In a large bowl, whisk egg whites until stiff, then fold in remaining sugar. Pile meringue on pudding and return to oven about 20 minutes, until meringue is crisp and golden. Serve warm or cold. Garnish with orange slices, fresh raspberries and herbs, if desired.

Makes 4 servings.

Note: Sieve raspberry jam to remove seeds, if desired.

MERINGUES WITH HONEY & ALMONDS

MERINGUES
4 egg whites
1/2 cup superfine sugar
TO SERVE
2 tablespoons honey
2 tablespoons toasted sliced almonds
1-1/4 cups whipping cream, if desired
TO DECORATE
Fresh herbs, if desired

Preheat oven to 300F (150C). Line 2 baking sheets with parchment paper. To prepare meringues, in a large bowl, whisk egg whites until stiff but not dry.

Sprinkle 1 tablespoon of sugar over egg whites and whisk 1 minute more. Sprinkle 1/2 of remaining sugar over egg whites and, using a metal spoon, fold in carefully. Then fold in remaining sugar. Using a pastry bag fitted with a plain or star nozzle, pipe 12 to 16 small circles or ovals onto prepared baking sheets, or drop 12 to 16 spoonfuls of meringue onto prepared baking sheets.

Bake meringues 1 to 1-1/2 hours, until crisp on outside. Cool on a wire rack. When cold, pile onto a serving plate. Drizzle with honey and sprinkle with toasted almonds. If desired, whip cream until stiff and serve separately. Decorate with fresh herbs, if desired.

Makes 12 to 16 meringues.

Note: An electric mixer can be used to make meringues. Separate eggs carefully; whites will not whip if there is any yolk in them.

GINGER MARRONS GLACÉS

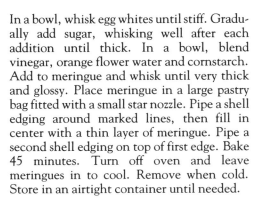

PAVLOVA
3 egg whites
1 cup superfine sugar
1 teaspoon white vinegar
1 teaspoon orange flower water
1 teaspoon cornstarch
FILLING
1-1/4 cups whipping cream
3 pieces preserved stem ginger in syrup, chopped
10 whole marrons glacés, cut in pieces
Vanilla ice cream

Preheat oven to 275F (135C). Line 2 baking sheets with parchment paper. Mark 10 (3-inch) circles and invert paper.

In a bowl, whisk egg whites until stiff. Gradually add sugar, whisking well after each addition until thick. In a bowl, blend vinegar, orange flower water and cornstarch. Add to meringue and whisk until very thick and glossy. Place meringue in a large pastry bag fitted with a small star nozzle. Pipe a shell edging around marked lines, then fill in center with a thin layer of meringue. Pipe a second shell edging on top of first edge. Bake 45 minutes. Turn off oven and leave meringues in to cool. Remove when cold. Store in an airtight container until needed.

In a bowl, whip cream until thick. Place 1/2 of whipped cream into pastry bag fitted with a nozzle. Fold chopped ginger into remaining whipped cream and spoon into center of each meringue. Just before serving, top each with balls of ice cream and a marron glacé. Decorate with mint sprigs.

Makes 10 servings.

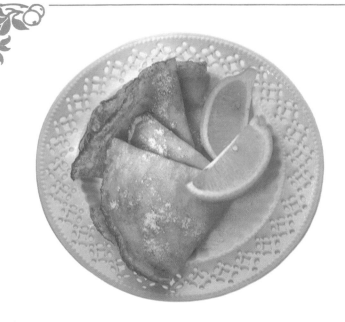

PANCAKES

1 cup all-purpose flour
Pinch of salt
1 egg plus 1 egg yolk
1-1/4 cups milk
2 tablespoons vegetable oil or butter, melted
TO SERVE
Lemon wedges and superfine sugar

Sift flour and salt together. In a food processor fitted with the metal blade, process flour and salt, egg, egg yolk and 1/2 of milk until well blended. Add remaining milk and oil or melted butter and blend again. Let stand 30 minutes. Process again before using.

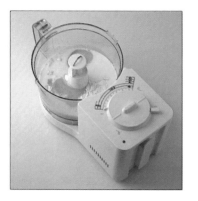

To prepare batter by hand, sift flour and salt into a large bowl. Make a well in center. In a small bowl, beat egg, egg yolk and 1/2 of milk and pour into well. Using a wooden spoon, stir flour into liquid gradually, keeping batter smooth. Add remaining milk and beat well until bubbles appear around surface of batter. Let stand 30 minutes; this allows flour to swell. Beat again before using.

Heat a 6- or 7-inch heavy-bottomed skillet and grease lightly. Pour in enough batter to cover bottom of skillet. Cook over medium heat 1 to 2 minutes, until lightly browned. Turn or toss pancake and cook other side 1 to 2 minutes, until lightly browned. Repeat procedure with remaining batter; keep warm stacked on a plate. Serve with lemon wedges and sprinkle with sugar.

Makes 4 servings.

ORANGE ROLL

5 eggs, separated
3/4 cup superfine sugar
Grated peel and juice of 2 oranges
Powdered sugar
1-1/4 cups whipping cream
Additional superfine sugar to taste
Fresh orange sections and fresh herbs to garnish,
    if desired
1 recipe Raspberry Sauce, page 230, if desired

Preheat oven to 350F (175C). Line a jelly-roll pan with a double thickness of foil and grease generously. In a bowl, whisk egg yolks, 3/4 cup superfine sugar and orange peel until thick.

In a large bowl, whisk egg whites until stiff but not dry. Fold 1 tablespoon of whipped egg whites into egg yolk mixture, then pour egg yolk mixture onto whites and fold in carefully. Pour into prepared pan and spread evenly. Bake 30 minutes, remove from oven and immediately cover with a damp tea towel. When cold, turn onto a piece of foil dusted thickly with powdered sugar. Peel off bottom layer of foil, tearing in long thin strips.

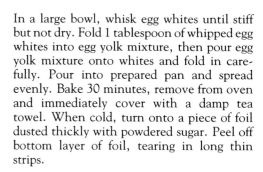

In a bowl, whip cream lightly and sweeten to taste with additional superfine sugar. Add orange juice gradually, whisking constantly until stiff. Reserve a small amount of whipped cream for decoration and spread remainder evenly over sponge cake. Roll up, using foil to help, and transfer to a serving plate. Using a pastry bag fitted with a star nozzle, pipe rosettes of reserved whipped cream along sides of roll. Garnish, and serve with Raspberry Sauce, if desired.

Makes 6 servings.

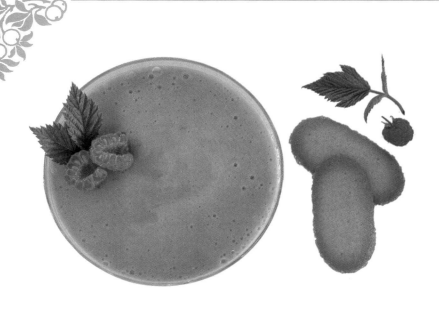

FRAMBOISE ZABAGLIONE

4 egg yolks
3/4 cup plus 2 tablespoons framboise liqueur
1 tablespoon plus 2 teaspoons superfine sugar
Fresh strawberries and leaves to garnish, if desired
Langue de chats cookies to serve.

Combine egg yolks, liqueur and sugar in a double boiler or a bowl set over a pan of simmering water.

Whisk mixture over medium heat until very thick and mousse-like, about 20 minutes.

Pour mixture into serving dishes. Garnish with strawberries and leaves, if desired, and serve immediately with cookies.

Makes 4 servings.

Note: It is important to use a whisk for this recipe. An electric mixer increases the volume of the eggs too quickly so that they do not have a chance to cook. The mixture will then collapse when poured into the serving dishes.

SOUFFLÉ LIME & CHOC LAYER

4 eggs, separated
1/3 cup superfine sugar
1 tablespoon plain gelatin
3 tablespoons water
Finely grated peel and juice 1 lime
2 (1-oz.) squares semi-sweet chocolate, melted
1-1/4 cups whipping cream
Chocolate curls and lime peel to decorate

In a bowl, combine egg yolks and sugar. Set over a saucepan of simmering water. Whisk until pale and thick. Remove bowl from pan. Continue to whisk until mixture leaves a trail when whisk is lifted.

In a small bowl, sprinkle gelatin over water and let soften 2 to 3 minutes. Stand bowl in saucepan of hot water and stir until dissolved and quite hot. Stir gelatin into egg yolk mixture until well blended. Pour 1/2 of mixture into another bowl. Stir grated lime peel and juice into 1 mixture and chocolate into remaining mixture until well blended. In a small bowl, whisk egg whites until stiff. In another small bowl, whip cream until thick. Add 1/2 of egg whites and cream to each mixture and fold in carefully until evenly blended.

Place alternate spoonfuls of each mixture into 8 small glasses. Let stand until set, then decorate with chocolate curls and lime twists.

Makes 8 servings.

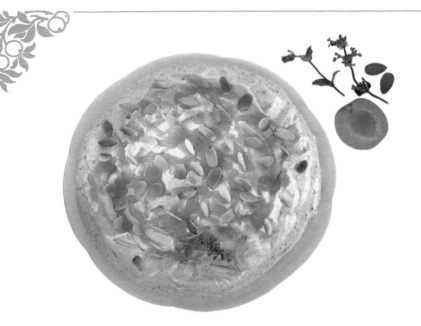

DACQUOISE

1 cup whole blanched almonds
5 egg whites
1-1/2 cups superfine sugar
2-3/4 cups dried apricots
Juice of 1 lemon
Water
1-1/2 cups whipping cream
Toasted sliced almonds and fresh herbs to decorate, if desired.

Toast whole almonds under a broiler, until evenly browned. Cool, then grind finely in a coffee grinder or a food processor fitted with the metal blade. Set aside.

Peheat oven to 300F (150C). Line a baking sheet with parchment paper. In a large bowl, whisk egg whites until stiff but not dry. Sprinkle with 2 tablespoons of sugar and whisk 1 minute. Using a metal spoon, fold in ground almonds and remaining sugar. Spoon meringue onto prepared baking sheet and spread evenly to a 10-inch circle. Bake 1-1/2 to 2 hours, until dry and light brown. Peel off paper and cool on a wire rack.

Place apricots and lemon juice in a saucepan. Cover with water and simmer over medium heat about 30 minutes, until tender; cool. In a food processor, process apricots and a small amount of cooking liquid to make a thick puree. In a small bowl, whip cream stiffly and fold 1/2 of puree into whipped cream. Pile onto meringue and drizzle remaining puree over top. If necessary, thin puree with additional cooking liquid. Decorate with toasted almonds and fresh herbs, if desired.

Makes 6 to 8 servings.

CHERRY CLAFOUTI

1-1/2 pounds pitted dark sweet cherries, thawed and drained if frozen
3/4 cup all-purpose flour
Pinch of salt
3 eggs
1/3 cup superfine sugar
2 cups milk
1 tablespoon cherry brandy or kirsch
Powdered sugar

Preheat oven to 400F (205C). Butter an oval baking dish and place cherries in it.

Sift flour and salt into a small bowl. In a large bowl, beat eggs and sugar until creamy, then fold in flour and salt. In a saucepan, warm milk slightly over low heat and stir milk and cherry brandy or kirsch into egg mixture. Beat well until batter is smooth, then pour batter over cherries.

Bake 30 minutes, until set and golden. Serve warm dusted with powdered sugar.

Makes 6 servings.

Note: Fresh cherries can taste a little bland when cooked. Add 1 to 2 drops almond extract to improve the flavor, if desired.

WHITE & DARK CHOCOLATE TERRINE

WHITE CHOCOLATE MOUSSE
9 ounces white chocolate
1/2 (1/4-oz.) envelope unflavored gelatin
1 tablespoon light corn syrup
2 egg yolks
2/3 cup whipping cream
2/3 cup dairy sour cream
DARK CHOCOLATE MOUSSE
6 ounces semisweet chocolate
1/4 cup strong coffee
2/3 (1/4-oz.) envelope unflavored gelatin
8 tablespoons butter, cubed
2 egg yolks
1-1/4 cups whipping cream

To prepare dark chocolate mousse, in top of a double boiler or bowl set over a pan of simmering water, melt chocolate with coffee. In a small bowl, sprinkle gelatin over 2 tablespoons water and let stand 2 to 3 minutes, until softened. Set bowl of gelatin in a saucepan of hot water and stir until dissolved. Stir gelatin and butter into chocolate mixture and beat until butter has melted and mixture is smooth. Cool, then beat in egg yolks. In a bowl, whip cream lightly and fold into chocolate mixture.

Line an 8 x 4-inch loaf pan with plastic wrap to overlap edges. To prepare white chocolate mousse, break white chocolate in small pieces and set aside. In a small bowl, sprinkle gelatin over 2 tablespoons of water and let stand 2 to 3 minutes, until softened. In a saucepan, combine 3 tablespoons water and corn syrup and bring to boil. Remove from heat and stir in gelatin until dissolved. Add chocolate pieces and beat until chocolate is melted and mixture is smooth.

Pour dark chocolate mixture over set white chocolate mousse. Refrigerate until set, then cover with overlapping plastic wrap and refrigerate overnight.

Beat in egg yolks, 1 at a time. In a bowl, whip whipping cream and sour cream lightly and fold into chocolate mixture. Pour into prepared loaf pan and refrigerate until set.

To serve, unfold plastic wrap from top and turn out onto a serving dish. Carefully peel off plastic wrap. Decorate with whipped cream and grated chocolate, if desired, and cut in slices.

Makes 8 to 10 servings.

CHOCOLATE CHERRY SLICE

6 (1-oz.) squares semi-sweet chocolate
4 eggs
1/4 superfine sugar
1/3 cup all-purpose flour
FILLING
1 cup unsweetened marron purée
4 (1-oz.) squares semi-sweet chocolate, melted
1-1/4 cups whipping cream
3 tablespoons cherry jam
1 cup sweet cherries, pitted, halved

Preheat oven to 350F (175C). Line a 13" x 9" jelly roll pan with waxed paper. Melt chocolate in a bowl over a saucepan of hand-hot water. Stir until melted and smooth.

In a bowl, whisk eggs and sugar until thick and pale. Stir in chocolate. Sift in flour and fold in gently until evenly mixed. Pour mixture into prepared pan and shake to level. Bake in oven 20 to 25 minutes or until firm to touch. Cover with a damp tea towel and let stand until cold. To prepare filling, process marron and chocolate in a food processor fitted with a metal blade to a purée. In a small bowl, whip cream until thick. Fold 2/3 cream into chocolate mixture. Place remaining cream into a pastry bag fitted with small star nozzle.

Remove cake from pan. Remove paper, trim edges and cut into 3 short strips across width. Spread 2 strips of cake with jam. Cover each with 1/3 of filling. Spread smoothly. Arrange 1/3 of cherry halves on each and stack layers on a serving plate. Top with remaining cake layer. Spread top and sides of cake evenly with remaining filling and pipe scrolls of whipping cream around top edge. Decorate with remaining cherry halves. Chill until needed.

Makes 10 servings.

RICH CHOCOLATE LOG

1 (14-oz.) can sweetened condensed milk
3 ounces semisweet chocolate
3 tablespoons butter
1 pound plain sponge cake
2/3 cup glacé cherries, halved
1/2 cup walnuts, chopped
3 tablespoons chopped pitted dates
CHOCOLATE FUDGE ICING
3 tablespoons butter
1/4 cup superfine sugar
1/2 cup powdered sugar
1/4 cup unsweetened cocoa powder
Glacé cherries, cut in strips, and walnut halves to
 garnish, if desired

In a saucepan, combine milk, chocolate and butter. Stir over low heat until chocolate and butter have melted and ingredients are well combined. Remove from heat. In a blender or food processor fitted with the metal blade, process cake to crumbs. Stir crumbs into chocolate mixture. Stir in cherries, walnuts and dates. Spoon mixture onto a large piece of waxed paper and form in a log shape. Roll up in waxed paper. Chill overnight.

Two hours before serving, unwrap log and place on a serving dish. To prepare icing, in a saucepan, combine butter, superfine sugar and 2 tablespoons water. Bring to a boil. Sift powdered sugar and cocoa into pan and beat well. Cool until fudgy, then spread over roll. Mark lines along roll with a fork. Garnish with glacé cherry strips and walnut halves, if desired.

Makes 8 to 10 servings.

CHOCOLATE PEARS

2 ounces amaretti cookies (macaroons)
3 to 4 tablespoons Cointreau
4 ounces semisweet chocolate
3 tablespoons strong coffee
1 tablespoon orange juice
2 tablespoons butter
2 eggs, separated
4 ripe medium-size pears
Orange peel curls and fresh mint to garnish, if desired.

Place amaretti cookies in a bowl. Pour liqueur over cookies. Using end of a rolling pin, crush cookies to rough crumbs.

In top of a double boiler or a bowl set over a pan of simmering water, melt chocolate with coffee and orange juice, stirring until smooth. Remove from heat and beat in butter and egg yolks. In a separate bowl, whisk egg whites until stiff and fold chocolate mixture into them. Set aside. Peel pears, leaving them whole with stems intact. Hollow out as much core as possible from bottom and fill cavity with crumb mixture.

Set pears on a wire rack, cutting off a small slice to make them stand upright, if necessary. Spoon chocolate mixture over pears to coat evenly. Chill several hours or overnight. To serve, place on individual plates. Garnish with orange peel and mint, if desired.

Makes 4 servings.

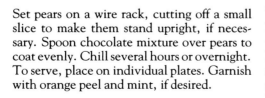

MINTY CHOCOLATE MOUSSE

6 ounces semisweet chocolate
1-1/4 cups whipping cream
1 egg
Pinch of salt
Few drops peppermint extract
Coarsely grated semisweet chocolate to decorate, if desired
SUGARED MINT LEAVES
Mint leaves
1 small egg white
Superfine sugar

Break up chocolate in small pieces and place in a blender or food processor fitted with the metal blade.

In a small saucepan, heat whipping cream until almost boiling. Pour cream over chocolate and blend 1 minute. Add egg, salt and peppermint extract and blend 1 minute more. Pour into individual ramekin dishes or chocolate cups, if desired, and refrigerate overnight.

To prepare decoration, wash and dry mint leaves. In a shallow bowl, lightly whisk egg white and dip in mint leaves to cover. Dip leaves into sugar, shake off any excess and let stand on waxed paper until hardened. To serve, decorate mousses with sugared mint leaves and grated chocolate, if desired.

Makes 4 to 6 servings.

Note: Peppermint extract has a very strong flavor; use it sparingly.

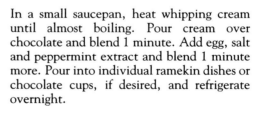

ROUND CHRISTMAS PUDDING

PEARS IN DESSERT WINE

3 cups mixed dried fruit
1/2 cup chopped prunes
1/3 cup chopped glacé cherries
1/2 cup chopped almonds
1/4 cup grated carrot
1/4 cup grated cooking apple
Finely grated peel and juice 1 orange
1 tablespoon molasses
1 tablespoon brandy plus extra for serving
1/3 cup stout
1 egg, beaten
1/4 cup butter, melted
1/3 cup dark-brown sugar
3/4 teaspoon ground allspice
1/2 cup all-purpose flour
1 cup soft white bread crumbs

2 medium-size pears
1-1/4 cups sweet dessert wine
1/2 orange
1/2 lemon
1/4 cup superfine sugar
Whipping cream to decorate, if desired

Using a vegetable peeler, peel pears, leaving stalks intact. Cut out as much core as possible from flower end. In a small saucepan, lay pears on their sides; they should fit snugly. Pour dessert wine over pears.

Combine mixed fruit, prunes, cherries, almonds, carrot, apple, orange peel and juice, molasses, brandy and stout. Stir in egg, butter, brown sugar, allspice, flour and bread crumbs. Cover with plastic wrap and refrigerate. Using a 5-inch buttered spherical mold or a rice steamer mold lined with a double thickness of foil, fill each half of the mold with mixture. Place 2 halves together, securing mold tightly.

Thinly peel orange and lemon, then cut peel in julienne strips. Squeeze juice from orange and lemon. Add peel, juices and sugar to pears. Poach pears, covered, over low heat until just tender.

Half-fill a saucepan with water. Bring to a boil and place mold in so water comes just below seam of mold. Cover and simmer 6 hours. Cool in mold, then turn out. When cold, wrap in foil. To reheat, unwrap and replace in mold. Cook as before in simmering water 2 to 3 hours. Decorate with holly. Warm brandy, spoon over pudding and light.

Makes 8 servings.

Remove with a slotted spoon to a bowl. Cover with cooking liquid, cool and chill 2 hours. In a saucepan, boil cooking liquid vigorously until syrupy and reduced by half. Place pears on individual serving plates and pour syrup over pears. Decorate syrup with dabs of whipping cream, if desired.

Makes 2 servings.

Note: Use leftover wine to pour over dried fruit. Keep in a covered container. The fruit gives flavor to fruit cakes and puddings.

FRUIT FRITTERS

TART LEMON MOLD

4 baking or crisp tart eating apples
2 to 3 tablespoons calvados or cognac
3 tablespoons superfine sugar
1 cup all-purpose flour
Pinch of salt
2 eggs, separated
2/3 cup milk
1 tablespoon vegetable oil
Vegetable oil for deep-frying
Powdered sugar

2-1/2 cups milk
1/3 cup granulated sugar
1 (1/4-oz.) envelope unflavored gelatin (1 tablespoon)
3 small egg yolks
Grated peel and juice of 1 large lemon
1/3 cup superfine sugar
Twists of lemon and fresh herbs to garnish, if desired

Peel, core and cut apples in rings.

In a small saucepan, combine milk, granulated sugar and gelatin. Cook over low heat, stirring constantly, until almost to boiling point; do not boil. Remove from heat.

In a shallow dish, mix calvados or cognac with 1/2 of sugar. Add apples, turning to coat. Let stand 30 minutes. Sift flour and salt into a large bowl and mix in remaining sugar. Make a well in center and drop in egg yolks. Using a wooden spoon, draw flour into yolks while gradually adding milk. Beat to a smooth batter, then let stand 30 minutes. In a separate bowl, whisk egg whites until stiff and fold into batter with 1 tablespoon oil.

In a bowl, beat egg yolks lightly. Gradually pour hot milk over beaten egg yolks, stirring constantly. Pour into a 3-3/4-cup mold. Chill until set.

Heat oil for deep frying to 385F (195C). Drain fruit and dip each ring into batter to coat. Deep-fry a few at a time, turning once, until puffed up and golden-brown. Drain on paper towels. Sprinkle with powdered sugar. Serve hot.

Meanwhile, in a small saucepan, combine grated lemon peel and juice with superfine sugar and stir over low heat until sugar dissolves; cool. To serve, turn out mold onto a serving plate and pour cold lemon syrup around mold. Garnish with lemon twists and fresh herbs, if desired.

Makes 4 servings.

Makes 4 servings.

Variations: Use pineapple, pears or bananas in place of apples, soaking fruit in an appropriate liqueur 30 minutes.

APPLE CHARLOTTE

SUMMER PUDDINGS

1-1/2 pounds tart eating apples
1/2 cup packed light-brown sugar
8 tablespoons butter
Grated peel of 1 lemon
2-1/2 cups coarse fresh bread crumbs
Apple slices and fresh mint to decorate, if desired

Peel, core and slice apples. In a saucepan, place sliced apples, 1/3 cup of brown sugar, 2 tablespoons of butter and grated lemon peel. Simmer, covered, over low heat until soft. Beat until pureed.

8 ounces red currants
8 ounces black currants
Juice of 1/2 orange
1/2 cup superfine sugar
1-2/3 cups fresh raspberries
12 to 16 thin slices white bread
Additional red currants to garnish, if desired

In a saucepan, combine currants, orange juice and sugar. Cook over low heat, stirring occasionally, until currants are juicy and just tender. Gently stir in 1-2/3 cups raspberries; cool.

In a skillet, melt remaining butter and sauté bread crumbs until golden-brown, stirring constantly to prevent burning. Stir in remaining brown sugar and cool.

Cut crusts from bread. From 6 slices, line 6 ramekin dishes or dariole molds, overlapping bread to line dishes completely. From remaining bread, cut circles same size as top of small ramekin dishes or dariole molds. Strain fruit, reserving juice, and spoon fruit into bread-lined dishes, pressing down quite firmly. Cover with bread circles. Pour some of reserved juice into dishes to soak bread. Place a small weight on top of each pudding.

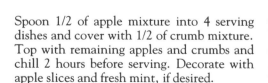

Spoon 1/2 of apple mixture into 4 serving dishes and cover with 1/2 of crumb mixture. Top with remaining apples and crumbs and chill 2 hours before serving. Decorate with apple slices and fresh mint, if desired.

Makes 4 servings.

Note: To prevent brown sugar from hardening when stored, place a slice of apple in the container with it, and the brown sugar will stay soft.

Chill puddings and remaining juice several hours or overnight. To serve, turn puddings out onto individual plates and spoon a small amount of reserved juices over them. Garnish with additional red currants, if desired.

Makes 6 servings.

Note: A dariole mold is a small cylindrical mold used for cooking pastries or vegetables.

FLAMING FRUIT SALAD

1 pound (7-1/2 cups) mixed dried fruit such as prunes, apricots, figs, apples, pears and peaches
2-1/2 cups water
2 tablespoons sherry
Juice of 1/2 lemon
2 tablespoons honey
1/2 (3-inch) cinnamon stick
1/4 cup brandy
3/4 cup toasted sliced almonds
1/2 cup walnuts, coarsely chopped

Soak dried fruit overnight in water and sherry.

In a saucepan, place fruit and soaking liquid, lemon juice, honey and cinnamon stick. Cover and simmer over low heat until fruit is just tender. Discard cinnamon stick, transfer fruit to a serving dish and keep warm.

In a small pan, heat brandy and light. While still flaming, pour over fruit and sprinkle with almonds and walnuts. Serve immediately.

Makes 5 to 6 servings.

Note: The effect of flaming brandy is to burn off the alcohol and so concentrate the flavor. It is important to warm brandy first or it will not light.

PORT GELATIN WITH FROSTED FRUIT

Peel and juice of 1/2 orange
Peel and juice of 1 lemon
2-1/2 cups ruby port
1/3 cup superfine sugar
1 (3-inch) cinnamon stick
1-2/3 (1/4-oz.) envelopes unflavored gelatin (1 tablespoon plus 2 teaspoons)
FROSTED FRUIT
1 egg white
Small bunches of red currants and seedless grapes
Superfine sugar

Using a vegetable peeler, thinly peel orange and lemon. In a saucepan, combine fruit peel, port, lemon juice and squeezed lemon shell.

Add sugar and cinnamon stick and heat gently until sugar dissolves. Let stand 20 minutes to infuse. In a small bowl, sprinkle gelatin into orange juice and let stand 2 to 3 minutes, until softened. Set bowl of gelatin in a saucepan of hot water and stir until dissolved. Stir gelatin into port, then strain mixture through a fine sieve into a wetted 3-1/4-cup mold.

Chill until set. To prepare frosted fruit, lightly whisk egg white in a shallow dish. Wash and dry fruit. Dip into whisked egg white and then into sugar to coat thoroughly. Place on waxed paper to dry. To serve, turn out mold onto a serving dish and decorate with frosted fruit.

Makes 4 to 6 servings.

HOT ORANGE CAKE

8 tablespoons butter, softened
1/2 cup superfine sugar
2 large eggs, separated
1 cup self-rising flour
Grated peel and juice of 3 small oranges
1 cup whipping cream
Powdered sugar and fresh orange sections to decorate

Preheat oven to 350F (175C). In a large bowl, cream butter and superfine sugar until light and fluffy. Beat egg yolks into mixture with 1 tablespoon of flour and grated peel and juice of 1 orange.

In a separate bowl, whisk egg whites until stiff but not dry; fold into creamed mixture with remaining flour. Spoon into a deep 8-inch nonstick cake pan. Bake 20 to 30 minutes, until golden-brown and springy to touch.

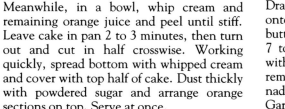

Meanwhile, in a bowl, whip cream and remaining orange juice and peel until stiff. Leave cake in pan 2 to 3 minutes, then turn out and cut in half crosswise. Working quickly, spread bottom with whipped cream and cover with top half of cake. Dust thickly with powdered sugar and arrange orange sections on top. Serve at once.

Makes 6 servings.

Note: The whipped cream will melt, so serve as quickly as possible.

CARAMEL FRUIT KABOBS

Selection of fruit such as 2 bananas, 2 pears, 1 small
 pineapple, 2 peaches, grapes and strawberries
4 tablespoons butter, melted
2 tablespoons superfine sugar
MARINADE
1 tablespoon lemon juice
3 tablespoons brandy
1 to 2 tablespoons honey
1/2 cup orange juice
1 (3-inch) cinnamon stick, broken in pieces

In a large bowl, combine all marinade ingredients.

Cut bananas in 1-inch pieces. Peel and core pears and cut in chunks. Cut pineapple in thick slices; peel and discard core and cut pulp in chunks. Peel and pit peaches and cut pulp in chunks. Leave grapes whole. Add prepared fruit to marinade and stir very gently to coat evenly. Let stand 2 hours. Add whole strawberries to marinade 15 minutes before end of marinating time.

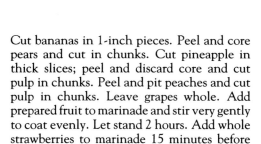

Drain fruit, reserving marinade. Thread fruit onto 6 skewers. Brush with some of melted butter and sprinkle with some of sugar. Broil 7 to 8 minutes, turning frequently. Brush with remaining butter and sprinkle with remaining sugar while turning. Strain marinade into a saucepan and heat gently. Garnish kabobs with edible flowers and fresh herbs, if desired, and serve with marinade and sauce, if desired.

Makes 6 servings.

GOLDEN CREAM FLAN

SHORTCRUST PASTRY
2 cups all-purpose flour
8 tablespoons butter, cut in cubes
1 teaspoon sugar, if desired
2 to 3 tablespoons chilled water or milk
FILLING
1/2 cup corn syrup
3 tablespoons butter, cut in cubes
1/4 cup dairy sour cream
Grated peel of 1 lemon
2 eggs, beaten

Sift flour and pinch of salt into large bowl and add butter. Using fingertips, cut butter into flour until mixture resembles bread crumbs.

Stir in sugar, if desired. Stir in enough water or milk to make a firm but not sticky dough. Knead lightly on a floured surface. Wrap pastry in foil and chill 30 minutes; this allows flour to expand and helps to prevent pastry shrinking during baking. Meanwhile, preheat oven to 375F (190C).

Roll out pastry 1 inch larger than an 8-inch flan pan. Using a rolling pin, lift pastry and lower into flan pan. Press gently into sides and trim off any excess with a sharp knife.

To bake blind, fold foil in 1-inch strips, using several thicknesses, and press around sides. Prick bottom and bake 15 to 20 minutes, until dry and lightly colored.

To prepare filling, in a medium-size saucepan, warm corn syrup over low heat. Remove from heat and add butter. Stir until butter has melted. Stir in sour cream and lemon peel. Whisk eggs into mixture, until thoroughly incorporated. Pour mixture in pastry shell.

Bake 45 to 55 minutes, until filling is golden-brown and puffed up. Garnish with lemon slices and fresh herbs, if desired. Serve warm or cold with whipped cream, if desired.

Makes 6 servings.

PECAN PIE

1 recipe Shortcrust Pastry, page 181
3 eggs
2 cups packed light-brown sugar
1 tablespoon honey
2 tablespoons butter, melted
2 tablespoons whipping cream
Pinch of salt
1-1/2 cups pecans, coarsely chopped
Powdered sugar

Prepare pastry as directed and line a 10-inch flan pan. Bake blind as directed. Leave oven temperature at 375F (190C).

In a large bowl, whisk eggs and brown sugar until pale and thick. Stir in honey, butter, whipping cream and salt and mix thoroughly. Fold in chopped pecans.

Pour mixture evenly into baked pastry shell and bake 20 minutes. Lower oven temperature to 325F (165C) and bake 45 to 50 minutes more, until set. Dust with powdered sugar and serve warm or chilled.

Makes 6 servings.

Variation: Substitute walnuts for pecans, if desired.

KUMQUAT CRANBERRY TARTS

FILLING
3/4 cup superfine sugar
1 cup water
8 oz. kumquats, sliced
1-1/2 cups cranberries
2 (3-oz.) pkgs. cream cheese, softened
1/3 cup plain yogurt
1 teaspoon arrowroot
WALNUT PASTRY
1-1/2 cups all-purpose flour
1/2 cup butter
1/2 cup chopped walnuts
1/4 cup superfine sugar
1 egg, beaten

To prepare pastry, sift flour into a bowl.

Cut butter into flour finely. Stir in walnuts, sugar and egg. With a fork, mix to form a soft dough. Knead on a lightly floured surface. Roll out and line 6 (4-1/2-inch) fluted flan pans. Trim edges, prick bottom and chill 30 minutes. Preheat oven to 375F (190C). Gently heat sugar and water in a saucepan until dissolved. Bring to a boil. Add kumquats and cook 3 minutes or until tender. Strain into a sieve. Return 1/3 of syrup to pan; reserve remaining syrup. Add cranberries to syrup in saucepan. Bring to a boil, cover and cook 3 minutes or until tender.

Strain into a sieve. Keep syrups and fruits separate. Bake pastries 10 to 15 minutes or until lightly browned. Let stand until cold. In a bowl, beat cream cheese and yogurt. Spread over bottom of pastries. Arrange alternate circles of kumquats and cranberries on cream cheese mixture. Blend 1/2 teaspoon of arrowroot into each syrup and bring each to boil separately. Glaze kumquats with clear syrup and cranberries with red syrup. Let stand until set.

Makes 8 servings.

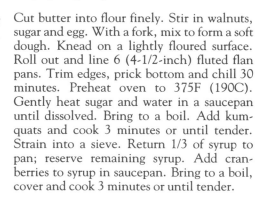

TARTE FRANCAISE

ORANGE MERINGUE PIE

13 ounces fresh or frozen puff pastry
1 egg yolk, beaten
1/4 cup plus 2 tablespoons apricot jam, sieved
2 tablespoons lemon juice
1-1/2 pounds mixed fresh fruit such as grapes, strawberries, raspberries and bananas
Additional strawberries and leaves to garnish, if desired

Thaw pastry, if frozen, and roll out to a 12 x 8 in. rectangle. Fold pastry in half. Cut a rectangle from folded edge 1-1/2 inches in from outside edges.

1 recipe Shortcrust Pastry, page 181
1/4 cup cornstarch
1-1/4 cups water
2 tablespoons butter
Grated peel and juice of 2 small oranges
Juice of 1 small lime
2 eggs, separated
3/4 cup superfine sugar
Orange and lime twists and mint leaves to garnish, if desired

Preheat oven to 375F (190C). Prepare pastry as directed and line a 10-inch flan pan. Bake blind as directed. Lower oven temperature to 325F (165C).

Unfold middle section and roll out to a 12 x 8 in. rectangle. Place on a baking sheet, dampen edges with water, then unfold frame and place carefully on top of pastry rectangle. Press edges of pastry together. Mark a pattern on frame and brush with beaten egg yolk. Prick center all over.

In a bowl, mix cornstarch and a small amount of water to a smooth paste. Stir in remaining water, then pour into a saucepan and add butter. Bring to a boil, stirring constantly. Simmer 2 to 3 minutes, stirring constantly, and remove from heat. Beat in citrus juices and grated orange peel, egg yolks and 1/3 of sugar. Spoon into baked pastry shell and cool slightly.

Preheat oven to 425F (220C). Chill pastry 10 minutes, then bake about 20 minutes, until golden-brown; cool. In a saucepan, heat jam and lemon juice gently until jam has melted. Halve and seed grapes. Leave strawberries and raspberries whole and peel and slice bananas. Brush bottom of tart lightly with jam and arrange prepared fruit in rows. Brush fruit with jam and garnish with additional strawberries and leaves, if desired. Serve as soon as possible.

Makes 6 servings.

In a large bowl, whisk egg whites until stiff but not dry. Add 1/2 of remaining sugar and whisk again until mixture holds its shape. Fold in remaining sugar. Using a pastry bag fitted with a star nozzle, pipe meringue on top of flan to cover filling and pastry. Bake 2 to 3 minutes, until meringue is set and lightly golden. Serve warm or cold, garnished with orange and lime twists and mint leaves, if desired.

Makes 6 to 8 servings.

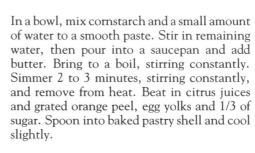

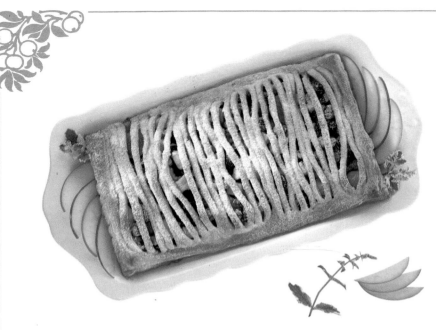

MINCEMEAT JALOUSIE

2/3 (17-1/4-oz.) package puff pastry, thawed
1 tablespoon milk
1 tablespoon superfine sugar
MINCEMEAT
2 eating apples
2 bananas
Juice and grated peel of 1/2 lemon and 1 orange
1/3 cup grapes
2/3 cup currants
1/2 cup golden raisins
1/2 cup dark raisins
1/4 cup almonds, coarsely chopped
1/3 cup walnuts, coarsely chopped
1/3 cup sugar
2 tablespoons brandy
3 tablespoons butter, melted

To prepare mincemeat, peel, core and chop apples. Peel and chop bananas. In a large bowl, quickly toss prepared fruit in lemon juice. Halve and seed grapes and add to fruit with orange juice and lemon and orange peels. Add currants and raisins. Add chopped nuts, sugar and brandy to mixture and mix well. Stir in melted butter.

Dampen a baking sheet. Roll out pastry to a 12 x 5 in. rectangle. Cut in half. Preheat oven to 425F (220C).

Place 1 pastry half on a dampened baking sheet and spread about 1/2 of mincemeat on top to within 1 inch of edges. Reserve remaining mincemeat for another use. Moisten edges with water. Roll out remaining pastry half 1 inch larger all around than other piece. Fold in half lengthwise and make cuts down from folded edge, 1/2 inch apart to within 1 inch of edge. Open and, lifting carefully, place over mincemeat and pastry.

Press edges of pastry together and flute edges. Chill jalousie 30 minutes. Brush jalousie lightly with milk and sprinkle with sugar. Bake 30 to 35 minutes, until pastry is puffed up and golden.

If pastry starts to brown too quickly, cover with foil. Garnish with apple slices and fresh herbs, if desired. Serve with whipped cream, if desired.

Makes 6 servings.

NECTARINE BAKLAVA

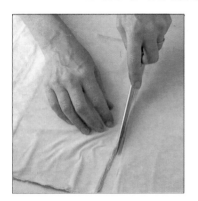

10 sheets filo pastry, thawed if frozen
2/3 cup butter, melted
1-3/4 cups chopped mixed nuts
1-1/2 teaspoons ground cinnamon
1/2 cup superfine sugar
Grated peel and juice of 2 lemons
1 tablespoon orange flower water
4 nectarines
Powdered sugar

Preheat oven to 350F (175C). Cut pastry sheets in half, then cut each half in quarters.

Working quickly, brush 1 cut sheet of pastry with melted butter. Line 8 individual 4-inch pans with 1 piece of pastry. Brush 3 more cut sheets with butter and lay cut pieces into pans, overlapping each other at different angles. In a bowl, combine nuts, cinnamon and 1/2 of sugar; spread 1/2 of nut mixture over pastry. Cover with 2 more layers of pastry, each brushed with butter, then top with remaining nut mixture. Cover with remaining pastry, brushed with butter.

Press down pastry in pans and bake 20 to 25 minutes, until golden-brown. Meanwhile, in a saucepan, combine remaining sugar and lemon juice. Cook, over low heat, until sugar dissolves. Stir in lemon peel and orange flower water. Bring to a boil and simmer 3 minutes; cool slightly. Slice nectarines into syrup, turning carefully to coat. Spooon into center of pastries and dust edges with powdered sugar. Serve lukewarm or cold, when pastries have absorbed some syrup.

Makes 8 servings.

APRICOT HAZELNUT GALETTE

1/2 cup hazelnuts, skins removed
1/3 cup butter, softened
1/3 cup superfine sugar
1 cup all-purpose flour
8 ounces fresh apricots, halved, pitted
3 tablespoons water
1-1/4 cups whipping cream
Powdered sugar

Toast hazelnuts under broiler to brown evenly. Reserve 8 nuts and grind remainder finely in a coffee grinder. Preheat oven to 350F (175C). Lightly grease 2 baking sheets.

In a bowl, beat butter and 2/3 of superfine sugar until light and fluffy. Fold in ground nuts and flour, then beat to a firm dough. Knead lightly on a lightly floured surface, wrap in foil and chill 30 minutes. Unwrap dough and cut in half. Roll each half out to an 8-inch circle. Carefully place on greased baking sheets and bake about 20 minutes, until golden. Cut 1 circle in 8 wedges and cool all pastry on wire racks.

Poach apricots and remaining superfine sugar gently in water, until just soft; cool. In a bowl, whip cream until stiff. Transfer pastry circle to a serving plate and spread with 1/2 of whipped cream. Remove apricots from pan with a slotted spoon and arrange over whipped cream. Top with pastry wedges and dust lightly with powdered sugar. Using a pastry tube fitted with a star nozzle, pipe a rosette of remaining whipped cream onto each wedge and decorate with hazelnuts. Serve within 1 hour.

Makes 8 servings.

INDIVIDUAL PEAR PUFFS

STRAWBERRY MILLE-FEUILLE

8 ounces fresh or frozen puff pastry
2 large ripe pears
1 egg yolk
1 tablespoon milk
Superfine sugar
Fresh herbs to garnish, if desired
Poire William Liqueur, if desired

Preheat oven to 425F (220C). Thaw pastry, if frozen, and roll out to a rectangle about 1/4 inch thick. Using half a pear as a guide, cut out pastry pear shapes 1/2 inch larger than pears, then cut around pear leaving a pear-shaped frame.

Roll out solid pear shape to same size as frame, dampen edges with water and fit frame on top. Press edges together lightly. Prepare 3 more pastry pear shapes in same way. Peel and halve pears. Core pears and cut crosswise in thin slices. Place in pastry shapes.

Place pear puffs on a baking sheet. In a small bowl, beat egg yolk and milk and brush edges of pastry. Bake 15 to 20 minutes, until pears are tender and pastry edges are puffed up and golden. Remove from oven, sprinkle with sugar and broil 1 minute. Transfer to serving plates. Garnish with fresh herbs, if desired. If desired, heat liqueur in a small saucepan, light and pour flaming over puffs. Serve at once

Makes 4 servings.

13 ounces fresh or frozen puff pastry
1 pound strawberries
1-1/4 cups whipping cream
1 to 2 drops vanilla extract
Sugar to taste
1/4 cup plus 1 tablespoon red currant jelly
2 tablespoons water

Thaw pastry, if frozen. Preheat oven to 425F (220C). Roll out pastry to a thin rectangle and cut in 3 equal sections.

Place sections on baking sheets and prick all over with a fork. Bake 15 to 20 minutes, until golden-brown and crisp. Cool on a wire rack. When cold, trim edges with a very sharp knife to make even. Reserve trimmings. Cut 1/2 of strawberries in half, using even-sized ones. Slice remainder. In a bowl, whip cream until fairly stiff and flavor with vanilla and sugar. Fold sliced strawberries into whipped cream.

Place 1 pastry slice on a serving plate and spread with 1/2 of whipped cream mixture. Lay another slice on top and spread with remaining cream mixture. Top with remaining slice. In a small saucepan, heat jelly and water gently until jelly has dissolved. Brush top slice with jelly and arrange halved strawberries on top. Brush with remainder of jelly. Crush reserved pastry trimmings and press into sides of mille-feuille.

Makes 6 to 8 servings.

COOKIES & CAKES

ALMOND MACAROONS

2 egg whites
3/4 cup ground blanched almonds
1/2 cup sugar
2 teaspoons cornstarch
1/4 teaspoon almond extract
12 blanched almond halves

Preheat oven to 350F (175C). Line 2 baking sheets with parchment paper or waxed paper. Reserve 2 teaspoons egg white. In a large bowl, put remaining egg whites and beat until soft peaks form.

Fold in ground almonds, sugar, cornstarch and almond extract until mixture is smooth. Put 6 spoonfuls of mixture onto each baking sheet and flatten slightly. Place an almond half in center of each macaroon. Brush lightly with reserved egg white.

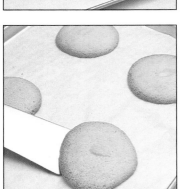

Bake 20 minutes, until very lightly browned. Cool on baking sheets. When cold, remove macaroons from paper.

Makes 12.

GINGER SNAPS

1/3 cup unsalted butter
1/2 cup packed brown sugar
1/4 cup light corn syrup
1/4 cup black molasses
2 cups self-rising flour
1 teaspoon baking soda
2 teaspoons ground ginger
1 teaspoon ground allspice

Preheat oven to 350F (175C). Grease 2 baking sheets with butter. Put butter, sugar, corn syrup and molasses in a small saucepan; stir over low heat until butter is melted. Cool slightly.

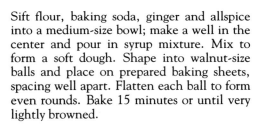

Sift flour, baking soda, ginger and allspice into a medium-size bowl; make a well in the center and pour in syrup mixture. Mix to form a soft dough. Shape into walnut-size balls and place on prepared baking sheets, spacing well apart. Flatten each ball to form even rounds. Bake 15 minutes or until very lightly browned.

Remove Ginger Snaps from oven, allow to cool 2 to 3 minutes on baking sheets then remove to a wire rack to cool completely. As the ginger snaps cool they will beome very crisp. Store in an airtight container in a cool place for 2 to 3 days.

Makes about 30.

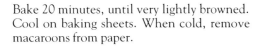

DOUBLE CHOCOLATE COOKIES

1/2 cup butter
1/4 cup granulated sugar
1/3 cup packed brown sugar
1 egg, beaten
1/2 teaspoon vanilla extract
1 cup plus 2 tablespoons all-purpose flour
2 tablespoons unsweetened cocoa powder
1/2 teaspoon baking soda
5 ounces white chocolate pieces, cut into pieces

Preheat oven to 350F (175C). Butter several baking sheets.

In a bowl, beat butter with sugars until creamy. Gradually beat in egg and vanilla extract. Into another bowl, sift flour, cocoa powder and baking soda. Mix well, then stir in chocolate pieces.

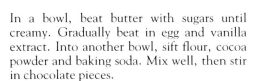

Drop teaspoonfuls of dough, well spaced out, onto prepared baking sheets. Bake 10 to 12 minutes, until firm. Cool on baking sheets a few minutes, then remove to wire racks to cool completely.

Makes about 48.

–WHOLE-WHEAT NUT BISCOTTI–

2 eggs
1/3 cup sugar
1-3/4 cups whole-wheat flour
1-1/2 teaspoons baking powder
Pinch of salt
1 tablespoon light olive oil
3/4 cup Brazil nuts, toasted and ground
1/2 teaspoon caraway seeds
1/2 teaspoon freshly grated lemon peel

Preheat oven to 350F (175C). Lightly grease a baking sheet. Beat eggs and sugar together until very thick and pale.

Beat in flour, baking powder and salt to form a soft, sticky dough. Stir in remaining ingredients. Turn out onto a clean surface. Divide dough in half and roll into 2 logs about 8 inches long. Transfer to prepared baking sheet. Bake 20 minutes. Remove from oven and increase oven temperature to 400F (205C).

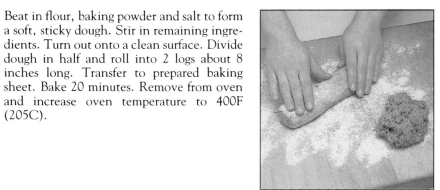

Using a serrated knife, cut logs into 1/2-inch cookies, slicing diagonally. Place cookies, cut-sides down, on the baking sheet. Bake 8 to 10 minutes or until browned around edges. Cool on a wire rack.

Makes 32 cookies.

Note: Sprinkle the cookies with a little confectioners' sugar, if desired.

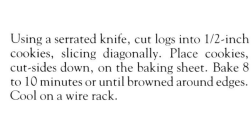

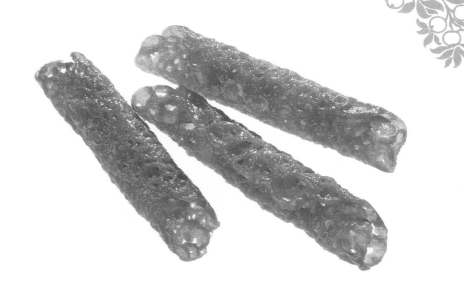

TUILES

1/4 cup unsalted butter
Finely grated peel of 1 medium-size orange
2 teaspoons Grand Marnier
2 egg whites
2/3 cup powdered sugar, sifted
1/2 cup all-purpose flour, sifted
1/3 cup (2 oz.) blanched almonds, halved and cut in
    thin slivers
TO FINISH
Sifted powdered sugar for sprinkling

Preheat oven to 450F (230C). Grease several baking sheets with butter.

In a small saucepan, melt butter; stir in orange peel and Grand Marnier. Set aside to cool. In a medium-size bowl beat egg whites until soft peaks form; beat in powdered sugar. Fold in flour, then butter mixture. Mix almonds into batter. Drop small teaspoonfuls of mixture onto prepared baking sheets, spacing well apart. Using a fork dipped in cold water, flatten each mound to make a thin round. Bake in batches 5 minutes or until lightly browned around edges.

Once the cookies are removed from the oven, quickly place them over a rolling pin to give them a gently curved shape. Sprinkle with powdered sugar.

Makes about 30.

BRANDY SNAPS

1/2 cup butter
3/4 cup packed brown sugar
1/3 cup light corn syrup
4 teaspoons lemon juice
4 teaspoons brandy
1 cup all-purpose flour
1 teaspoon ground ginger

Put butter, sugar, corn syrup, lemon juice and brandy in a medium-size saucepan; stir over medium heat until butter melts and sugar dissolves. Remove from heat; sift flour and ginger into saucepan. Mix well. Allow mixture to cool completely.

Preheat oven to 375F (190C). Grease several baking sheets; line with parchment or waxed paper. For ease of handling, bake only 6 Brandy Snaps at a time, placing baking sheets in oven at 5 minute intervals. Parchment paper may be reused; wipe with a paper towel before spooning on more mixture. Drop small teaspoonfuls of mixture onto prepared baking sheets, spacing well apart. Bake 8 to 10 minutes or until very lightly browned. Have 6 wooden spoon handles or chopsticks ready to use for shaping cookies.

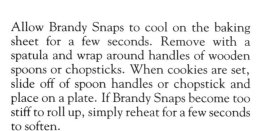

Allow Brandy Snaps to cool on the baking sheet for a few seconds. Remove with a spatula and wrap around handles of wooden spoons or chopsticks. When cookies are set, slide off of spoon handles or chopstick and place on a plate. If Brandy Snaps become too stiff to roll up, simply reheat for a few seconds to soften.

Makes about 36.

MARBLED SHORTBREAD

FRUIT BARS

SHORTBREAD
2 cups all-purpose flour
Pinch of salt
1/4 cup sugar
3/4 cup butter, softened
CARAMEL
1/2 cup unsalted butter
1 (14-oz.) can condensed milk
2 teaspoons instant coffee granules
1/4 cup sugar
2 tablespoons light corn syrup
TOPPING
6 oz. semisweet chocolate, melted
1 oz. white chocolate, melted

3/4 cup butter
1/4 cup packed brown sugar
1/4 cup light corn syrup
2-3/4 cups rolled oats
2/3 cup (3 oz.) dried apricots, chopped
1/2 cup (3 oz.) pitted dates, chopped
1/2 cup (3 oz.) pitted prunes, chopped

Preheat oven to 400F (205C). Grease a shallow 11 x 7 in. baking pan with butter. Put butter, sugar and corn syrup in a large saucepan; stir continuously over medium heat until melted. Remove from heat.

Preheat oven to 350F (175C). To make shortbread, sift flour, salt and sugar into a medium-size bowl. Cut in butter until mixture forms coarse crumbs; mix together to form a soft dough. Roll out dough on a floured surface to a rectangle slightly smaller than a 13 x 9 in. baking pan. Place in pan; press to fit. Prick well. Chill 30 minutes. Bake about 25 minutes or until lightly browned; cool.

Stir rolled oats into melted mixture. Spread half of mixture in bottom of pan to form a thin layer. Press with the back of a spoon to compact the mixture and smooth the top. In a medium-size bowl, mix apricots, dates and prunes together. Sprinkle evenly over top of packed mixture. Spread remaining mixture on top of fruit; press with spoon again.

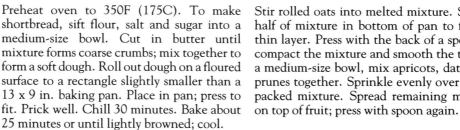

To make caramel, place all ingredients in a heavy saucepan. Stir over medium heat until butter melts. Continuing to stir, bring to a gentle boil; boil 6 to 8 minutes or until mixture retains its shape for a few seconds after a spoon is drawn through it. Spread over shortbread; cool. Spread semisweet chocolate over caramel. Pipe lines of white chocolate across semisweet chocolate, 1/2 inch apart. Pull a metal skewer through lines to create marbling. Allow chocolate to set. Cut in 48 squares.

Makes 48 small squares.

Bake about 20 minutes or until lightly browned. Cool 5 minutes. Using a knife, mark surface of mixture with lines to use as a guide for cutting. Leave in pan to cool completely. Cut in squares, then lift out with a small spatula. Store in an airtight container in a cool place for up to 1 week.

Makes 24.

JUMBLES

2/3 cup butter, softened
1/2 cup plus 2 tablespoons sugar
1 egg, beaten
2 cups all-purpose flour
1/2 cup ground blanched almonds
Shredded zest of 1 lemon
GLAZE:
2 tablespoons honey
2 tablespoons brown sugar

In a bowl, beat butter with sugar until creamy. Gradually beat in egg.

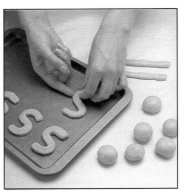

Sift flour onto creamed mixture. Add ground almonds and lemon zest. Mix well to make a firm dough. Knead lightly, then wrap in plastic wrap and refrigerate 30 minutes. Meanwhile, preheat oven to 350F (175C). Grease several baking sheets. Divide dough into 32 equal pieces. Roll each piece into a pencil-thin strip 4 inches long. Twist into an S-shape and place on a baking sheet. Bake 15 minutes, until very lightly browned.

To glaze, in small saucepan, warm honey. Brush warm jumbles with honey, then sprinkle with brown sugar. Return to oven 2 minutes. Cool on baking sheets a few minutes, then remove to wire racks to cool completely.

Makes 32.

SHREWSBURY COOKIES

2/3 cup butter, softened
2/3 cup sugar
1 egg
1 teaspoon vanilla extract
3 cups all-purpose flour
1 teaspoon baking powder
Pinch of salt

In a large bowl, beat butter with sugar until creamy. Beat in egg and vanilla. Sift flour, baking powder and salt into bowl; blend in with a spoon then mix with your hand to form a dough. Knead lightly to make a smooth dough.

Wrap dough in plastic wrap or waxed paper. Chill 45 minutes. Grease several baking sheets with butter. Roll out dough on a floured surface to 1/8-inch thickness. Using a round 2-1/2-inch-fluted cookie cutter, cut out circles from dough. Place circles, slightly apart, on prepared baking sheets. Knead and roll out trimmings; cut out more circles. Refrigerate unbaked 30 minutes. Preheat oven to 350F (175C).

Bake cookies about 15 minutes or until very lightly browned. Using a spatula, carefully remove cookies from baking sheets to wire racks; cool. Store in an airtight container.

Makes about 44.

CHERRY PRALINE RINGS

1/2 cup (2 oz.) hazelnuts
2/3 cup sugar
1/2 cup butter, softened
1 egg
3 cups all-purpose flour
Pinch of salt
1 teaspoon baking powder
1 cup candied cherries, halved and thinly sliced
GLAZE
1 small egg, beaten
1 tablespoon milk
2 teaspoons sugar
TO FINISH
Sugar for sprinkling

Lightly grease a small baking sheet. Put hazelnuts and 1/4 cup of the sugar in a small saucepan; stir over low heat until sugar caramelizes. Pour onto baking sheet; cool. Break into rough pieces and grind finely in a food processor or blender. Preheat oven to 350F (175C). Grease several baking sheets with butter. In a large bowl, cream butter with remaining sugar; beat in egg then praline. Sift flour, salt and baking powder into bowl; blend in with a spoon then mix with your hand to form a dough. Knead lightly to make a smooth dough.

Roll out dough on a floured surface to 1/8-inch thickness. Using a round 2-1/2-inch-fluted cookie cutter, cut out circles from dough; remove centers from circles with a round 1/2-inch-fluted cookie cutter. Place circles, slightly apart, on prepared baking sheets. Knead and roll out trimmings; cut out more circles. Mix all ingredients for glaze together; brush over circles. Decorate with candied cherries. Bake about 15 minutes or until lightly browned; sprinkle with sugar. Remove to wire racks; cool.

Makes 38 to 40.

PINWHEELS

3/4 cup (12 tablespoons) butter, softened
3/4 cup (12 tablespoons) sugar
1 teaspoon vanilla extract
2 eggs
4-1/2 cups all-purpose flour
2 teaspoons baking powder
2 pinches of salt
2 tablespoons unsweetened cocoa
1 teaspoon brandy
1 egg white, very lightly beaten

Divide butter and sugar equally between 2 separate bowls.

To make vanilla dough, beat 1/2 of butter and sugar until creamy; beat in vanilla and 1 egg. Sift 1/2 of flour, 1/2 of baking powder and a pinch of salt into bowl. Blend in with a spoon then mix with your hand to form a dough. Wrap in plastic wrap; chill 45 minutes. Make chocolate dough in same way, using remaining butter, sugar, egg, flour, baking powder and salt, sifting cocoa in with remaining flour and baking powder. Add brandy to chocolate dough. Wrap and chill 45 minutes. Preheat oven to 350F (175C).

Roll out doughs separately on a floured surface to 13 x 11 in. rectangles. Brush vanilla dough with beaten egg white; place chocolate dough on top. Trim edges to make straight. Brush chocolate dough with egg white. Roll up, starting from one long side, to form a tight roll. Wrap in plastic wrap; chill 1 hour. Grease several baking sheets. Cut roll in 1/4-inch thick slices; place on prepared baking sheets. Bake 20 minutes or until lightly browned. Remove to wire racks; cool.

Makes about 48.

HAZELNUT SPECULAAS

2 cups (8 oz.) hazelnuts
1-1/4 cups (4 oz.) ground almonds
3/4 cup sugar
1 cup powdered sugar, sifted
2 teaspoons lemon juice
1 egg, beaten
SPICY DOUGH
2 cups all-purpose flour
3/4 teaspoon baking powder
1 teaspoon ground allspice
1/2 cup packed brown sugar
1/2 cup butter, softened
2 small eggs
1 tablespoon milk
2 teaspoons sugar
20 blanched almonds, split in half

Skin hazelnuts, then lightly toast and grind finely. Put hazelnuts in a medium-size bowl with almonds and sugars; mix well. Add lemon juice and egg; mix to make a firm paste. On a surface sprinkled with powdered sugar, knead paste until smooth. Divide in half; shape each piece into a neat roll about 12 inches long. Wrap in plastic wrap and chill.

To make dough, mix flour, baking powder, a pinch of salt, allspice and brown sugar in a medium-size bowl; cut in butter until mixture resembles fine bread crumbs. Mix in 1 beaten egg to form a dough; knead lightly until smooth. Wrap in plastic wrap; chill 30 minutes. Preheat oven to 350F (175C). Grease a large baking sheet with butter.

Roll out dough on a lightly floured surface to a square slightly larger than 12 inches; trim edges to make straight. Cut square in half to make two (6-inch-wide) strips. Beat a second egg; brush over pastry strips. Place one roll of hazelnut paste on each strip; roll up neatly to enclose paste. Place rolls on prepared baking sheets, seam-side-down.

Mix remaining beaten egg with milk and sugar. Brush rolls with glaze. Decorate with almonds, placed slightly at an angle in a long line on top. Brush almonds with glaze.

Bake about 30 minutes or until golden. Using two large spatulas, very carefully remove rolls from baking sheet to a wire rack; cool. When cool, cut each roll diagonally in thin slices, cutting between almonds.

Makes about 40.

LEMON SHORTBREAD

1/2 cup butter, softened
1/4 cup sugar
1-3/4 cups all-purpose flour
1/4 teaspoon grated nutmeg
2 tablespoons cornstarch
Shredded zest of 1 lemon
TO FINISH:
Sugar and grated nutmeg for sprinkling

In a bowl, beat butter with sugar until creamy. Into another bowl, sift flour and nutmeg, then add cornstarch and lemon zest. Blend in creamed butter and sugar with a spoon, then work with your hands to form a soft dough.

On a lightly floured surface, knead until smooth. Roll out to a smooth circle, about 6 inches in diameter. Very lightly flour a 7-inch shortbread mold. Place shortbread, smooth side down, in mold. Press out to fit mold exactly. Very carefully unmold shortbread onto a baking sheet. Refrigerate 1 hour. (If you do not have a shortbread mold, shape dough into a neat circle. Place on baking sheet, prick well with a fork, then pinch edge to decorate.)

Preheat oven to 325F (165C). Bake shortbread 35 to 40 minutes, until cooked through, but still pale in color. As soon as shortbread is removed from oven, sprinkle lightly with sugar and nutmeg. Cool on baking sheet about 20 minutes, then very carefully transfer to a wire rack to cool completely.

Makes 1.

FLORENTINES

1/4 cup unsalted butter
1/3 cup whipping cream
1/3 cup sugar
Finely shredded zest of 1 lemon
1 teaspoon lemon juice
1/2 cup all-purpose flour, sifted
1/2 cup slivered blanched almonds
3/4 cup chopped mixed candied citrus peel
1/3 cup chopped candied cherries
2 tablespoons golden raisins
2 tablespoons chopped angelica
TO FINISH:
3 ounces semisweet chocolate, chopped
3 ounces white chocolate, chopped

Preheat oven to 350F (175C). Grease several baking sheets. Line with parchment paper. Into a saucepan, put butter, cream, sugar, lemon zest and juice. Stir over medium heat until butter melts. Remove from heat and stir in flour, almonds, mixed peel, cherries, golden raisins and angelica. Drop teaspoonfuls of mixture onto baking sheets, spacing well apart. Using a fork dipped in cold water, flatten each mound to a circle about 2-1/2 inches in diameter.

Bake 10 to 12 minutes, until lightly browned around edges. Cool on baking sheets a few minutes, then remove with a spatula to wire racks to cool completely. Melt semisweet and white chocolate separately in 2 heatproof bowls placed over pans of simmering water. Spread flat sides of half the florentines with semisweet chocolate and the remaining florentines with white chocolate. Using a fork, mark chocolate into wavy lines. Leave to set, chocolate sides up.

Makes 28.

VIENNESE FINGERS

1 cup butter, softened
1/3 cup powdered sugar, sifted
1 teaspoon vanilla extract
2 cups all-purpose flour
Pinch of salt
1 tablespoon pistachio nuts, chopped
TO FINISH
2 oz. semisweet chocolate pieces

Preheat oven to 350F (175C). Grease several baking sheets with butter; dust lightly with flour.

In a medium-size bowl, beat butter with powdered sugar until very light and creamy. Beat in vanilla. Sift flour and salt into bowl; mix into butter with a wooden spoon to form a soft dough. Put dough in a piping bag fitted with a 1/2-inch (10-point-star) tip. Pipe 2-1/2-inch lengths of mixture onto prepared baking sheets, spacing apart. Cut dough off at tip with a small knife when required length is reached. Sprinkle with pistachio nuts.

Bake about 20 minutes or until very lightly browned. Cool on baking sheets a few minutes then move to wire racks to cool completely. Put chocolate in a small bowl and place over a pan of simmering water; stir until melted and smooth. Dip both ends of fingers in melted chocolate, scraping off excess on side of bowl; place on foil. Leave in a cool place until chocolate sets.

Makes about 24.

LANGUES DE CHAT

1/4 cup butter, softened
1/3 cup sugar
1 egg, beaten
1 teaspoon vanilla extract
1/2 cup all-purpose flour

Preheat oven to 425F (220C). Grease several baking sheets; line with parchment or waxed paper. In a medium-size bowl, beat butter with sugar until very light and fluffy. Gradually beat in egg and vanilla. Sift flour into bowl; fold in to form a soft dough.

Put dough in a piping bag fitted with a 3/8-inch-plain tip. Pipe 3-inch lengths of mixture onto prepared baking sheets, spacing well apart and cutting dough off at tip with a small knife when required length is reached.

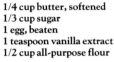
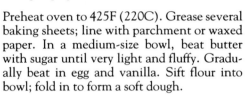
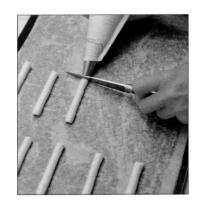

Bake 6 to 8 minutes or until golden brown around edges. Cool on baking sheets a few minutes. Using a spatula, very carefully remove cookies to a wire rack to cool completely.

Makes 36 to 40.

AMARETTI

1 egg white
2 teaspoons Amaretto
A few drops almond extract
1-2/3 cups (6 oz.) ground almonds
1-1/2 cups powdered sugar, sifted
TO FINISH
Sifted powdered sugar for sprinkling

Preheat oven to 350F (175C). Grease several baking sheets; line with parchment or waxed paper. In a small bowl, very lightly beat egg white, Amaretto and almond extract together.

Put almonds and sugar in a large bowl and mix well. Make well in center. Pour egg white mixture into well; mix to form a paste.

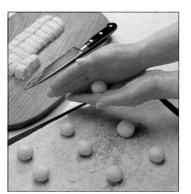

Shape mixture into 36 equal-size balls; place on prepared baking sheets. Bake about 15 minutes or until just lightly browned. As soon as cookies are removed from oven, sprinkle with powdered sugar. Cool Amaretti on baking sheets.

Makes about 36.

LINZER HEARTS

1/2 cup butter, softened
1/4 cup sugar
1 egg, beaten
1/4 teaspoon almond extract
1-3/4 cups all-purpose flour
3 tablespoons cornstarch
1/2 teaspoon baking powder
FILLING:
6 tablespoons seedless raspberry jam
TO FINISH:
Powdered sugar for sifting

In a bowl, beat butter and sugar together until creamy. Gradually beat in egg, then beat in almond extract.

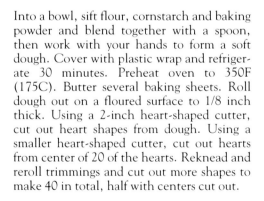

Into a bowl, sift flour, cornstarch and baking powder and blend together with a spoon, then work with your hands to form a soft dough. Cover with plastic wrap and refrigerate 30 minutes. Preheat oven to 350F (175C). Butter several baking sheets. Roll dough out on a floured surface to 1/8 inch thick. Using a 2-inch heart-shaped cutter, cut out heart shapes from dough. Using a smaller heart-shaped cutter, cut out hearts from center of 20 of the hearts. Reknead and reroll trimmings and cut out more shapes to make 40 in total, half with centers cut out.

Bake 15 minutes, until very lightly browned. Remove from baking sheets to wire racks to cool. Dust cookies with cut-out centers with powdered sugar. Spread whole hearts with raspberry jam, then top with cut-out cookies.

Makes 20.

ADVENT CRESCENTS

2 cups all-purpose flour
Pinch of salt
1/2 cup sugar
1-1/3 cups (5 oz.) ground almonds
1 cup butter, cut in small cubes
3 egg yolks
A few drops almond extract
TO FINISH
Sifted powdered sugar for sprinkling

Sift flour and salt into a large bowl; mix in sugar and ground almonds. Make a well in the center.

Add butter, egg yolks and almond extract to the well. Using your fingertips, gently mix butter with egg yolks, gradually incorporating flour mixture until a soft dough forms. Wrap dough in plastic wrap; refrigerate 30 minutes. Preheat oven to 350F (175C).

Shape dough into walnut-size balls, then into thin rolls each about 4 inches long. Curve rolls into a crescent shape. Place on ungreased baking sheets. Bake crescents 15 minutes or until lightly browned. Cool on baking sheets. Sprinkle heavily with powdered sugar. Remove from baking sheets to a serving plate.

Makes about 42.

EASTER COOKIES

2/3 cup walnuts
1/2 cup sunflower oil
1/2 cup superfine sugar
2 tablespoons dried currants
1 egg
1-1/2 cups all-purpose flour
1 teaspoon baking powder
1/4 teaspoon vanilla extract
Powdered sugar

Preheat oven to 350F (175C). Grease 2 baking sheets. In a food processor, chop walnuts finely. In a bowl, mix together walnuts, sunflower oil, sugar, currants and egg.

Sift in flour and baking powder. Add vanilla extract. Stir together to form a firm paste, adding more flour if too soft.

Roll mixture into small walnut-size balls, flatten slightly and place on prepared baking sheets. Bake 10 minutes, or until crisp and golden. Transfer to wire racks to cool. Dust with powdered sugar as they cool.

Makes about 14.

FESTIVAL CRESCENTS

LEBKUCHEN HEART

4-1/2 ounces hazelnuts
1-1/4 cups unsalted butter, softened
1/4 cup superfine sugar
1 egg yolk
2 tablespoons brandy
1/2 cup cornstarch
2-1/2 cups all-purpose flour
Orange-flower water
Powdered sugar

In a food processor, chop nuts finely, without reducing to ground hazelnuts. Preheat oven to 350F (175C). Butter 2 or 3 baking sheets.

3 cups self-rising flour
2 teaspoons ground allspice
Pinch of salt
1/4 cup clear honey
1 cup packed dark brown sugar
3 tablespoons butter
1 egg, beaten
Finely grated peel of 1 lemon
1 tablespoon lemon juice
TO DECORATE
8 oz. semisweet chocolate, melted
1 egg white
1-1/2 cups powdered sugar, sifted
Silver dragées

In a bowl, cream butter and superfine sugar until pale and fluffy. Beat in egg yolk and brandy. Stir in hazelnuts. Sift cornstarch and flour over mixture. Stir in, adding more flour, if necessary, to make a firm dough. With floured hands, break off small pieces of dough and roll into 3-inch pieces, tapering into pointed ends. Shape into crescents; place on baking sheets. Bake 20 to 25 minutes or until firm. Reduce heat if cookies brown. Transfer to wire racks to cool.

Preheat oven to 350F (175C). Grease a large baking sheet with butter. Sift flour, allspice and salt into a large bowl; make a well in the center. Put honey, brown sugar and butter in a small saucepan; stir over low heat until melted. Cool slightly. Pour into well; add beaten egg, lemon peel and juice. Mix to form a soft dough. Knead on a floured surface until smooth. Roll out dough to an 11 x 9 in. rectangle. Place on prepared baking sheet. Using a paper or cardboard template, cut out a large heart shape.

Into a small bowl, pour orange-flower water. Into a large bowl, put powdered sugar. Dip crescents very briefly into orange-flower water, then into powdered sugar, to coat completely. Pack loosely in a pan to avoid cookies sticking together.

Makes about 40.

Remove trimmings from around heart. Bake heart 20 to 25 minutes or until lightly browned. Remove to wire rack; cool. When cool, place rack over a large baking sheet; coat heart with melted chocolate. Allow chocolate to set. In a medium-size bowl, beat egg white with powdered sugar until mixture forms stiff peaks. Decorate heart, simply or elaborately, with icing and silver dragées.

Makes 1.

PALMIERS

1/2 pound puff pastry dough, thawed if frozen
1/4 cup sugar, plus extra for rolling out
FILLING:
1/2 cup whipping cream
4 teaspoons red jelly (such as red currant jelly)

Preheat oven to 425F (220C). On a surface sprinkled with sugar, roll out dough to a 12-inch square. Sprinkle dough with half of the sugar. Fold sides of dough into center, sprinkle with half of remaining sugar, then fold sides into center again.

Sprinkle dough with remaining sugar and fold in half down center. Press lightly together to seal the edges. Cut dough into 24 slices. Place slices, cut edges down, on dampened baking sheets. With palm of your hand, press to flatten slightly. Bake 10 minutes, or until crisp and a light golden-brown. Turn over and bake 2 to 3 minutes more, until second side is golden-brown. Remove from baking sheets immediately and cool on wire racks.

In a bowl, whip cream until soft peaks form. Spread a little jelly on 12 of the palmiers. Spread cream over jelly, then top with remaining 12 palmiers.

Makes 12.

LITTLE GEMS

1/3 cup butter, softened
1/3 cup powdered sugar, sifted
1 egg yolk
1 teaspoon vanilla extract
1 cup all-purpose flour
A pinch of salt
ICING
1 egg white
1-1/2 cups powdered sugar, sifted
Food coloring, as desired

In a medium-size bowl, cream butter with powdered sugar; beat in egg yolk and vanilla.

Sift flour and salt into bowl; blend in with a spoon then mix with your hand to form a smooth dough. Wrap in plastic wrap; chill until firm. Preheat oven to 350F (175C). Grease 2 large baking sheets with butter. Roll out dough on a floured surface to 1/8-inch thickness. Using a round 3/4-inch-fluted cookie cutter, cut out small circles. Place on prepared baking sheets. Knead and roll out trimmings; cut out more circles. Bake 8 to 10 minutes or until very lightly browned. Remove from baking sheets to wire racks; cool.

To make icing, lightly beat egg white in a small bowl. Beat in powdered sugar until very white and icing forms stiff peaks. Divide icing between three or four small bowls; color as desired. Spoon icings into small paper piping bags, each one fitted with a small star tip. Pipe a rosette of icing on each cookie. Let icing set.

Makes about 110.

EGGNOG BROWNIES

2 eggs
1 tablespoon brandy
1 teaspoon vanilla extract
1/2 cup butter
4 oz. unsweetened chocolate
1 cup sugar
1-1/3 cups packed brown sugar
1-1/4 cups all-purpose flour
1 cup (4 oz.) pecans, chopped

Grease a shallow 11 x 7 in. baking pan with butter; line base with parchment or waxed paper. Preheat oven to 350F (175C).

In a small bowl, lightly beat eggs with brandy and vanilla; set aside. Put butter and chocolate in a large saucepan; stir continuously over a medium heat until melted. Remove from heat; stir in sugars, flour, pecans and egg mixture. Pour into prepared pan; spread evenly. Bake 30 minutes or until a wooden pick inserted into the center comes out clean.

Allow brownies to cool in pan. When cool, cut in 24 squares. Remove from pan with a small flexible spatula. Brownies will keep well for up to a week stored in an airtight container in a cool place. These brownies taste better when they have sat for 2 to 3 days.

Makes 24.

MADELEINES

4 eggs
3/4 cup sugar
1/2 teaspoon vanilla extract
1/2 teaspoon orange flower water
1-1/2 cups all-purpose flour
1/3 cup unsalted butter, melted, cooled
TO FINISH
Superfine sugar for sprinkling

Preheat oven to 400F (205C). Grease 1 or 2 madeleine molds with melted butter and dust with flour.

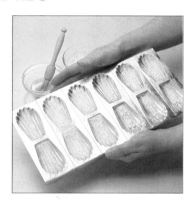

Put eggs, sugar, vanilla and orange flower water in a medium-size bowl. Place over a pan of gently simmering water; beat until very thick. Remove from heat. Continue beating until cool and the mixture retains its shape for a few seconds after a spoon is drawn through it. Carefully fold in flour; then gently fold in 1/2 cup melted butter.

Fill each madeleine mold 3/4 full with mixture. Bake 12 to 15 minutes or until lightly browned and springy to the touch. Remove from pans onto a wire rack, patterned-side up. Sprinkle with superfine sugar immediately. Continue to bake Madeleines, in batches, until all mixture is used.

Makes about 42.

DATE & WALNUT LOAF

1/2 pound pitted dates
Grated zest and juice of 1 lemon
1/3 cup water
3/4 cup butter, softened
1 cup packed light brown sugar
3 eggs, beaten
1-1/2 cups self-rising flour
1/2 cup chopped walnuts
TO FINISH:
8 walnut halves

Preheat oven to 325F (165C). Grease and line the bottom of a 9″ × 5″ loaf pan with waxed paper. Chop dates.

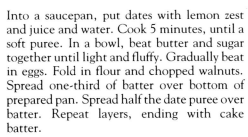

Into a saucepan, put dates with lemon zest and juice and water. Cook 5 minutes, until a soft puree. In a bowl, beat butter and sugar together until light and fluffy. Gradually beat in eggs. Fold in flour and chopped walnuts. Spread one-third of batter over bottom of prepared pan. Spread half the date puree over batter. Repeat layers, ending with cake batter.

Arrange halved walnuts in a line down center of loaf. Bake 1 to 1-1/2 hours, until well risen and firm to the touch. Cool loaf in pan 10 minutes, then turn out loaf, peel off lining paper and transfer to a wire rack to cool completely. Serve sliced.

Makes 10 to 12 slices.

BLACKBERRY MUFFINS

2-1/2 cups all-purpose flour
1 tablespoon baking powder
1/2 cup sugar
1 egg
1-1/3 cups milk
6 tablespoons vegetable oil
1 teaspoon vanilla extract
6 ounces blackberries
TO FINISH:
2 tablespoons granulated brown sugar

Preheat oven to 400F (205C). Grease a 12-cup muffin pan. Into a bowl, sift flour and baking powder. Stir in sugar.

In another bowl, beat together egg, milk, oil and vanilla. Add to dry ingredients all at once. Stir just until blended. Gently stir in blackberries.

Spoon batter into prepared muffin pan. Sprinkle with brown sugar. Bake 15 to 20 minutes, until well risen and golden-brown. Cool in pan 5 minutes, then turn out muffins onto a wire rack to cool completely.

Makes 12.

LEMON CRUNCH CAKE

1/2 cup butter or margarine, softened
3/4 cup sugar
2 eggs, beaten
Finely grated zest of 1 lemon
1-1/2 cups self-rising flour, sifted
1/4 cup milk
TOPPING:
Juice of 1 lemon
1/2 cup sugar

Preheat oven to 350F (175C). Grease a 9″ × 7″ or an 8-inch square baking pan and line with waxed paper. In a bowl, beat together butter and sugar until light and fluffy.

Gradually beat in eggs. Stir in lemon zest. Fold in sifted flour, alternately with milk. Pour batter into prepared pan and level surface with a metal spatula. Bake about 50 minutes, until well risen and pale golden.

While cake is baking, make topping. In a bowl, mix together lemon juice and sugar. Spoon topping over hot cake. Leave cake in pan until completely cold, then turn out cake and cut into squares or diamonds.

Makes 12 squares or diamonds.

GINGER CAKE

2 cups self-rising flour
1 tablespoon ground ginger
1 teaspoon ground cinnamon
1/2 teaspoon baking soda
1/2 cup butter or margarine, chilled
3/4 cup packed light brown sugar
2 eggs
5 teaspoons light corn syrup
5 teaspoons milk
TOPPING:
3 pieces stem ginger
3/4 cup powdered sugar
4 teaspoons stem ginger syrup

Preheat oven to 325F (165C). Grease an 11″ × 7″ baking pan and line with waxed paper. Into a bowl, sift flour, ginger, cinnamon and baking soda. Cut in butter, then stir in sugar. In another bowl, beat together eggs, syrup and milk. Pour into dry ingredients and beat until smooth and glossy. Pour batter into pan. Bake 45 to 50 minutes, until well risen and firm to the touch. Cool in pan 30 minutes, then transfer to a wire rack to cool completely.

Cut each piece of stem ginger into quarters and arrange on top of cake. In a bowl, mix together powdered sugar, ginger syrup and enough water to make a smooth frosting. Put frosting into a waxed-paper pastry bag and drizzle frosting over top of cake. Let set. Cut cake into squares.

Makes 12 pieces.

DUNDEE CAKE

1 cup butter, softened
1-1/2 cups packed brown sugar
4 eggs, beaten
2-1/2 cups all-purpose flour, sifted
1/4 cup milk
1/2 cup ground blanched almonds
3/4 cup dried currants
3/4 cup golden raisins
3/4 cup dark raisins
1/3 cup chopped mixed candied citrus peel
1/3 cup candied cherries, halved
Grated zests of 1 small orange and 1 small lemon
1/2 teaspoon baking soda, dissolved in 1 teaspoon milk
1/3 cup whole blanched almonds

Preheat oven to 325F (165C). Grease and line an 8-inch springform cake pan with waxed paper. In a bowl, beat butter and sugar until light and fluffy. Gradually beat in eggs. Fold in flour alternately with milk. Carefully fold in ground almonds, currants, golden raisins, raisins, peel, cherries and orange and lemon zests. Add baking soda dissolved in milk. Stir to mix.

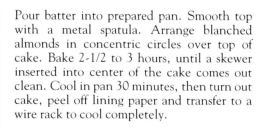

Pour batter into prepared pan. Smooth top with a metal spatula. Arrange blanched almonds in concentric circles over top of cake. Bake 2-1/2 to 3 hours, until a skewer inserted into center of the cake comes out clean. Cool in pan 30 minutes, then turn out cake, peel off lining paper and transfer to a wire rack to cool completely.

Makes about 12 slices.

COCONUT & CHERRY CAKE

1 cup butter, softened
1-1/4 cups sugar
4 eggs and 1 egg yolk
2 cups self-rising flour, sifted
2/3 cup shredded coconut
1 cup candied cherries, quartered
TOPPING:
1 egg white
1/2 cup powdered sugar, sifted
1-1/4 cups unsweetened thin coconut slices

Preheat oven to 350F (175C). Grease an 8-inch springform cake pan and line with waxed paper.

In a bowl, beat butter and sugar until light and fluffy. In another bowl, beat together eggs and egg yolk. Gradually beat into creamed mixture. Fold in flour, coconut and cherries. Spoon mixture into prepared pan. Bake 45 to 50 minutes, until just firm to the touch. To make the topping, in a bowl, beat egg white until soft peaks form; gradually beat in powdered sugar until stiff peaks form.

Spread topping over top of cake. Sprinkle with coconut. Return cake to oven and bake 20 minutes, until golden-brown and a skewer inserted into center comes out clean. Cover lightly with foil if topping is browning too quickly. Cool cake in pan 10 minutes, then remove from pan, peel off lining paper and transfer to a wire rack to cool.

Makes 8 to 10 slices.

Note: Thin, dried slices of unsweetened coconut are available in natural food stores.

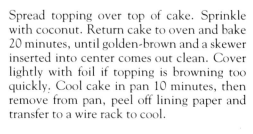

JEWEL-TOPPED MADEIRA CAKE

—CHOCOLATE MARBLE CAKE—

1 cup butter, softened
1-1/4 cups sugar
Grated zest of 1 lemon
4 eggs, beaten
2 cups self-rising flour, sifted
3 tablespoons milk
TOPPING:
2-2/3 tablespoons honey
1/2 pound glacéd fruits and angelica

2 ounces semisweet chocolate
1 tablespoon strong coffee
2 cups self-rising flour
1 teaspoon baking powder
1 cup margarine, softened
1-1/4 cups sugar
4 eggs, beaten
1/2 cup ground blanched almonds
2 tablespoons milk
FROSTING:
4-1/2 ounces semisweet chocolate
2 tablespoons butter
2 tablespoons water

Preheat oven to 325F (165C). Grease and line an 8-inch springform cake pan with waxed paper. In a bowl, beat together butter, sugar and lemon zest until light and fluffy. Gradually beat in eggs. Fold in flour, alternately with milk. Spoon batter into prepared pan. Bake 1-1/2 to 1-3/4 hours, until a skewer inserted into center of cake comes out clean.

Preheat oven to 350F (175C). Grease a ring mold with a 7-1/2-cup capacity. In a heat-proof bowl set over a pan of simmering water, break chocolate and add coffee. Heat until melted. Let cool. Into a bowl, sift flour and baking powder. Add margarine, sugar, eggs, ground almonds and milk. Beat well until smooth. Spoon half the batter evenly into prepared pan. Stir cooled, soft chocolate into the remaining batter, then spoon into pan. Draw a knife through batter in a spiral. Smooth the surface.

Cool cake in pan 5 minutes, then turn out onto a wire rack to cool completely. In a saucepan, gently heat honey. Brush over cake and arrange fruits and angelica on top.

Makes 8 to 10 slices.

Variation: A traditional Madeira cake has thin sliced candied peel on top. This should be placed on cake after it has been baking about 1 hour.

Bake 50 to 60 minutes, until well risen and a skewer inserted into center comes out clean. Cool in pan 5 minutes, then turn out cake and transfer to a wire rack to cool completely. To make frosting, into a heatproof bowl set over a pan of simmering water, put chocolate, butter and water; heat until melted. Stir frosting and pour over cake on a rack, working quickly to coat top and sides. Let set before serving.

Makes 10 to 12 slices.

SUMMER CAKE

3/4 cup butter, softened
3/4 cup sugar
3 eggs, beaten
1-1/2 cups self-rising flour
4 teaspoons boiling water
FILLING:
1/3 cup unsalted butter, softened
3/4 cup powdered sugar, sifted
1 teaspoon vanilla extract
FROSTING:
1 cup powdered sugar, sifted
2 teaspoons lemon juice
TO DECORATE:
Crystallized flowers

Preheat oven to 350F (175C). Grease two 8-inch round cake pans and line bottoms with waxed paper. In a bowl, beat together butter and sugar until light and fluffy. Gradually beat in eggs, then fold in flour. Stir in the boiling water to make a soft batter. Divide batter between prepared pans. Bake 25 to 30 minutes, until cakes are lightly browned and spring back when pressed. Cool in pans 5 minutes, then turn out cakes, peel off lining paper and transfer to wire racks to cool.

To make filling, in a bowl, beat together butter and powdered sugar. Stir in vanilla. Sandwich cakes together with filling. To make icing, in a bowl, mix together powdered sugar, lemon juice and enough water to make a good consistency for spreading. Spread frosting over cake top and decorate with crystallized flowers.

Makes 8 slices.

APPLE CAKE

2 cups plus 2 tablespoons self-rising flour
3/4 teaspoon ground cinnamon
1/3 cup sugar
Finely grated zest and juice 1 lemon
2 eggs, beaten
3 tablespoons sweet sherry
2/3 cup olive oil
1 pound Granny Smith apples

Preheat oven to 350F (175C). Grease a 7-inch pan. In a bowl, stir together flour, cinnamon, sugar and lemon zest. Make a well in the center and gradually add eggs, sherry, olive oil and lemon juice, stirring to make a smooth batter.

With a sharp knife, peel, core and chop apples. Fold into cake batter, then spoon batter into prepared pan. Bake 40 to 45 minutes or until golden-brown and firm to the touch in center. Cool in pan a few minutes, then turn out onto a wire rack to cool completely.

Makes 8 servings.

DOUBLE CHOCOLATE GÂTEAU

1 cup butter, softened
1-1/4 cups sugar
4 eggs, beaten
1-1/2 cups self-rising flour
1/2 cup unsweetened cocoa powder
FILLING:
1 cup whipping cream
5 ounces white chocolate
FROSTING:
12 ounces semisweet chocolate
1/2 cup butter
6 tablespoons whipping cream
TO DECORATE:
4 ounces semisweet chocolate
2 teaspoons each powdered sugar and unsweetened
    cocoa powder mixed

Preheat oven to 350F (175C). Grease an 8-inch springform cake pan and line bottom with waxed paper. In a bowl, beat together butter and sugar until light and fluffy. Gradually beat in eggs. Into another bowl, sift together flour and cocoa powder. Fold into mixture, then spoon into pan. Bake 45 to 50 minutes, until cake springs back when lightly pressed and a skewer inserted into center comes out clean. Cool in pan 5 minutes, then turn out cake, remove lining paper and transfer to a wire rack to cool completely.

To make the filling, in a saucepan, heat cream to just below boiling point. In a food processor, chop white chocolate. With motor running, pour hot cream through feed tube and process 10 to 15 seconds, until smooth. Transfer to a bowl, cover with plastic wrap and chill overnight. The next day after cake is ready to fill, beat filling until just beginning to hold soft peaks.

To make frosting, in a heatproof bowl over a pan of simmering water, melt chocolate. Stir in butter and cream. Cool, stirring occasionally, until mixture is a thick spreading consistency.

To make chocolate curls for decoration, in a heatproof bowl over a pan of simmering water, melt chocolate. Spread one-quarter of chocolate over a baking sheet. Refrigerate sheet a few minutes until chocolate loses its gloss and is just set, but not hard. Using a metal spatula, scrape off large curls of chocolate, transferring them to a baking sheet lined with waxed paper. Refrigerate until set. Make 3 more batches of curls in the same way.

With a serrated knife, slice the cake horizontally into 3 layers. Sandwich layers together with white chocolate filling. Cover top and sides of cake with chocolate frosting. Arrange chocolate curls over top of cake. Sift mixed powdered sugar and cocoa powder over cake.

Makes 10 slices.

ARTEMIS CAKE

14 ounces semisweet chocolate
5 eggs, separated
1 cup butter, softened
3/4 cup powdered sugar, sifted
2 tablespoons all-purpose flour, sifted
1 teaspoon ground cinnamon
Extra powdered sugar, to decorate

Preheat oven to 350C (175C). Butter and line an 8-inch cake pan with waxed paper (preferably a loose-bottomed pan). Into a bowl, break chocolate. Stand bowl over a pan of hot water until melted. Leave until almost cold.

In a bowl, whisk egg whites until stiff but not dry. In another bowl, beat butter and powdered sugar until light and creamy. Beat in egg yolks. Stir in chocolate. It does not need to be thoroughly mixed.

Stir in flour and cinnamon, then fold in egg whites. Pour mixture into prepared pan. Bake 45 minutes or until firm to the touch. Leave in pan until almost cool, then transfer to a wire rack. Sift powdered sugar over the top and place on a serving plate.

Makes 8 servings.

FROSTED WALNUT CAKE

3/4 cup butter, softened
3/4 cup sugar
3 eggs, beaten
1/2 cup chopped walnuts
1-1/2 cups self-rising flour, sifted
FROSTING:
1-1/4 cups sugar
1/3 cup water
2 egg whites
6 walnut halves

Preheat oven to 350F (175C). Grease 2 (8-inch) round cake pans and line bottoms with waxed paper. In a bowl, beat together butter and sugar until light and fluffy.

Gradually beat in eggs. Fold in walnuts and flour. Divide batter between prepared pans. Bake 25 to 35 minutes, until risen and golden-brown. Cool in pans 5 minutes, then turn out cakes, peel off lining papers and transfer to wire racks to cool. To make frosting, in a saucepan, put sugar and 1/3 cup water. Stir over low heat until sugar has dissolved.

Bring to a boil and boil to 240F (115C) on a candy thermometer. Remove from heat. In a bowl, beat egg whites until stiff peaks form. Pour hot syrup onto egg whites, beating constantly. Continue beating as mixture cools. Use some frosting to sandwich cakes together; cover cake with remaining frosting. Decorate with walnut halves. Let frosting set overnight.

Makes 8 servings.

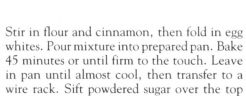

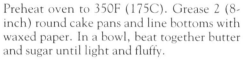

COFFEE-CARAMEL CAKE

2 cups self-rising flour
3/4 cup butter, softened
3/4 cup sugar
3 eggs, beaten
7 tablespoons strong coffee
FROSTING AND DECORATION:
1/2 cup half and half
3/4 cup plus 1 tablespoon butter
3 tablespoons sugar
3-3/4 cups powdered sugar
Chocolate-covered coffee beans

Preheat oven to 350F (175C). Grease 2 (8-inch) round cake pans and line the bottoms with waxed paper.

Into a bowl, sift flour 3 times and set aside. In another bowl, beat together butter and sugar until light and fluffy. Gradually beat in eggs. Fold in flour alternately with coffee. Divide batter between prepared pans and bake 30 minutes, until slightly shrinking from sides of pans. Cool cakes in pans 5 minutes, then turn out cakes and transfer to wire racks to cool completely. To make frosting, in a saucepan, warm half and half and butter.

In another heavy-bottomed saucepan, heat sugar over low heat until it dissolves and turns a golden caramel. Off the heat, stir in warm half and half mixture, taking care as it may splatter. Return to the heat and stir until caramel has dissolved. Remove from heat. Gradually stir in powdered sugar, beating until frosting is a smooth spreading consistency. Sandwich cakes together with some frosting; spread remaining frosting over top and side. Decorate with coffee beans.

Makes 8 servings.

CHOCOLATE-ORANGE CAKE

2 small oranges
3 ounces semisweet chocolate
1-3/4 cups self-rising flour
1-1/2 teaspoons baking powder
3/4 cup margarine, softened
3/4 cup sugar
3 eggs, beaten
TO GLAZE:
1-1/2 cups powdered sugar
2 tablespoons orange juice
2 ounces semisweet chocolate

Preheat oven to 325F (165C). Thoroughly grease a fluted or plain ring mold with a 3-3/4-cup capacity.

With a sharp knife, cut peel and pith from oranges. Cut oranges into sections by cutting down between membranes. Chop sections into small pieces, reserving as much juice as possible. Grate chocolate coarsely. Into a bowl, sift flour and baking powder. Add margarine, sugar, eggs and any reserved orange juice. Beat thoroughly until batter is smooth. Fold in chopped oranges and grated chocolate. Spoon batter into prepared mold.

Bake 40 minutes, until well risen and golden-brown. Cool in mold 5 minutes, then turn out cake and transfer to a wire rack to cool completely. To make frosting, into a bowl, sift powdered sugar. Stir in enough orange juice to make a thin frosting. Using a spoon, drizzle frosting over cake. Into a heatproof bowl over a pan of simmering water, break chocolate. Melt. Drizzle chocolate over cake. Let set.

Makes 8 to 10 slices.

In another bowl, combine flour, mixed spice, ground almonds, brown sugar, butter, molasses and eggs with a wooden spoon, then beat until smooth and glossy. Add mixed fruit to cake mixture; stir until evenly mixed.

Spoon mixture into prepared pan. Level top with back of a metal spoon, making a slight depression in center. Bake in oven 3-1/4 to 3-1/2 hours. Test with a skewer; when inserted in center, skewer should come out clean. Cool in pan. Invert cake, remove paper and place on a cake plate.

CHRISTMAS CAKE

CAKE
6-3/4 cups mixed dried fruit
3/4 cup quartered glacé cherries
1/2 cup cut mixed peel
3/4 cup flaked almonds
Finely grated peel and juice 1 orange
1/2 cup brandy or sherry
3 cups all-purpose flour
1 tablespoon ground mixed spice
2/3 cup ground almonds
1-1/2 cups dark-brown sugar
1-1/2 cups butter, softened
2 tablespoons molasses
5 eggs
DECORATION
3 tablespoons apricot jam, boiled, sieved
1-3/4 lb. marzipan
2-lb. ready-to-roll fondant icing (sugar paste)
Red and green food colorings
Red and green ribbon

Brush top and side of cake with apricot jam. Knead marzipan and roll out to 1/4-inch thickness. Cover top and sides of cake; trim to fit at bottom. Roll out fondant icing on a lightly sugared surface. Cover cake. Press icing over top and down side of cake. Trim off excess icing at bottom.

Preheat oven to 275F (135C). Line a 2-1/2-inch deep 8-inch-square or 2-1/2-inch deep 9-inch-round cake pan with a double thickness of greased parchment paper, extending parchment paper above sides of pan. Place pan on a double parchment paper-lined baking sheet. In a large bowl, combine dried fruit, cherries, mixed peel and flaked almonds until well mixed. Add orange peel and juice and brandy or sherry; mix well.

Knead trimmings together; color 1/3 red and remainder green with food colorings. Make tiny berries with some of the red icing. Roll and cut out holly leaves from green icing. Mark in veins with knife; let stand until set. Arrange on top of cake with berries. Cut out 'NOEL' from red icing and place on cake. Let cake stand until dry. Tie with ribbon.

Makes 40 servings.

RUM TRUFFLE CAKE

7 (1-oz.) squares semi-sweet chocolate
1/2 cup unsalted butter
1/4 cup dark rum
3 eggs, separated
1/2 cup superfine sugar
3/4 cup all-purpose flour
1/2 cup ground almonds
ICING
7 (1-oz.) squares semi-sweet chocolate
1-1/4 cups whipping cream
1 tablespoon dark rum
2 (1-oz.) squares white chocolate, grated

Preheat oven to 350F (175C).

In a bowl, whisk egg whites until stiff. Fold 1/3 at a time into chocolate mixture until all egg whites are incorporated. Pour mixture into prepared pan. Bake in oven 45 to 55 minutes or until firm to touch in center. Turn out of pan and cool on a wire rack.

Butter and flour a 2-1/2-inch deep 8-inch-round cake pan. Line with waxed paper. Place chocolate and butter in a bowl over hand-hot water. Stir occasionally until melted. Add rum and stir well.

To prepare filling, melt 4 squares of chocolate with 1/4 cup of whipping cream in a bowl set over hot water. Stir in rum until well blended. Let stand until cool. To prepare icing, whip 1/2 cup of whipping cream in a bowl until thick. Add 1/2 of rum-chocolate to whipped cream and fold in until smooth.

Place egg yolks and sugar in a bowl over a saucepan of simmering water. Whisk until thick and pale. Remove bowl from saucepan. Continue to whisk until mixture leaves a trail when whisk has been lifted. Stir chocolate mixture into egg yolk mixture until evenly blended. In a small bowl, mix flour and ground almonds. Add to chocolate mixture; fold in carefully using a spatula.

Cut cake in half. Sandwich together with chocolate icing and spread remainder over top and sides. Chill cake and remaining rum-chocolate mixture in bowl. Melt remaining chocolate with whipping cream in a bowl set over hot water. Stir until smooth and cool until thick. Spread chocolate mixture over cake to cover evenly. Shape rum-chocolate mixture into 16 truffles. Coat in grated white chocolate. Arrange truffles on top of cake and chill to set.

Makes 10 servings.

—CHOC-ALMOND MERINGUE—

MERINGUE:
4 egg whites
1-1/4 cups sugar
1-1/4 cups ground blanched almonds
FILLING:
6 ounces semisweet chocolate
3 tablespoons unsalted butter
3 tablespoons strong coffee
3 tablespoons brandy
3/4 cup whipping cream
TO DECORATE:
Chopped, toasted almonds

Preheat oven to 275F (80C). Line 2 baking sheets with waxed paper.

To make meringue, in a bowl, beat egg whites until soft peaks form. Beat in half of the sugar until stiff peaks form. In another bowl, mix together remaining sugar and ground almonds. Carefully fold into meringue mixture. Pipe or spread meringue into 2 (8-inch) circles on prepared baking sheets. Bake about 1-1/2 hours, until completely dry and crisp. Carefully remove from baking sheets and transfer to wire racks to cool completely.

To make filling, into a heatproof bowl set over a pan of simmering water, break chocolate. Add butter, coffee and brandy. When melted, stir and set aside to cool. Whip cream until soft peaks form; stir in cooled chocolate mixture. Sandwich meringue circles together with most of the chocolate cream. Put remaining cream into a pastry bag and pipe whirls on top of cake. Decorate with toasted almonds.

Makes 8 servings.

—LIME & TANGERINE GÂTEAU—

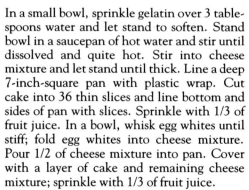

3 eggs, separated
2 (4-oz.) pkgs. cream cheese, softened
1/2 cup superfine sugar
Finely grated peel and juice 2 tangerines
Finely grated peel and juice 2 limes
1 tablespoon plus 2 teaspoons plain gelatin
1 pound cake
2/3 cup whipping cream
3 tablespoons fromage frais
1/4 cup chopped pistachio nuts
Lime and tangerine wedges to decorate

Beat egg yolks, cream cheese and sugar in a bowl with a wooden spoon until smooth. Stir in grated fruit peel and 1/2 of juices.

In a small bowl, sprinkle gelatin over 3 tablespoons water and let stand to soften. Stand bowl in a saucepan of hot water and stir until dissolved and quite hot. Stir into cheese mixture and let stand until thick. Line a deep 7-inch-square pan with plastic wrap. Cut cake into 36 thin slices and line bottom and sides of pan with slices. Sprinkle with 1/3 of fruit juice. In a bowl, whisk egg whites until stiff; fold egg whites into cheese mixture. Pour 1/2 of cheese mixture into pan. Cover with a layer of cake and remaining cheese mixture; sprinkle with 1/3 of fruit juice.

Top with remaining cake and fruit juice. Cover with plastic wrap and chill until set; leave in pan until required. Remove gâteau from pan and remove plastic wrap carefully. In a bowl, whip cream and fromage frais until thick. Spoon 1/4 of mixture into a pastry bag fitted with a small star nozzle. Spread remaining cream evenly over gâteau and press pistachio nuts onto all sides to coat evenly. Pipe a shell border around top of gâteau and decorate with fruit wedges.

Makes 12 servings.

BREADS

CRUMPETS

4 cups bread flour
1 teaspoon salt
1 teaspoon sugar
2 teaspoons active dry yeast
2-1/2 cups lukewarm milk (130F, 55C)
2/3 cup lukewarm water (130F, 55C)
Vegetable oil for cooking
TO SERVE:
Butter and jam

Into a bowl, sift flour. Stir in salt, sugar and yeast.

Make a well in center of flour and pour in milk and water. With a wooden spoon, gradually work flour into liquid, then beat vigorously to make a smooth batter. Cover bowl with a cloth and leave in a warm place 1 hour or until batter has doubled in bulk.

Thoroughly grease a heavy skillet or griddle and several crumpet rings or round cookie cutters. Arrange as many rings as possible in pan. Heat pan, then pour in enough batter to half fill each ring. Cook crumpets 5 to 6 minutes, until bubbles appear and burst on the surface. Remove rings and turn crumpets over. Cook on other side 2 to 3 minutes longer. Return rings to skillet to heat and repeat with remaining batter. Serve crumpets hot, generously buttered, with jam.

Makes about 16.

SEEDED BREAD STICKS

1 tablespoon dried yeast
4 teaspoons honey
1/2 cup butter, chopped
1 teaspoon salt
1 egg, beaten
3-1/4 cups all-purpose flour
1 egg
Caraway, sesame and poppy seeds

In a small bowl mix together yeast, 1/2 cup warm water and 1 teaspoon honey. Set aside and allow yeast to become foamy. In a sauce-pan, combine butter, remaining honey, salt and 1/2 cup water. Heat gently until butter and honey melt.

Pour liquid into large warmed bowl. Stir beaten egg and yeast into mixture. Beat in flour. Do not knead dough. Cover and place in refrigerator until cold. Divide dough into 12 pieces. On a floured board, roll each piece to a 12-inch length. Cut in halves length-ways. Place lengths on greased cookie sheets about 4-inches apart.

In a small bowl beat remaining eggs with 1 teaspoon water. Brush egg over lengths. Sprinkle with seeds. Let rise in a warm place for 30 minutes, or until not quite doubled in size. Preheat oven to 425F (220C). Bake bread sticks 15 minutes, or until golden brown. Cool on a wire rack.

Makes 24 sticks.

SPANISH COUNTRY BREAD

2 cups bread flour
2 teaspoons salt
1 envelope active dried yeast (about 1 tablespoon)
3/4 cup warm water
Olive oil for brushing
Cornmeal for sprinkling

Into a large bowl, sift flour and salt. Stir in yeast and form a well in center. Slowly pour water into well, stirring with a wooden spoon, to make a dough. Beat well until dough comes away from sides of bowl.

Turn dough out onto a lightly floured surface and knead 10 to 15 minutes or until smooth and elastic; add a little more flour if dough is sticky. Put dough in an oiled bowl, cover and leave in a warm place, about 2-1/2 hours or until doubled in volume. Lightly sprinkle a baking sheet with cornmeal. Turn dough onto lightly floured surface and punch down, then roll to a 16" x 6" rectangle. Roll up like a jellyroll and pinch seam to seal.

Place roll, seam-side down, on baking sheet. Using a very sharp knife, make 3 diagonal slashes on roll at equal distances. Brush top lightly with water. Leave in a warm place about 1 hour or until doubled in volume. Preheat oven to 450F (225C). Place a pan of water in the bottom of oven. Brush loaf again with water and bake 5 minutes. Remove pan of water. Brush loaf once more with water. Bake about 20 minutes or until loaf sounds hollow when tapped on bottom.

Makes 1 loaf.

PITA BREAD

7 cups bread flour
1 envelope active dry yeast (about 1 tablespoon)
2 teaspoons salt
2 tablespoons extra-virgin olive oil

Into a large bowl, sift flour. Stir in yeast and salt. Add oil and mix in enough water to make a soft dough. Turn dough out onto a floured surface.

Knead dough thoroughly 10 minutes or until smooth and elastic. Cut into 12 equal-size pieces. Roll each piece into a ball, then roll out to an oval shape 7 inches long. Place on floured trays, cover with a cloth and leave in a warm place 1 hour or until doubled in size.

Preheat oven to 475F (240C). Oil 2 baking sheets and place in the oven to heat. Place 3 pita breads on each baking sheet and sprinkle with water. Bake 5 minutes or until puffed and lightly browned. Remove from baking sheets and wrap in a cloth while baking remaining bread.

Makes 12.

CHAPATI

1-1/4 cups all-purpose flour
1-1/4 cups whole-wheat flour
Salt to taste
About 3/4 cup water
1/4 cup butter or ghee, melted, plus extra for serving

Sift together flours and salt into a medium bowl, add any bran remaining in sifter. Mix in enough water to make a soft dough.

Knead dough on a lightly floured surface about 5 minutes, until smooth and pliable, then with wet hands, knead dough 1 minute more to make it extra smooth. Wrap in plastic wrap; refrigerate 30 minutes. Divide dough into 12 pieces and roll each out on a lightly floured surface to a 5-inch round.

Heat a griddle or heavy skillet over medium heat; cook rounds one at a time, floured side down, 1 to 2 minutes, until beginning to bubble on surface. Turn over and cook 30 to 60 seconds, pressing with a folded dry cloth during cooking to make them puff up. Wrap chapatis in a dry cloth as they are ready. Serve warm, brushed with extra melted butter.

Makes 12.

NAAN

4 cups all-purpose flour
1 teaspoon baking powder
1/2 teaspoon baking soda
Salt to taste
1 egg, beaten
6 tablespoons plain yogurt
3 tablespoons butter or ghee, melted
About 1 cup milk
1 tablespoon poppy seeds

Sift together flour, baking powder, baking soda and salt into a medium bowl.

Stir in egg, yogurt and 2 tablespoons butter. Gradually mix in enough milk to make a soft dough. Cover bowl with a damp cloth and put in a warm place 2 hours. Preheat oven to 400F (205C). Knead dough on a lightly floured surface for 2 to 3 minutes until smooth, then divide dough into 8 pieces.

Roll each piece into a ball, then roll out to make ovals about 6 inches long, pulling ends to stretch dough into shape. Brush ovals with water and place wet side down on greased baking sheets. Brush dry side with melted butter, sprinkle with poppy seeds. Bake 8 to 10 minutes, until puffy and golden brown.

Makes 8.

WALNUT BREAD

1 (1/4-oz.) package active dry yeast
1 tablespoon honey
2/3 cup warm milk (110F, 45C)
3 cups bread flour or all-purpose flour
3 cups whole-wheat flour
1-1/2 teaspoons salt
2 tablespoons butter, diced
1-1/4 cups chopped walnuts
2 teaspoons fennel seeds, lightly crushed
1/2 teaspoon grated nutmeg
About 1 cup warm water
Milk to glaze

In a small bowl, dissolve yeast and honey in milk. Let stand 5 to 10 minutes until frothy.

Sift flours and salt into a large bowl. Rub butter into flour. Stir in walnuts, 1 teaspoon of the fennel seeds and the grated nutmeg.

Using a wooden spoon, stir yeast mixture into flour mixture, then gradually beat in enough water to form a soft, but not sticky, dough.

Knead dough on a lightly floured surface 5 minutes until elastic. Put dough into an oiled large bowl, cover and let rise in a warm place 35 to 40 minutes until doubled in size. Turn out onto a lightly floured surface and knead 5 minutes.

Preheat oven to 425F (220C). Oil a 6-inch round pan. Divide dough into 7 equal pieces and shape into balls. Arrange balls in oiled pan. Brush tops with milk and sprinkle with remaining 1 teaspoon fennel seeds. Let rise in a warm place 25 minutes. Bake in preheated oven about 45 minutes until browned and bottom sounds hollow when tapped.

Turn bread out onto a wire rack and cool. Serve as part of the antipasti.

Makes 1 large loaf.

Note: This bread is delicious served with cheese and fish dishes, for soaking up olive oil dressings and is particularly good toasted.

FOCACCIA

4 cups bread flour or all-purpose flour
Pinch of salt
1 (1/4-oz.) package active dry yeast (about 1
    tablespoon)
1 teaspoon sugar
1 cup warm milk (110F, 45C)
1/4 cup extra-virgin olive oil, plus extra for brushing
2 teaspoons rosemary
Coarse sea salt

Sift flour and salt into a large bowl.

In a small bowl, dissolve yeast and sugar in milk. Let stand 5 to 10 minutes until frothy. Stir in the 1/4 cup olive oil. Using a wooden spoon, gradually beat yeast mixture into flour mixture to give a soft, but not sticky, dough. Knead on a lightly floured surface 5 minutes until smooth and elastic. Place in an oiled medium-size bowl, cover and let rise in a warm place about 40 minutes until doubled in size. Turn out onto a lightly floured surface and knead 5 minutes.

Oil a baking sheet. Roll out dough to a large circle about 1/2 inch thick and transfer to baking sheet. Brush dough with olive oil, sprinkle with rosemary and sea salt and lightly press into surface. With your finger make deep indentations over surface. Let rise 25 minutes. Preheat oven to 450F (230C). Bake in preheated oven 20 to 25 minutes until golden. Brush again with olive oil. Serve warm.

Makes 1 loaf.

OLIVE BREAD

1/3 cup extra-virgin olive oil
1 onion, finely chopped
7 cups bread flour
1 envelope active dry yeast (about 1 tablespoon)
2 teaspoons salt
About 1 cup warm water
1-1/3 cups ripe olives, pitted and chopped

In a skillet, heat oil. Add onion and cook until soft. Let cool. Into a large bowl, sift flour. Stir in yeast and salt. Add 2 table-spoons of the cooking oil and mix in enough water to make a soft dough. Turn dough out onto a floured surface.

Knead dough thoroughly 10 minutes or until smooth and elastic. Knead in 1 tablespoon of the cooking oil, the fried onion, reserving remaining oil, and chopped olives. Cut dough in half and shape into 2 round loaves. Place on lightly oiled baking sheets.

Cover with oiled plastic wrap and leave in a warm place 1 hour, or until doubled in size. Preheat oven to 350F (175C). Brush loaves with a little of the cooking oil. Bake loaves 30 to 40 minutes or until bottom of each sounds hollow when tapped. Brush tops of loaves with remaining oil. Return to the oven 2 minutes, then transfer to wire racks to cool.

Makes 2 loaves.

LEEK & BACON KNOTS

1 leek, finely chopped
1/4 cup butter, chilled
6 ounces bacon slices, chopped
2 cups bread flour
2 cups whole-wheat flour
1 teaspoon salt
1 teaspoon sugar
2 teaspoons active dry yeast
2/3 cup lukewarm milk (130F, 55C)
3/4 cup lukewarm water (130F, 55C)
TO FINISH:
1 egg, beaten, and sesame seeds

Into a skillet, put leek and half the butter. Cook over low heat until leek is softened.

Remove leek from pan and cool. In same skillet, cook bacon until slightly crisp. Let cool. Into a bowl, sift bread flour. Stir in whole-wheat flour, salt, sugar and yeast. Cut in remaining butter. Stir in leek and bacon. Make a well in center. Pour in milk and water. Stir until a soft dough is formed. Turn dough out onto a floured surface and knead about 10 minutes, until smooth. Put in an oiled bowl, cover and leave in a warm place until doubled in bulk.

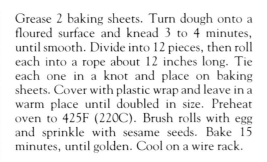

Grease 2 baking sheets. Turn dough onto a floured surface and knead 3 to 4 minutes, until smooth. Divide into 12 pieces, then roll each into a rope about 12 inches long. Tie each one in a knot and place on baking sheets. Cover with plastic wrap and leave in a warm place until doubled in size. Preheat oven to 425F (220C). Brush rolls with egg and sprinkle with sesame seeds. Bake 15 minutes, until golden. Cool on a wire rack.

Makes 12.

CHEESE & CHIVE BRAID

4 cups bread flour
1 teaspoon salt
1 teaspoon sugar
1-1/2 teaspoons active dry yeast
2 tablespoons butter, chilled
1 cup shredded Cheddar cheese (4 ounces)
3 tablespoons snipped fresh chives
4 green onions, chopped
2/3 cup lukewarm milk (130F, 55C)
3/4 cup lukewarm water (130F, 55C)
Beaten egg, to glaze

Into a bowl, sift flour. Stir in salt, sugar and yeast. Cut in butter.

Stir in cheese, chives and green onions and make a well in the center. Mix milk with water, then pour into the well. Mix until a soft dough is formed. Turn out dough onto a lightly floured surface. Knead about 10 minutes, until smooth and elastic. Place in an oiled bowl, cover and leave in a warm place about 1 hour, until doubled in bulk. Turn dough out onto a floured surface and knead about 3 minutes.

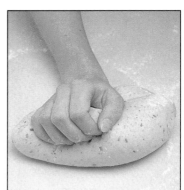

Divide dough into 3 pieces. Roll each one out to a long rope and braid together, pinching ends to seal. Place on a baking sheet, cover with oiled plastic wrap and leave in a warm place about 45 minutes, until doubled in bulk. Preheat oven to 425F (220C). Brush with beaten egg and bake 20 minutes. Reduce temperature to 350F (175C) and bake 15 minutes longer, until golden-brown and the bottom sounds hollow when tapped. Serve warm or cold with cheese and a salad.

Makes about 10 slices.

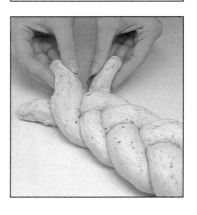

WHOLE CORN BREAD

EASTER BREAD

2/3 cup coarse cornmeal
2 cups all-purpose flour
1 teaspoon quick-rise dried yeast
1 teaspoon sugar
1/2 teaspoon salt
1 (8-oz.) can whole-kernel corn kernels
2/3 cup milk
2 tablespoons butter, melted

In a large bowl, combine cornmeal, flour, yeast, sugar and salt. Make a well in center.

7 cups bread flour
1 envelope active dry yeast (about 1 tablespoon)
1/4 cup superfine sugar
2 teaspoons caraway seeds
1/2 cup butter, melted
2 eggs, beaten
1 cup warm milk
1 egg, beaten, for glazing
2 tablespoons slivered almonds, to decorate

Into a large bowl, sift flour. Stir in yeast, sugar and caraway seeds. Stir in butter, eggs and milk. Mix together, then turn dough out onto a floured surface.

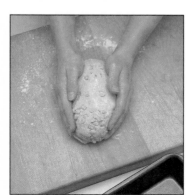

Drain corn, reserving juice. Into a small pan, pour juices. Add milk and heat gently until tepid. Stir into cornmeal mixture with melted butter and gradually work to form a soft dough. On a lightly floured surface, knead 6 to 8 minutes or until smooth. Carefully begin working in corn, adding a little more flour, if necessary. In an oiled bowl, place dough, cover and let rise in a warm place 45 minutes or until doubled in size.

Knead dough thoroughly 10 minutes or until smooth and elastic. Cut dough in half and divide each half into 3 pieces. Roll each piece into a rope 20 inches long. Braid 3 ropes, then shape the braid into a ring, pressing the ends together firmly. Braid remaining 3 ropes. Place the 2 rings on oiled baking sheets. Cover with a cloth and leave in a warm place 1 hour or until doubled in size. Preheat oven to 375F (190C).

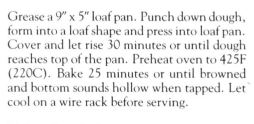

Grease a 9" x 5" loaf pan. Punch down dough, form into a loaf shape and press into loaf pan. Cover and let rise 30 minutes or until dough reaches top of the pan. Preheat oven to 425F (220C). Bake 25 minutes or until browned and bottom sounds hollow when tapped. Let cool on a wire rack before serving.

Makes 1 large loaf.

Brush loaves with beaten egg. Scatter slivered almonds over the top. Bake 40 minutes or until loaves are lightly browned and sound hollow when tapped on the bottoms. Leave on wire racks to cool. Serve sliced and buttered.

Makes 2 loaves.

Note: Traditionally these loaves have red-dyed eggs tucked into the braids before baking.

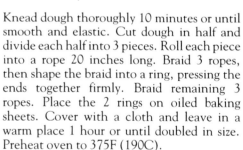

SAUCES & SALAD DRESSINGS

BASIC WHITE SAUCE

2 tablespoons low-fat margarine
1/4 cup all-purpose flour
1-1/4 cups low-fat milk
Salt and pepper

In a saucepan over low heat, melt low-fat margarine. Stir in flour and cook 1 minute, stirring.

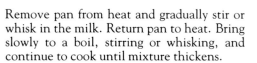

Remove pan from heat and gradually stir or whisk in the milk. Return pan to heat. Bring slowly to a boil, stirring or whisking, and continue to cook until mixture thickens.

Simmer 3 minutes. Remove pan from heat and season with salt and pepper. Serve with meat, poultry, fish, or vegetables.

Makes 1-1/4 cups/20 tablespoons.

WHITE SAUCE VARIATIONS

CHEESE SAUCE
Follow recipe for Basic White Sauce. Before seasoning with salt and pepper, stir in 1/2 cup shredded reduced-fat cheddar cheese and 1 teaspoon prepared mustard. Serve with fish, poultry, ham, vegetables, or egg dishes.

PARSLEY SAUCE
Follow recipe for Basic White Sauce. After seasoning with salt and pepper, stir in 2 tablespoons finely chopped fresh parsley. Serve with fish or ham.

CAPER SAUCE
Follow recipe for Basic White Sauce. Before seasoning with salt and pepper, stir in 2 tablespoons capers and 2 teaspoons vinegar from jar of capers. Reheat gently before serving. Serve with lamb or fish.

ESPAGNOLE SAUCE

1 slice Canadian bacon
2 tablespoons low-fat margarine
1 small onion or shallot
1 small carrot
2 ounces mushrooms
3 tablespoons all-purpose flour
2-1/2 cups beef stock
1 bouquet garni
4 black peppercorns
1 bay leaf
2 tablespoons tomato paste
Salt and pepper

Trim bacon, if needed, then finely chop bacon.

In a saucepan over low heat, melt margarine. Add bacon and cook 2 minutes, stirring. Finely chop onion or shallot, carrot, and mushrooms. Add vegetables to bacon and cook 5 to 10 minutes or until lightly browned, stirring occasionally. Stir in flour and cook until lightly browned, stirring constantly. Remove pan from heat and gradually stir in stock. Add all remaining ingredients, return to heat, and bring slowly to a boil, stirring, until mixture thickens. Cover and simmer 1 hour, stirring occasionally.

Strain sauce, remove bouquet garni, and rub pulp through a strainer. Discard remaining pulp in strainer and return sauce to clean saucepan. Reheat gently and adjust seasoning before serving. Serve with red meats or game.

Makes 1-3/4 cups/28 tablespoons.

BECHAMEL SAUCE

1 small onion or shallot
1 small carrot
1/2 stalk celery
1 bay leaf
6 black peppercorns
Several sprigs parsley
1-1/4 cups low-fat milk
2 tablespoons low-fat margarine
1/4 cup all-purpose flour
Salt and pepper

Slice onion or shallot and carrot. Chop celery roughly. Put vegetables, bay leaf, peppercorns, and parsley into a saucepan with milk and bring slowly to a boil.

Remove pan from heat, cover, and set aside to infuse 30 minutes. Strain into a measuring cup, reserving milk. In a saucepan over low heat, melt margarine. Stir in flour and cook 1 minute, stirring.

Remove pan from heat and gradually stir or whisk in flavored milk. Bring slowly to a boil, stirring or whisking, then continue to cook until mixture thickens. Simmer 3 minutes. Remove pan from heat and season with salt and pepper. Serve with poultry, fish, vegetables, or egg dishes.

Makes 1-1/4 cups/20 tablespoons.

ITALIAN GRAVY

ONION SAUCE

1 small onion
2 tablespoons low-fat margarine
1/4 cup all-purpose flour
1-1/4 cups beef stock
1 tablespoon tomato paste
1 teaspoon sugar
1 teaspoon Italian seasoning
Salt and pepper

Finely chop onion. In a saucepan, over low heat, melt margarine. Add onion and cook 5 minutes or until soft, stirring.

1 onion
2 tablespoons low-fat margarine
1/4 cup all-purpose flour
2 cups low-fat milk
Salt and pepper

Chop onion finely. In a saucepan over low heat, melt margarine. Add onion and cook 8 to 10 minutes or until soft, stirring occasionally.

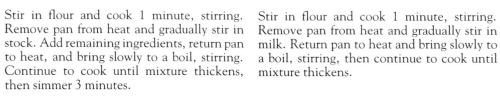

Stir in flour and cook 1 minute, stirring. Remove pan from heat and gradually stir in stock. Add remaining ingredients, return pan to heat, and bring slowly to a boil, stirring. Continue to cook until mixture thickens, then simmer 3 minutes.

Stir in flour and cook 1 minute, stirring. Remove pan from heat and gradually stir in milk. Return pan to heat and bring slowly to a boil, stirring, then continue to cook until mixture thickens.

Adjust seasoning and serve with broiled or roasted meats, such as beef, lamb, or pork.

Makes 1-3/4 cups/28 tablespoons.

Simmer gently 3 minutes. Remove pan from heat and season with salt and pepper. Serve with lamb or egg dishes.

Makes 2-1/4 cups/36 tablespoons.

Variation: Use chicken stock instead of beef stock, if serving the gravy with poultry.

MUSHROOM SAUCE

MUSTARD SAUCE

1 small onion
1 small carrot
1/2 stalk celery
1 bay leaf
6 black peppercorns
2 cups low-fat milk
6 ounces button mushrooms
1/4 cup low-fat margarine
1/2 cup all-purpose flour
Salt and pepper

Slice onion and carrot. Chop celery roughly. Put vegetables, bay leaf, and peppercorns into a saucepan. Add milk and slowly bring to a boil.

Remove pan from heat, cover, and set aside to infuse 30 minutes. Strain into a measuring cup, reserving milk. Slice mushrooms thinly. In a saucepan over low heat, melt margarine. Add mushrooms and cook 5 minutes or until soft, stirring occasionally. Stir in flour and cook 1 minute, stirring. Remove pan from heat and gradually stir in flavored milk.

Return pan to heat. Bring slowly to a boil, stirring, then continue to cook until mixture thickens. Simmer 3 minutes. Remove pan from heat and season with salt and pepper. Serve with fish or vegetables, such as broccoli or potatoes.

Makes 2-1/4 cups/36 tablespoons.

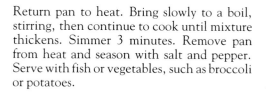

2 tablespoons low-fat margarine
1/4 cup all-purpose flour
1-1/4 cups low-fat milk
2 tablespoons whole-grain mustard
Salt and pepper

In a saucepan over low heat, melt margarine. Stir in flour and cook 1 minute, stirring.

Remove pan from heat and gradually stir or whisk in milk. Return pan to heat. Bring slowly to a boil, stirring or whisking, then continue to cook until mixture thickens. Simmer 3 minutes.

Stir in mustard and season with salt and pepper. Reheat gently before serving. Serve with oily fish, ham, bacon, vegetables, or cheese dishes.

Makes 1-1/2 cups/24 tablespoons.

ROMESCO SAUCE

3 garlic cloves, unpeeled
8 ounces beefsteak tomatoes
1 fresh red bell pepper
1/3 cup blanched almonds, lightly toasted
1 dried hot red chile, soaked in cold water 30 minutes, drained and seeded
3 tablespoons red-wine vinegar
About 2/3 cup olive oil
Salt

Preheat oven to its hottest setting. Roast garlic, tomatoes and bell pepper 20 to 30 minutes, removing tomatoes and garlic when soft and pepper when soft and lightly browned.

With a sharp knife, peel tomatoes and pepper and discard seeds. Peel garlic. In a blender or food processor with the metal blade, process vegetables with almonds and chile. With the motor running, slowly pour in vinegar and enough oil to make a thick sauce.

Add salt to taste. Cover and refrigerate 3 to 4 hours before serving with meat, fish and vegetable dishes.

Makes 6 servings.

Variation: True Romesco Sauce is made from romesco peppers. If available, substitute 2 dried romesco peppers for the red bell pepper and chile.

TOMATO SAUCE

2 tablespoons olive oil
1/2 Spanish onion, finely chopped
1/2 garlic clove, chopped
1 red bell pepper, seeded and chopped
6 cups peeled, seeded and chopped beefsteak tomatoes
Sugar or tomato paste (optional)
Salt and black pepper

In a skillet, heat oil. Add onion and cook over low heat 5 minutes.

Stir in garlic and bell pepper and cook 10 minutes, stirring occasionally.

Stir tomatoes into pan. Simmer 20 to 30 minutes, stirring occasionally, until thickened. Add sugar or tomato paste, if desired, and season with salt and black pepper. Process in a blender or food processor with the metal blade until pureed, or press through a non-metallic strainer, if desired.

Makes 4 to 6 servings.

BARBECUE SAUCE

3 tablespoons corn oil
1 small onion, finely chopped
1 clove garlic, crushed
1/2 teaspoon dry mustard
2 tablespoons malt vinegar
1 tablespoon Worcestershire sauce
2 tablespoons light-brown sugar
3 tablespoons catsup
1/2 teaspoon chili seasoning
3/4 cup chicken stock
Fresh Italian parsley sprig, if desired

Heat oil in a small saucepan. Add onion and garlic and cook gently 2 minutes, stirring frequently.

Stir in mustard, vinegar, Worcestershire sauce, sugar, catsup, chili seasoning and stock. Bring to a boil.

Cover and simmer sauce gently 7 to 8 minutes or until slightly thickened. Garnish with parsley sprig, if desired.

Makes 1-1/4 cups.

Note: Serve hot as a sauce with hamburgers, hot dogs or fried chicken. Or, if preferred, allow to cool and use to brush over meats, poultry and fish while baking or grilling.

SWEET SPICY CHILI SAUCE

1 clove garlic
1 Spanish onion, cut in fourths
2 fresh green chilies, seeded
2 tablespoons corn oil
1/2 teaspoon ground ginger
1 (8-oz.) can tomatoes in tomato juice
1/3 cup seedless raisins
1 tablespoon lemon juice
1 tablespoon dark soy sauce
2 tablespoons light-brown sugar
Salt and freshly ground pepper to taste
Fresh parsley sprig, if desired

In a blender or food processor, finely chop garlic, onion and chilies.

Heat oil in a saucepan. Add onion mixture and ginger and cook gently 3 minutes. Add tomatoes and break up with a spoon. Stir in raisins, lemon juice, soy sauce, brown sugar and water.

Bring to a boil, reduce heat and simmer 15 minutes, uncovered. Process in a blender or food processor to desired consistency. Reheat and season with salt and pepper. Garnish with parsley sprig, if desired.

Makes 2-1/2 cups.

Note: Serve hot with grilled steak, fried chicken or grilled whitefish.

HORSERADISH SAUCE

4 tablespoons grated fresh horseradish
1 teaspoon sugar
2 teaspoons Dijon mustard
Salt and pepper
2 tablespoons malt vinegar
3 tablespoons low-fat plain yogurt

Place the grated horseradish into a bowl. Add sugar, mustard, salt, and pepper and mix together well.

Stir in vinegar, then gently stir in yogurt, mixing together well. Leave horseradish sauce in a cool place 30 minutes before serving to let flavors develop.

Serve with beef or oily fish.

Makes 2/3 cup/10 tablespoons.

APPLESAUCE WITH MINT

1 small onion
1 pound cooking apples
Small bunch fresh mint
2 tablespoons sugar

Using a sharp knife, finely chop onion. Peel, core, and slice apples. Put onion, apples, and 2 tablespoons water into a saucepan.

Cover saucepan and simmer until apples and onion are soft, stirring occasionally. Remove pan from heat and mash apples and onion lightly together.

Using a sharp knife, finely chop mint. Add mint to saucepan with sugar, mixing together well. Reheat sauce gently, stirring until sugar dissolves. Serve hot or cold with lamb or pork.

Makes 1-2/3 cups/26 tablespoons.

CRANBERRY SAUCE

8 ounces cranberries
1/2 cup sugar
1/4 cup ruby port wine

Place cranberries into a saucepan with 2/3 cup water.

Bring to a boil and boil rapidly until cranberries are soft. Reduce heat and stir in sugar.

Heat gently until sugar dissolves, then stir in port wine. Reheat gently and serve with turkey or pork.

Makes 1-3/4 cups/28 tablespoons.

Variation: Substitute medium-dry sherry for ruby port wine.

BRANDY SAUCE

2 tablespoons cornstarch
1-1/4 cups low-fat milk
2 tablespoons sugar
3 tablespoons brandy

In a bowl, blend cornstarch with 2 tablespoons milk until smooth. Into a saucepan, put remaining milk and bring slowly to a boil.

Pour hot milk onto cornstarch mixture, whisking. Return sauce to saucepan and bring slowly to a boil, stirring constantly, until sauce thickens. Simmer 3 minutes.

Remove pan from heat and stir in sugar and brandy. Reheat sauce gently. Serve with plum pudding or apple tartlets.

Makes 1-1/4 cups/20 tablespoons.

Variation: Replace brandy with rum, sherry, or whiskey.

RASPBERRY SAUCE

DARK CHOCOLATE SAUCE

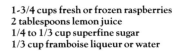

1-3/4 cups fresh or frozen raspberries
2 tablespoons lemon juice
1/4 to 1/3 cup superfine sugar
1/3 cup framboise liqueur or water

Combine all ingredients in a saucepan and bring slowly to a boil.

6 ounces semisweet chocolate
1/2 cup strong coffee or water
1/4 cup superfine sugar

Break chocolate in pieces and put into top of a double boiler or a bowl set over a pan of simmering water. Add coffee or water and sugar.

Simmer a few minutes. Serve immediately or, using a wooden spoon, press through a nylon sieve and serve cold.

Makes 4 to 6 servings

Stir over medium heat until chocolate melts and sauce is smooth and creamy. Serve hot or cold.

Makes 4 to 6 servings.

Note: Serve with Orange Roll, page 170, if desired.

Note: Serve with White & Dark Chocolate Terrine, page 173, if desired.

BLACK CURRANT SAUCE

HOT LEMON SAUCE

8 ounces fresh or frozen black currants
1/4 cup superfine sugar
1/2 cup water
2 tablespoons crème de cassis

In a saucepan, combine black currants, sugar and water. Cook over medium heat until currants are juicy and tender.

Grated peel and juice of 3 lemons
1/3 cup butter
1/3 cup superfine sugar
1 teaspoon cornstarch
Water

In a saucepan, combine lemon peel and juice, butter and sugar. Stir over gentle heat until butter melts and sugar dissolves.

Drain currants, reserving juice. Push currants through a sieve with a little juice to make a puree. Stir in liqueur and enough juice to desired consistency. Serve cold, if desired.

Makes 4 to 6 servings.

Mix cornstarch and a small amount of water to a smooth paste; stir into lemon mixture. Bring sauce to a boil, stirring constantly.

Note: Serve with Coeurs à la Crème, page 163, if desired.

Simmer 1 to 2 minutes, stirring constantly. Keep warm until ready to serve.

Makes 4 to 6 servings.

CARAMEL SAUCE

3/4 cup light brown sugar
1/2 cup sugar
1 tablespoon arrowroot

Into a saucepan, put sugars with 2 cups water. Heat mixture gently until sugar dissolves. Bring slowly to a boil, then simmer 10 minutes, stirring occasionally.

In a small bowl, blend arrowroot with 2 tablespoons water. Whisk arrowroot mixture into sugar mixture, mixing together well. Reheat sauce gently, until sauce thickens, stirring constantly.

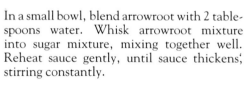

Serve with fruit such as oranges or bananas.

Makes 1-3/4 cups/28 tablespoons.

Variation: Once sauce has thickened, add 2 to 3 tablespoons brandy or a liqueur such as Cointreau to sauce and reheat gently.

BLACKBERRY & APPLE SAUCE

8 ounces cooking apples
8 ounces blackberries
1/4 cup sugar
1/2 cup low-fat cream cheese
2/3 cup reduced-fat light cream

Using a sharp knife, peel, core, and slice apples thinly. Into a saucepan, put apples and blackberries along with 3 tablespoons water. Cover and cook gently until fruit is soft, stirring occasionally.

Remove pan from heat and stir in sugar. Set aside to cool. When slightly cool, in a blender or food processor, puree fruit until smooth. Press fruit through a nylon strainer, discarding seeds.

Beat cream cheese and cream together, then whisk fruit in, mixing together thoroughly. Serve with steamed and baked puddings, meringues, or poached fruit such as peaches or pears.

Makes 2-1/4 cups/36 tablespoons.

Variation: In place of blackberries, use raspberries, loganberries, or black currants.

MINT & YOGURT DRESSING

1 garlic clove
1-1/4 cups low-fat plain yogurt
2 tablespoons low-fat milk
2 tablespoons chopped fresh mint
Salt and pepper

Peel and crush garlic. Into a bowl, put garlic, yogurt, milk, mint, salt, and pepper.

Whisk ingredients together until thoroughly mixed. Cover and leave dressing in a cool place 30 minutes before serving to let flavors develop. Adjust seasoning before serving.

Serve with a mixed bean salad or chicken salad.

Makes 1-1/2 cups/24 tablespoons.

Variation: In place of garlic and mint, add finely grated zest and juice of 1 lemon or 1 lime.

FRENCH DRESSING

1/4 cup olive oil
1/4 cup white-wine vinegar
1/4 cup tarragon vinegar
2/3 cup white grape juice
2 teaspoons chopped fresh mixed herbs, such as
    parsley, thyme, mint, and rosemary
2 teaspoons whole-grain mustard
Pinch sugar
Salt and pepper

Into a bowl, put olive oil, vinegars, grape juice, herbs, mustard, sugar, salt, and pepper. Beat ingredients together until thoroughly mixed.

Alternatively, put all ingredients in a clean jelly jar. Screw top on jar and shake until ingredients are thoroughly mixed.

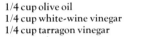

Adjust seasoning before serving. Serve with a fresh mixed salad or a selection of raw or cooked vegetables.

Makes 1-1/3 cups/21 tablespoons.

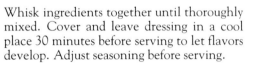

COCONUT-YOGURT DRESSING

1-1/4 cups low-fat plain yogurt
3 tablespoons shredded coconut
2 tablespoons honey
Juice of 1 lime

Into a bowl, put yogurt and coconut and mix together well.

Whisk in honey and lime juice, mixing together well. Cover and leave dressing in a cool place 30 minutes before serving to let flavors develop.

Serve with a bean salad or a mixed salad.

Makes 1-2/3 cups/26 tablespoons.

Variation: For a special dressing, add 2 tablespoons coconut liqueur, such as Malibu, to dressing with honey.

TARTAR SAUCE

7 or 8 cornichons (tiny sour pickles)
1 tablespoon capers, drained
1-1/4 cups reduced-calorie mayonnaise
1 tablespoon tarragon vinegar
1 tablespoon chopped fresh parsley
1 tablespoon snipped fresh chives
2 teaspoons chopped fresh tarragon
Salt and pepper

Using a sharp knife, finely chop cornichons (pickles) and capers.

Into a bowl, put cornichons (pickles) and capers and stir in mayonnaise, mixing together well.

Stir in vinegar, parsley, chives, tarragon, and salt and pepper and mix together thoroughly. Cover and leave in a cool place at least 30 minutes before serving to let flavors develop. Serve with grilled, broiled, or baked fish.

Makes 1-2/3 cups/26 tablespoons.

—THOUSAND ISLAND DRESSING—

—MILD CURRY MAYONNAISE—

1 medium-size dill pickle
2 tablespoons chopped red bell pepper
2 tablespoons chopped green bell pepper
1-1/4 cups reduced-calorie mayonnaise
1/4 cup low-fat plain yogurt
2 tablespoons tomato ketchup
1 tablespoon chopped fresh parsley
Salt and pepper

Using a sharp knife, chop pickle finely. In a bowl, mix together pickle and red and green bell peppers.

6 green onions
1 tablespoon low-fat margarine
2 tablespoons mango chutney
1 tablespoon mild curry powder
1 tablespoon shredded coconut
1-1/4 cups low-fat or nonfat mayonnaise
2/3 cup low-fat plain yogurt
Salt and pepper

Using a sharp knife, trim and chop green onions finely. In a saucepan over low heat, melt margarine. Add green onions and cook 5 minutes, stirring.

Stir in mayonnaise, yogurt, tomato ketchup, parsley, salt, and pepper and mix together thoroughly. Cover and leave in a cool place 30 minutes before serving to let flavors develop.

Remove pan from heat and stir in chutney, curry powder, and coconut, mixing together well. Set aside to cool.

Serve with a fresh mixed seafood salad.

Makes 2-1/2 cups/44 tablespoons.

Variation: Add 2 cold hard-boiled eggs, mashed or finely chopped, to dressing.

When cool, mix with mayonnaise, yogurt, salt, and pepper. Cover and leave the sauce in a cool place 30 minutes before serving to let flavors develop. Serve with potato salad or coleslaw.

Makes 2 cups/32 tablespoons.

RASPBERRY VINAIGRETTE

1 (14-oz.) can raspberries packed in light syrup
1/2 cup red-wine vinegar
5 tablespoons sunflower oil
1 teaspoon sugar
1 teaspoon dried sage
Salt and pepper

Into a blender or food processor, put raspberries and juice and blend until smooth.

Strain raspberry puree through a nylon strainer and discard seeds. Into a bowl, put raspberry juice, vinegar, oil, sugar, sage, salt, and pepper. Beat ingredients together until thoroughly mixed.

Alternatively, put all ingredients in a clean jelly jar. Screw top on jar and shake until ingredients are thoroughly mixed. Adjust seasoning before serving. Serve with fresh salad leaves, a rice salad, avocado, or cold, sliced cooked meats such as chicken.

Makes 2-1/4 cups/36 tablespoons.

GARLIC & GINGER DRESSING

2 garlic cloves
1 (1-inch) piece fresh gingerroot
7 tablespoons cider vinegar
2 tablespoons light soy sauce
1 tablespoon sunflower oil
1 tablespoon sesame oil
Salt and pepper

Peel and crush garlic cloves. Peel and chop or grate ginger finely.

Into a bowl, put garlic, ginger, vinegar, soy sauce, sunflower oil, sesame oil, salt, and pepper. Beat ingredients together until thoroughly mixed. Alternatively, put all ingredients in a clean jelly jar. Screw top on jar and shake until all the ingredients are thoroughly mixed.

Adjust seasoning before serving. Serve with a fresh mixed salad, root vegetables, a mixed bean salad, or broiled chicken or turkey.

Makes 3/4 cup/12 tablespoons.

PRESERVES

LEMON CURD

4 lemons
1-3/4 cups sugar
1-1/2 cups butter
4 eggs, beaten

Into a heatproof bowl, finely grate zest of lemons. Squeeze lemons and pour juice into bowl. Stir in sugar. Cut butter into small pieces and add to other ingredients.

Set bowl over a saucepan one-quarter filled with simmering water and stir until butter has melted and sugar dissolved. Strain eggs into lemon mixture.

Cook gently, stirring frequently, 10 to 15 minutes, until mixture is thick and creamy. Pour into clean, warm jars and seal while hot. Keep in the refrigerator.

Makes about 1-1/2 pounds.

Variations: For Lime Curd, use limes instead of lemons.

For Lemon & Elderflower Curd, add 2 handfuls of elderberry flowers, well shaken and flowers removed from stems, after adding butter.

APPLE BUTTER

5 cups dry cider
2-1/2 pounds Golden Delicious apples
1 pound Granny Smith apples
Sugar
Grated zest and juice of 1/2 orange
Grated zest and juice of 1/2 lemon
1/2 teaspoon ground cinnamon
1/2 teaspoon ground cloves

Into a large saucepan, put cider. Boil rapidly until reduced by one-third. With a knife, peel, core and slice apples, then add to pan.

If necessary, add enough water to just cover apples. Half cover pan and simmer until apples are very soft and pulpy and well reduced. Stir occasionally and crush pulp down in pan as it cooks. Measure pulp and process to a puree if it is lumpy. Return to saucepan. Add 1-1/2 cups sugar for every 2-1/2 cups of apple pulp. Stir in orange and lemon zests and juices, cinnamon and cloves.

Cook gently until sugar has dissolved. Simmer, stirring frequently, until most moisture has been driven off. The mixture is ready when a spoon drawn across the surface leaves an impression. Spoon into clean, warm jars and store in the refrigerator. Once a jar is opened, apple butter should be consumed within 3 to 4 days.

Makes 4 or 5 small jars.

GRAPEFRUIT MARMALADE

4 lb. grapefruit, well scrubbed
6 to 9 cups sugar

Cut grapefruit into quarters, remove seeds and pithy centers. Put the seeds and centers in a 6-inch square of cheesecloth, tie into a bag. Peel grapefruit. Cut peel into julienne strips. Slice peeled fruit crosswise into thin slices. Separate slices into individual sections. Place fruit and bag in a large bowl; just cover with water. Soak 12 hours. Remove bag.

In large preserving pan or saucepan, simmer fruit and soaking water 1 hour. For every cup of fruit and water add 3/4 cup sugar. Bring to a boil; boil about 20 minutes or to proper consistency. Test marmalade for doneness immediately after boiling. Proper consistency is reached when candy thermometer reaches 220F (105C). Or, test by spoon test. Pour a small amount of marmalade onto a cold plate. Let stand until cold. If marmalade forms a skin and wrinkles when pushed with a finger or spoon, it is ready.

Remove pan from heat while test preserve is cooling. Cool 10 minutes; stir gently to mix skin through the marmalade. Pour into sterilized jars to within 1/2-inch of top. Seal with sterilized lids. Invert jars for a few seconds. Cool in upright position. Store in cool, dark place.

Makes about 5 pints.

ROSE PETAL JAM

1/2 pound fragrant, red rose petals
2 cups sugar
4-1/2 cups water
Juice of 2 lemons

Cut off white area from bottom of each petal. Into a bowl, put petals and sprinkle with enough of the sugar to cover them. Leave overnight.

In a saucepan, put remaining sugar, the water and lemon juice. Heat gently until sugar has dissolved. Stir in rose petals and simmer 20 minutes. Bring to a boil and boil 5 minutes, until mixture thickens.

Pour jam into clean, warm jars. Cover and label. Store in a cool place.

Makes about 1 pound.

APRICOT & ALMOND CONSERVE —— SPICED CITRUS SLICES

1 lb. dried apricots, quartered
5 cups water
6 cups sugar
1/2 teaspoon almond liqueur or almond extract
1/2 cup blanched, slivered almonds

Soak apricots overnight in water. Strain apricots; reserve liquid.

3 thin-skinned oranges
4 thin-skinned lemons
5 limes
Water
2-1/2 cups white wine vinegar
4-1/2 cups sugar
2 (2-inch) cinnamon sticks
2 teaspoons whole cloves
6 blades mace

Scrub fruit thoroughly. Cut each fruit in 1/8-inch thick slices.

In a heavy-bottomed saucepan combine reserved liquid and sugar; bring to boil over a low heat stirring until sugar is dissolved. Add apricots and simmer until proper consistency is reached and candy thermometer reaches 220F (105C). Or test using spoon method described in Grapefruit Marmalade, page 239.

Lay slices in a stainless steel or enamel saucepan and just cover with water. Bring to a boil, cover and cook very gently about 10 minutes or until peel is tender. Drain slices and reserve liquor. In another saucepan, gently heat vinegar, sugar and spices, stirring occasionally, until sugar has dissolved. Bring to a boil. Lay fruit slices in syrup. Add reserved liquor to cover fruit, if necessary, and cook very genty 15 minutes or until peel looks transparent.

Immediately stir in liqueur and almonds. Remove from heat. Allow jam to stand at room temperature 10 minutes, stirring occasionally, to keep fruit and nuts in suspension. Pour conserve to within 1/8-inch of top of sterilized jars. Seal tightly with sterilized lids. Invert jars for a few seconds to complete seal. Cool in upright position. Store in a cool, dark place.

Makes 4 pints.

Meanwhile, sterilize 3 small jars and lids. Arrange fruit slices in warm jars, alternating slices or packing each separately. Bring syrup to a boil. Immediately fill each jar to top and seal with lids. When cold, label and store in a cool place.

Makes 3 small jars.

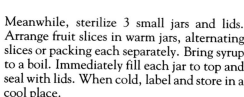

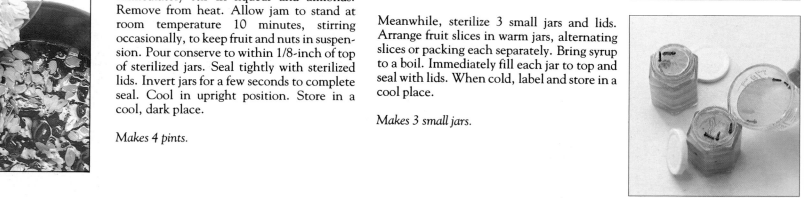

MIXED CURRANT JELLY

2 lb. red currants, washed
2 lb. black currants, washed
6 cups water
Sugar, see recipe

In a preserving pan combine fruit and water. Bring to boil and simmer until very soft.

Mash fruit with a wooden spoon and spoon into a jelly bag to drip overnight. Measure fruit juice and allow 1 cup sugar for each cup of juice.

Place sugar and liquid back in pan and bring to boil, stirring to dissolve sugar. Boil 7 minutes. Begin testing for proper consistency. Proper consistency is reached when candy thermometer reaches 220F (105C). Or test using spoon method described in Grapefruit Marmalade, page 239. Pour into sterilized jars. Seal tightly with sterilized lids. Invert jars for a few seconds to complete seal. Cool in upright position. Store in a cool, dark place.

Makes about 8 pints.

BRANDIED MINCEMEAT

6 cups raisins
3-1/3 cups currants
1 cup dried apricots
3/4 cup dates
1 cup candied peel
3/4 cup whole almonds
1 lb. tart apples, peeled, cored
Finely grated peel and juice 2 lemons
2-1/4 cups light-brown sugar
1 cup unsalted butter, melted
1 tablespoon ground mixed spice
2/3 cup brandy

In a large bowl, place raisins and currants.

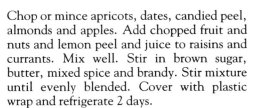

Chop or mince apricots, dates, candied peel, almonds and apples. Add chopped fruit and nuts and lemon peel and juice to raisins and currants. Mix well. Stir in brown sugar, butter, mixed spice and brandy. Stir mixture until evenly blended. Cover with plastic wrap and refrigerate 2 days.

Sterilize 6 (1-pint) jars and lids and keep warm. Stir mincemeat thoroughly, then spoon into hot jars, filling each to top. Cover each with paraffin and seal with lids.

Makes 6 (1-pint) jars.

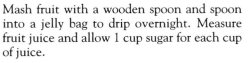

FIGS IN BRANDY

14 dried whole figs
1/2 cup sugar
1 cinnamon stick
Approximately 1 cup brandy

In a large saucepan or skillet, place figs in one layer with sugar and cinnamon stick. Just cover with water. Poach over low heat for 5 minutes. Discard cinnamon stick. Drain figs, reserve syrup.

Pack figs in sterilized jar. Reduce syrup to half by simmering uncovered.

Half fill jar of figs with brandy. Pour reduced syrup in jar to within 1/2-inch of top, cover. Store in a cool dark place – allow to mellow at least 1 month before using.

Makes 1-1/2 pints.

FRUITS IN CHARTREUSE

10 fresh lychees or 1 (15-oz.) can lychees
2 cups fresh sweet cherries or 1 (15-oz.) can cherries
1 cup sugar
1-1/4 cups Chartreuse or Benedectine liqueur

Sterilize 3 or 4 small jars and lids and keep warm. Peel lychees and carefully remove pits, keeping fruit whole. Remove cherry stalks and pits. Wash cherries or drain canned fruit and dry on paper towels. Pierce skins of cherries all over with a clean needle or fine skewer.

Arrange 1 layer of cherries in 1 warm jar and sprinkle with a layer of sugar. Arrange 1 layer of lychees on top and sprinkle with more sugar. Continue to layer cherries, sugar and lychees until jar is loosely filled to neck of jar. Do not pack fruit tightly. Sprinkle with a final layer of sugar.

Fill jar to top with liqueur and seal with a clean lid. Repeat to fill more small jars with remaining fruit, sugar and liqueur. Store in a cool dry place up to 6 months.

Makes 3 or 4 small jars.

MINT JELLY

TOMATO RELISH

6 lb. tart green apples, quartered
Juice of 4 lemons
2 cups loosely packed fresh mint leaves
1 cup white wine vinegar
Sugar, see recipe
Chopped fresh mint leaves
Green food coloring
Mint extract, if desired

In a large heavy-bottomed saucepan, combine apples, lemon juice, mint; just cover with water. Simmer until apples are very soft. Add vinegar; simmer 5 minutes more.

Strain mixture through a jelly bag or double thickness of cheesecloth; do not force mixture through, as this will cloud jelly. Measure fruit juice and add 1 cup sugar for every cup of juice. In a clean pan, cook juice and sugar over a low heat until sugar dissolves, stirring. Increase heat, boil briskly 5 minutes, without stirring, until temperature reaches 220F (105C). Or, test using spoon method, page 239.

Stir in chopped mint, a little coloring and 1 to 2 teaspoons mint extract if desired. Pour jelly to within 1/8-inch of top into sterilized jars. Cover, seal tightly with sterilized lids. Invert jars for a few seconds to complete seal. Cool in upright position. Store in a cool, dark place.

Makes 6 to 8 pints.

3 lb. tomatoes
4 large onions, coarsely chopped
1/2 cup salt
2-1/2 cups white wine vinegar
2 cups sugar
10 small red chilies (or fewer, if less spicy relish is preferred)
1 tablespoon curry powder
1 tablespoon turmeric
1-1/2 teaspoons dry mustard
1 teaspoon cumin
1 teaspoon fenugreek
2 tablespoons all-purpose flour

Peel, core and coarsely chop tomatoes.

Place in a ceramic or glass bowl, sprinkle generously with salt; cover; let stand overnight. In a large saucepan combine tomatoes, onions and vinegar. Bring to boil; simmer 10 minutes. Add sugar and chilies. Continue to cook, stirring occasionally, until sugar is dissolved. Simmer 5 minutes more. In a small bowl combine remaining ingredients and enough cold water to form a paste. Add to simmering vegetable mixture, stirring to avoid any lumps. Simmer 1-1/2 hours stirring occasionally.

Pour into sterilized jars. Seal with sterilized vinegar-proof lids. Process for 15 minutes in a boiling-water bath. (Place jars on rack in processing pan. Do not allow jars to touch. Keep covered with 2-inches boiling water while processing.) Store in a cool, dark place. Allow to mellow 4 weeks before using.

Makes about 4 pints.

FRESH MANGO CHUTNEY

SPICY APPLE CHUTNEY

2 mangoes
1 red chile, seeded, finely sliced
1/4 cup chopped cashew nuts
1/4 cup raisins
2 tablespoons chopped fresh mint
Pinch of asafetida
1/2 teaspoon ground cumin
1/4 teaspoon red (cayenne) pepper
1/2 teaspoon ground coriander
Mint sprigs, to garnish

Peel and seed mangoes, then very thinly slice flesh.

2 lb. tart green apples
2 tablespoons salt
1 whole head garlic
1-inch piece fresh gingerroot
4 fresh green or red chiles, chopped (use red if you want
   a very hot chutney)
2/3 cup vegetable oil
2 tablespoons white mustard seeds
1 teaspoon fenugreek
15 whole black peppercorns
2 teaspoons powdered cumin
1 teaspoon chili powder
1 teaspoon turmeric
2/3 cup vinegar
1/2 cup sugar

Put mango slices in a bowl with chile, cashew nuts, raisins and chopped mint; stir gently. In a small bowl, mix together asafetida, cumin, cayenne and coriander; sprinkle over mango mixture.

Peel, core and slice apples. In a large glass or ceramic bowl, place apples; cover with salt; set aside. Peel and chop garlic and ginger, chop chilies. In a large saucepan gently fry garlic and ginger in oil for 3 minutes. Add mustard seeds, fenugreek, peppercorns, cumin, chili powder, turmeric and fresh chilies to garlic and ginger. Cook 5 minutes longer.

Stir gently to coat mango mixture in spices, then cover and refrigerate 2 hours. Serve cold, garnished with mint sprigs.

Makes about 2 cups.

Add apples, vinegar and sugar; simmer until chutney becomes thick. Fill sterilized jars with chutney to within 1/2-inch of top. Seal with sterilized vinegar-proof lids. Process 15 minutes in boiling-water bath for 1-pint jars. (Place jars on rack in processing pan. Do not allow jars to touch. Keep covered with 2 inches boiling water while processing.) Store in a cool, dark place.

Makes about 3 pints.

CONFECTIONERY

—CHOCOLATE TRUFFLE CUPS—

—HAND-DIPPED CHOCOLATES—

16 (1-oz.) squares white chocolate
1/4 cup unsalted butter, melted
2 tablespoons whipping cream
1 tablespoon plus 1 teaspoon cherry brandy
1 tablespoon plus 1 teaspoon Chartreuse liqueur
1 tablespoon plus 1 teaspoon apricot brandy
Pink, green and yellow food colorings
6 pistachio nuts, chopped

Break up chocolate and place in a bowl set over a saucepan of hand-hot water. Stir occasionally until melted. Remove bowl from saucepan and cool. Place 36 foil cups on a tray. Spoon a little chocolate into each.

Using a fine brush, coat inside of each cup and refrigerate to set. Add melted butter and cream to remaining chocolate and stir until smooth. Divide mixture evenly among 3 bowls. Flavor 1 with cherry brandy and tint pink with food coloring; stir until well blended. Repeat to flavor and color 1 chocolate with Chartreuse and green food coloring and remaining chocolate with apricot brandy and yellow and pink food coloring.

When chocolate mixtures are set enough to peak softly, place each into a pastry bag fitted with a small star nozzle. Pipe swirls of each flavored chocolate into 12 chocolate cups. Sprinkle with pistachio nuts and let set. Pack into pretty boxes, baskets or dishes and cover with pretty paper and ribbon.

Makes 36 pieces.

3 oz. ready-to-roll fondant icing (sugar paste)
Rose and violet flavorings
Pink and violet food colorings
2 oz. white marzipan
6 Brazil nuts
6 whole almonds
6 (1-oz.) squares semi-sweet chocolate
6 (1-oz.) squares white chocolate
6 (1-oz.) squares milk chocolate
6 maraschino cherries
6 creme de menthe cherries
Crystalized rose and violet petals

Cut fondant in 2 pieces. Flavor 1 piece rose and color pale pink with food coloring.

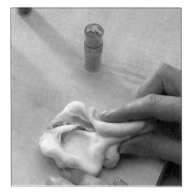

Flavor remaining piece violet and color pale mauve with food coloring. Roll out fondant to 1/2-inch thickness. Cut in shapes using cocktail cutters. Place on a waxed paper-lined baking sheet. Shape marzipan in various shapes by rolling bite-sized pieces between hands in balls, logs or ovals. Arrange on a baking sheet. Let dry several hours or overnight. Toast nuts until golden brown.

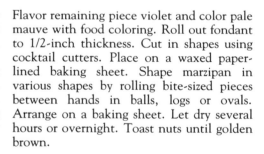

Melt each chocolate in different bowls over hand-hot water, stirring until melted. Using a fork, dip 1 center at a time into chocolate. Tap to remove excess and place chocolate on parchment paper-lined baking sheets. Leave plain, mark top with a fork or decorate rose and violet centers with crystallized petals. Continue to dip all centers, using white, dark or milk chocolate. Using a pastry bag, pipe some chocolates with threads of chocolate.

Makes 30 pieces.

CHOCOLATE TRUFFLES

ORANGE TRUFFLES

1/3 cup sliced almonds
1/3 cup sugar
1-1/2 lbs. semi-sweet or bittersweet chocolate, chopped
1 tablespoon strong coffee
1/3 cup butter, softened
2 tablespoons whipping cream
2 liqueurs of your choice
Dutch processed cocoa powder

In a small heavy-bottomed pan, combine almonds and sugar. On a low heat, slowly cook until golden brown, stirring with a wooden spoon. Remove from heat immediately and pour mixture onto an oiled plate. Allow to harden.

In a food processor or blender, crush nut mixture to a coarse powder. Melt 8 oz. chocolate in a bowl or top of a double boiler set over a pan of simmering water. Stir in coffee; cool slightly. Beat in butter; stir in cream and crushed nut mixture. Divide mixture in half, flavor each half with 1 or 2 tablespoons of liqueur.

1/4 cup butter, chopped
1/3 cup whipping cream
7 oz. semisweet chocolate, chopped
1 egg yolk
1 teaspoon grated orange peel
2 tablespoons finely chopped mixed citrus peel
2 tablespoons Grand Marnier
Unsweetened cocoa powder

In a small saucepan, combine butter and cream. Cook on low heat until butter melts and cream bubbles around edge. Remove from heat; add chocolate. Cover and let stand until chocolate melts. Stir until smooth.

Stir in egg yolk. Mix in orange peel, citrus peel, and Grand Marnier. Chill until firm.

Gently roll heaping teaspoons of truffle mixture into balls. Work quickly as chocolate sets fast. Set aside on wax paper; refrigerate until firm. Melt remaining chocolate; dip some truffles and place on wax paper to set. Roll others in cocoa when almost set. Place in paper cups. Store, covered, in a cool place.

Makes about 1-1/2 lb.

Form into 40 balls. Roll in cocoa. Refrigerate in an airtight container up to 2 weeks. To serve, place in small paper or aluminum cases.

Makes 40.

RUM BALLS

CHOCOLATE COVERED PRUNES

RUM BALLS
3/4 cup crushed vanilla wafers
1/4 cup powdered sugar
1/4 cup ground almonds
2 teaspoons dark rum
1 teaspoon lemon juice
1-1/2 oz. semisweet chocolate, chopped
2 tablespoons whipping cream
ICING
1/3 cup powdered sugar
2 tablespoons butter, chopped
1 oz. semisweet chocolate, grated
2 teaspoons dark rum
Warm water
Chocolate sprinkles

12 whole pitted prunes
12 whole Brazil nuts
8 oz semi-sweet or bittersweet chocolate, chopped

Fill cavity of prunes with Brazil nuts.

In a medium bowl, combine crushed vanilla wafers, sugar, almonds, rum and lemon juice. Melt chocolate in a bowl or top of a double boiler set over a pan of simmering water. Add to rum mixture with sufficient cream for mixture to hold together when pressed between fingers. Form teaspoonfuls of mixture into 18 balls. Refrigerate until firm. For icing, combine sugar, butter, chocolate and rum in a small saucepan. When chocolate and butter softens, add a tablespoon of water. Warm again and add sufficient water to liquify.

In a heatproof bowl or top of a double boiler placed over a saucepan of hot water, melt the chocolate, stirring.

To coat rum balls, insert a poultry skewer in center of a rum ball. Tilt pan of icing and dip each ball. Let excess drip. To decorate, roll in chocolate sprinkles to coat completely. Refrigerate in a covered container with waxed paper between layers up to 10 days.

Makes 18.

Dip prunes into chocolate. Place on wax paper to set. Store, covered, in the refrigerator.

Makes 12 chocolates.

— CHERRY NUT CHOCOLATES —

— PISTACHIO HALVA —

3-1/2 oz. semisweet chocolate
1/4 cup macadamia nuts or blanched almonds, coarsely
    chopped
8 glacé cherries, quartered

Grate or chop chocolate.

Toast nuts in a dry skillet until golden brown. Stir occasionally. Cool. Melt chocolate in a bowl or top of a double boiler set over a pan of simmering water. Stir until smooth. Drop by teaspoonfuls on waxed paper and flatten to form thick small buttons. Let partly set.

Sprinkle nuts on outside rim of chocolate. Press cherry piece in center. Let set; peel from waxed paper. Refrigerate in a covered container with waxed paper between layers up to 3 weeks.

Makes 30.

1-1/4 cups shelled pistachios
1 cup boiling water
2 tablespoons milk
1/2 cup sugar
1-1/2 tablespoons butter or ghee
1 teaspoon vanilla extract

Put pistachios in a bowl, top with boiling water and soak 30 minutes. Grease and line an 8-inch square pan with waxed paper.

Drain pistachios thoroughly and put in a blender or food processor fitted with the metal blade. Add milk and process until finely chopped, scraping mixture down from sides once or twice. Stir in sugar. Heat a large non-stick skillet, add butter and melt over medium-low heat. Add nut paste and cook about 15 minutes, stirring constantly, until mixture is very thick.

Stir in vanilla extract, then spoon into prepared pan and spread evenly. Cool completely, then cut into 20 squares using a sharp knife.

Makes about 20 squares.

Note: This halva will keep 2 to 3 weeks, covered and stored in the refrigerator.

—TOASTED ALMOND TOFFEE—

—CASHEW NUT FUDGE—

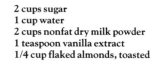

2 cups sugar
1 cup water
2 cups nonfat dry milk powder
1 teaspoon vanilla extract
1/4 cup flaked almonds, toasted

Grease and line an 8-inch square pan with waxed paper. Put sugar and water in a large heavy saucepan. Heat gently, stirring occasionally, until sugar is dissolved.

1-1/2 cups unsalted cashew nuts
1-1/2 cups boiling water
2 tablespoons milk
2/3 cup sugar
1 tablespoon butter or ghee
1 teaspoon vanilla extract
Few sheets of silver leaf

Put cashew nuts in a bowl, top with boiling water and soak 1 hour. Grease and line an 8-inch square pan with waxed paper.

Increase heat and bring to a boil, and boil over medium-high heat until a few drops of mixture will form a soft ball in cold water. Stir in milk powder and cook 3 to 4 minutes more, stirring all the time, until mixture begins to dry on spoon. Stir in vanilla.

Drain cashew nuts thoroughly and put in a blender or food processor fitted with the metal blade. Add milk and process until smooth, scraping mixture down from side once or twice. Stir in sugar. Heat a large non-stick skillet, add butter and melt over medium-low heat. Add nut paste and cook about 20 minutes, stirring constantly, until mixture is very thick.

Pour into prepared pan and spread evenly. Scatter almonds over top and press into surface. Leave to cool slightly, then cut into 25 squares with a sharp knife while still warm. Leave in pan until cold and firm.

Makes 25 squares.

Stir in vanilla extract, then spoon into prepared pan and spread evenly. Cool completely, then press silver leaf onto surface. Cut fudge into about 25 diamond shapes using a wet sharp knife.

Makes about 25 pieces.

Note: This fudge will keep for two to three weeks if stored in an airtight container.

MARZIPAN FRUITS

CHOCOLATE MARZIPAN LOG

1-1/4 cups finely ground almonds
3/4 cup powdered sugar (or more, if a sweeter flavor is desired)
1 egg white
Red, green, blue and yellow food coloring
A few cloves

In a heatproof bowl or top of a double boiler placed over a saucepan of hot water, place almonds; heat gently stirring occasionally until warmed. Remove double boiler from heat, add sugar and egg white.

On a work surface, knead almond mixture until a smooth, fairly dry paste. Roll into a ball, cover with a cloth and let stand at room temperature for 15 minutes. Break off small portions and shape into desired 'fruit'. The exact size of the fruit is up to you, but they should never be larger than a small walnut.

You will need a couple of fine-pointed brushes, a saucer for mixing colors, a cup of water and a cloth for wiping brushes between color changes. Remember, red and yellow make orange, diluted orange will put the base color on peaches, red and green make brown for the stripes on bananas. Use cloves for the stem ends of oranges, pears and apples. You may make leaves from marzipan or use angelica.

Makes about 1/2 lb.

4 oz. marzipan, crumbled
1/4 cup powdered sugar
1 egg white
3/4 cup shredded coconut
Angelica strips or glacé apricots, halved
1-1/2 oz. semisweet chocolate, chopped

In a medium bowl, mix marzipan and sugar. Knead small amounts of egg white into marzipan mixture. Add additional egg white until a sticky paste forms. Add coconut and knead for 1 minute. If too sticky, knead on a powdered sugar surface. Chill mixture 30 minutes.

Form a long roll 12 x 6 in on plastic wrap. Place angelica strips or glacé apricots along one side. Roll marzipan over to enclose fruit. Wrap well; chill 12 hours.

Melt chocolate in a bowl or top of a double boiler set over a pan of simmering water. Stir until smooth. Unwrap almond roll and spread one side with chocolate. When set, turn log over and spread chocolate on other side. When set, wrap and chill. Refrigerate whole up to 3 weeks. To serve, cut into slices as needed.

Makes 24 slices.

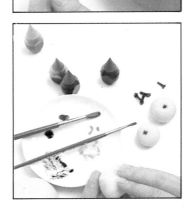

GLAZED APRICOT PECANS

CARAMELIZED FRUITS

40 pecan or walnut halves
APRICOT PURÉE
1/4 cup (2 oz.) plus 2 tablespoons dried apricots
2 tablespoons powdered sugar
1/4 cup (1 oz.) ground almonds
1 teaspoon brandy
TOFFEE
1 cup sugar
1/3 cup water

In a small saucepan, cook apricots covered with water until soft. Drain; and purée apricots.

In a medium bowl, combine apricots, powdered sugar, almonds and brandy. Chill 2 hours before using. Refrigerate up to 2 days. Place a teaspoon of apricot mixture on a nut; top with another nut. Press together gently. Remove excess apricot mixture.

Grease a wire rack and baking sheet. Place wire rack over baking sheet. In a small saucepan, cook sugar and water over low heat. Swirl mixture occasionally until sugar dissolves. Adjust heat to medium. Cook until mixture is a light golden brown. Remove from heat. Quickly drop nuts, one-by-one, into toffee. Using a small spoon, remove immediately; cool on wire rack. Refrigerate in a covered container up to 12 hours.

Makes 20 pieces.

2/3 cup sugar
5 tablespoons water
About 2 cups fresh assorted fruit, such as grapes, tangerine sections and strawberries, rinsed if necessary

In a heavy-bottomed saucepan combine sugar and water. Cook over a gentle heat, stirring occasionally until sugar is dissolved.

Bring to boil without stirring; boil until mixture turns a pale caramel color. Remove immediately from heat; place in a bowl of warm water.

Carefully place individual pieces of fruit in caramel, coating completely. Set fruit onto lightly greased cookie sheet or wire rack. Allow to cool and harden. To serve, place in petit four cases. Fruit must be eaten within 24 hours. Do not refrigerate.

Makes about 1-1/2 lbs.

FONDANT SWEETS

8 oz. ready-to-roll fondant icing (sugar paste)
Pink, green, yellow, violet and orange food colorings
FLAVORINGS
3 pieces marrons glacés
3 pieces crystallized ginger
1/2 teaspoon peppermint oil
1 teaspoon finely grated orange peel
1 teaspoon finely grated lemon peel
1 teaspoon finely grated lime peel.

Cut fondant in 6 pieces. Tint 5 pieces very pale pink, green, yellow, violet and orange.

Cut 2 marrons glacés and pink fondant in 8 pieces. Wrap each piece of marron glacé in pink fondant and shape in a smooth ball. Repeat with violet fondant and crystallized ginger to make oval shaped sweets. Decorate tops with remaining marron glacé and crystallized ginger.

Flavor white fondant with a few drops of peppermint oil. Roll out to 1/4-inch thickness. Using a small round or crescent cutter, cut out about 8 to 10 shapes. Knead orange peel into orange fondant, lemon peel into yellow fondant and lime peel into green fondant. Shape each piece in tiny pinwheels, squares or diamond shapes. Place all fondants on a parchment paper-lined baking sheet to dry out completely.

Makes 40 pieces.

KIWI FRUIT JELLIES

2 lb. kiwi fruit, peeled and chopped
Juice of 1 lemon
3 cups sugar
2 tablespoons unsalted butter
1 cup liquid pectin
Green food coloring, if desired
Superfine sugar

Line an 8 x 10-inch pan with wax or parchment paper. In a food processor or blender, combine fruit, lemon juice and 1 cup sugar.

Purée. It may be necessary to do this in batches. Pass the liquid through a food mill or fine strainer into a large saucepan. Add remaining sugar; stirring constantly, bring to boil. Boil for 3 minutes; add butter; still stirring, boil 3 minutes more. Remove from heat and stir in pectin and a few drops of coloring, if desired.

Pour into prepared pan and allow to set overnight in cool place. Cut into attractive shapes and roll in sugar. Store in a cool place in airtight containers with wax paper separating the layers. Will keep up to 1 week.

Makes about 2 lb.

INDEX